Reading in a Second Language

APPLIED LINGUISTICS AND LANGUAGE STUDY

GENERAL EDITOR

CHRISTOPHER N. CANDLIN,
Chair Professor of Applied Linguistics
City University of Hong Kong, Hong Kong

For a complete list of books in this series see pages *v–vi*.

Reading in a Second Language: Process, Product and Practice

A.H. Urquhart and C.J. Weir

Longman

London and New York

Addison Wesley Longman Limited
Edinburgh Gate
Harlow
Essex CM20 2JE
United Kingdom
and Associated Companies throughout the world

Published in the United States of America
by Addison Wesley Longman, New York

© Addison Wesley Longman Limited 1998

First published 1998

ISBN 0 582 298369 Paper

Visit Addison Wesley Longman on the world wide web at http://www.awl-he.com

British Library Cataloguing-in-Publication Data

A catalogue record for this book is available from the British Library

Library of Congress Cataloging-in-Publication Data

Urquhart, A.H.
      Reading in a second language : process, product, and practice /
A.H. Urquhart and C.J. Weir.
         p.   cm. — (Applied linguistics and language study)
      Includes bibliographical references and index.
      ISBN (invalid) 0–582–29836–9 (pbk.)
      1. Language and languages—Study and teaching.   2. Reading.
   3. Language and languages—Ability testing.   I. Weir, Cyril J.
   II. Title.   III. Series.
   P53.75.W45   1998
   418′.4—dc21   98–7949
                                                                        CIP

Set by 35 in 10/12pt Baskerville
Printed in Malaysia, LSP

APPLIED LINGUISTICS AND LANGUAGE STUDY

GENERAL EDITOR

CHRISTOPHER N. CANDLIN

Chair Professor of Applied Linguistics
City University of Hong Kong
Hong Kong

Contents

xi

Editors' acknowledgements

The authors would like to thank Chris Candlin for his support and guidance throughout the writing of this book. His insightful comments and firm grasp of the whole domain of applied linguistics have been invaluable. They would also like to thank Jin Yan and Luo Peng from Shanghai Jiaotong University, PRC, and other members of the reading research group at CALS, University of Reading, for their constructive feedback and help in clarifying our thoughts on the new blueprint for reading developed in this book, and in particular for their help in developing our taxonomy of reading skills and strategies.

Cyril Weir offers his gratitude to all his colleagues in CALS for their understanding over the past few years and, in particular, to Don Porter and Eddie Williams for their support and encouragement. He would also like to thank Lois Archer, Shigeko Amano and Jessica Wu for their close reading of the manuscript. Ron White deserves a special acknowledgement for being one of the rare breed of managers who is both liked and respected by his colleagues. His view of the role of management as bringing the best out of his staff rather than trying to get the most out of them is much appreciated. CALS generously awarded this author sabbatical leave both to start and finish this book.

Sandy Urquhart would like to thank his family for their support.

Publisher's acknowledgements

We are indebted to Kluwer Academic Publishers for permission to reproduce a version of the contribution 'The Testing of Reading in a Second Language' by Cyril Weir in *Encyclopedia of Language and Education* edited by David Corson et al. © 1998.

General Editor's preface

The subtitle of this new contribution to the *Applied Linguistics and Language Study Series* is significant. Reading is a matter of interaction. Products for reading in the form of texts are not only themselves outcomes of writer processes, cognitive, linguistic, and social, but invite and activate those processes in their readers. Not that the engagement of writer and reader only begins when the reader picks up or otherwise accesses a text. Writers always have readers in mind, and we know that expert writers tailor their writing to their readers' presumed cognitive and linguistic capacities, partly by establishing some common social context for the interaction. We may trace in writing evidence of the degree to which this accommodation takes place, and by monitoring reading processes we can appraise its effectiveness. Thus, as readers evaluate writers, so do writers envisage readers. Reading is in this way a kind of sympathetic and unscripted writing. Seen this way, the instructing and appraisal of reading is linked to those of writing, providing an example of how teaching and testing can go hand in hand. They do so explicitly in this innovative book by Sandy Urquhart and Cyril Weir. It is not axiomatic that teaching and testing enjoy this synergy. Indeed, it is often argued that they are adversarial. Testing is held by some to inhibit teaching, or through washback to come to dominate and direct it. Exploring the interaction between teaching and testing is one of the distinctive features of this book.

There are further interactions to be noted. Reading and writing invite in their relationship comparisons between listening and speaking. The authors establish this parallelism in their *Preliminaries* in the first chapter of the book. It is a compelling association since it embraces the cognitive, the linguistic and the social, within the speaking/listening connection and between that of reading and speaking. Reading, writing, listening and speaking not only interactively involve these processes, they are also in themselves social practices. They occur in contexts. The authors are sensitive to this but they are also cautious. They warn against too easy an assumption of transfer from one context to another. Reading in one context may not be the same as in another, and transferability and generalisability of effective reading strategies cannot be taken for granted. Testing is one way in which we may explore this issue. Here, too, testing and teaching are interlinked.

Reading as a social practice is, however, not only a little 'c' context matter. As a social practice it always also invokes the bigger 'C' Context, what sociologists refer to as the institutional matrices within which particular reading practices are embedded. Such ways of going about reading contribute to our understanding of the role reading plays in the definition of the institution as a particular social and cultural world. The receptive conditions governing the act of reading are important, as are the productive conditions governing writing. The experience and expertise of the authors is crucial at this point, as elsewhere in the book. Their close familiarity with the contexts and Contexts of reading ensures that there is no light assumption of transferability, nor any ignoring of the impact of the social interactivity of reading on its cognitive interactivity within the reader. Nonetheless, exploring reading from the perspective of mind and that of social relationships requires discrete discussion. Here the interplay in the book among theoretical, instructional and evaluative concepts and practices allows each its place, but, in the end, they interact. They do more than that. They are expressly positioned in the book to engage each other. Theories and models of reading and their components are tested against the constraints imposed by testing, and against the exigencies of instruction. Readers of the book are thus not led up some garden path. Nor are they allowed to forget that reading, as I say earlier, is essentially an engagement with text. How one describes such texts, as a reading specialist or as a testing specialist, will not be the same as if one described the text from the perspective of a linguist or a cognitive psychologist, or indeed as a sociologist. This is not always fully appreciated. Grammar is not disciplinarily neutral. The authors recognise this. Indeed, they are very explicit about boundaries in this case, as the section on *Future Research* makes clear. Nevertheless, they do not isolate these perspectives in practice. How one processes the grammar of a text does have some connection with the way the text is structured grammatically. Grammar, after all, acts to stimulate particular processes of exploring meaning potential.

Understanding such processes requires us to accommodate different strategies and styles of reading. There is no one way of reading a text, and reading variability depends on a range of factors: what one is reading, who one is as a reader, who or what one may be reading for and why, what level of linguistic competence one has, what relationships one may have with the writer, and for a host of other reasons. Such a range of variables imposes a challenge to testers, who have their own criteria and standards to meet, ones which urge convergence and normativeness. Thus, analysts of text, analysts of mind, and analysts of social context necessarily interact in the analysis of reading. Adding testing to this mixture causes a redefinition of the roles and boundaries of each. So, too does teaching, but not in the same way. Teaching, after all, is about divergence as well as convergence.

Interaction involves actors. An issue of importance for the book is the tension that arises between considering the reader as individual and the reader as a member of a social group. The authors believe that a current bias towards the social act of reading needs to be corrected so that the cognitive capacity of the reading individual is not lost, and his or her personal contribution to the activity of reading thereby underestimated. Here, again, the individualised focus of testing provides a useful corrective. Not that large scale testing of reading, such as that conducted over several years by expert teams advised by Cyril Weir in the almost ungraspable context of several million testees in China, does not provide some valuable collective and aggregative information. Nonetheless, examination halls, the authors' default environment, are but collections of individuals, whose capacities need personalised assessment, and the enhancement of whose strategies and skills in classrooms through instruction, they conclude, is currently best assessed cognitively rather than socially. Yet, authenticating reading remains a significant instructional goal. It is a measure of the wisdom of this clearly argued and sympathetic book that the authors conclude that it will only be through the interaction of theory, instruction and assessment that the challenge of this authentication can be addressed in classrooms, or indeed, in examination halls, and the legitimate pressures of the textual, the cognitive and the social can be accommodated by researchers, teachers and testers.

Professor Christopher N Candlin
General Editor
English Language Education and Communication Research
City University of Hong Kong

Introduction

The book is primarily intended for those professionally concerned with the teaching and testing of reading in a foreign language. We take this to include teachers, both practising and in training, teacher-trainers, materials writers, and those concerned with the production of reading tests, or with training testers.

Borrowing a term used by anthropologists and semanticists, we will refer to our *prototypical* teaching situation as an L2 classroom in a school, college or university. This does not mean that we are ignorant of the fact that reading may be taught, or learned, in other contexts, e.g. the home, the workplace, or that a teacher will always be present. We adopt this as our prototype simply in order to establish a point of reference. Similarly, our prototypical testing situation is the examination hall. Again we are fully aware that individuals can test themselves, or, perhaps more important, that classroom teachers can make use of informal tests to check reading performance. Again, though, we need a reference point for the discussion below and throughout the book. We hope that readers will be able to transfer what we say to their own particular situation.

Literacy

The teacher of reading is in the business of attempting to improve literacy. Literacy has been the focus of a great deal of work over the last few decades. By discussing, however briefly, some of this work, we shall hopefully set this book against a broad and meaningful context.

The definition of literacy is crucial (cf. Baynham, 1995 and Venezky et al., 1990). One implied definition, touching in its optimism, can be found in the US Census of 1940, where a person is judged literate if they are 10 years of age or older and has completed 5 or more years in school (Newman and Beverstock, 1990). For serious discussion nowadays, the starting point must be UNESCO proposals of the 1950s that literacy should be defined in terms of *minimal* and *functional* literacy (see Venezky et al., 1990). The former refers to the ability to read and write a simple message; the latter to a level of literacy sufficiently high for a person to function in a social setting. Prior to this, attempts were made to define what Street (1995: 76) refers to as 'autonomous literacy', that is, literacy divorced from any context. Such a hypothetical level is impossible to establish and is inappropriate in many situations. As Venezky et al. (1990: ix) say:

> the diverse communities that make up contemporary America are so variegated that simple dichotomies such as literate–illiterate fail to capture what are real differences in what people know and how they behave in certain situations.

The decision to take into account the social relevance of literacy has been momentous, leading as it has to modern notions of multiple '*literacies*'. The concept can apply both to *attitudes* towards the value of literacy, and to the *role* of literacy in the society as a whole. Street (1995) comments on problems caused by a clash in such values between outside educators and local values in Melanesia and among Amish communities in the USA.

In many parts of modern Western society, illiteracy in an adult is seen as a stigma, which the person concerned is often at pains to disguise. In a novel by Ruth Rendell, a character becomes alienated from society as a result of such subterfuges, grows up devoid of normal social emotions, and eventually murders her employers in order to disguise the fact that she cannot take a message.[1] In contrast, in a well-known article, Fingeret (1983) describes how, in urban communities in the USA, illiteracy is not a stigma, help with filling in forms, etc., being exchanged for other skills like car repairing.[2] It is likely that large and important cultures exist which view literacy in a way very different from our own. Certainly it has been our experience in the L2 classroom that some students do not seem to view written material as a potential source of information accessible to the individual reader. If this observation is valid, the students' behaviour may be a result of views of the role of literacy in their society. To remedy this, an intensified training in reading skills may not be sufficient; possibly more generalised approaches to the uses of written material might work.

The different levels of literacy required by different groups can be seen when one considers different occupations or professions in the same society. It seems obvious that different occupations make greater professional demands of the written word than others. Tudge – arguing in *New Scientist* that the population divides into those who like reading and those who do not, and that the education system should take this into account – notes that trainee surgeons do not need to make much use of the printed word (they can rely on video-tapes, computer simulations, etc.) whereas lawyers do (Tudge, 1987). It is also obvious that the required level of professional literacy varies radically over time. It seems likely that, in the last century, plumbers, for example, had comparatively low professional requirements for literacy. This is not likely to be the case now.

L2 students in the language class are often preparing to study on academic or other courses conducted in the L2. Such courses, e.g. engineering, nursing, can be assumed to have their own literacy requirements and criterion levels. It is clearly of vital importance that test and syllabus designers take these different requirements and levels into account. In Chapter 3 we discuss this topic under task- and text-based factors. Particularly in LSP, *Needs Analysis* has long been part of the design of courses (cf. Munby, 1978; Nunan, 1993). It is our opinion, however, that detailed ethnographic case studies of the needs of different study areas have not been conducted, or at least published. The difficulty of conducting such studies should not be underestimated.

Related to this is the notion of *transfer* of literacy from one area to another. Implicit in what has been said above, reading skills acquired in the reading class should be transferred to the student's eventual study area. However, the literature on transfer tends to be pessimistic. Mikulecky (1990) claims that a major misconception in literacy studies is that 'mastering literacy in one context substantially transfers to other contexts', and adds 'Transfer of literacy abilities is severely limited by differences in format, social support networks, and required background information as one moves from context to context' (p. 25). He contrasts 'literacy in schools' involving 'independent reading for answering questions at the end of the chapter, or, on some occasions, carefully studying material to remember, synthesize, or evaluate it [what we later refer to as "careful local" or "careful global" reading]' and claims that these activities differ from 'those used to read a troubleshooting manual on the job or gather information to fill in a form' (p. 25). Sticht (1980) has also claimed that there is little transfer from general reading ability, and reading in specific situations. He contrasts 'reading to learn' in school, with 'reading to do' in the workplace, or 'reading toward a goal of locating information for immediate use that need not be recalled later'. While transfer is always a potential problem, we see behind some of this discussion rather conventional and unimaginative limitations on the types of reading which should be practised in the reading class, and point below (Chapter 4) to a wider range of tasks and behaviours.

Returning now to multiple literacies, the notion extends to individuals. A reader may be highly literate in one area but minimally literate in another. The present authors are not functionally literate with respect to, for example, professional scientific texts, and only marginally so *vis-à-vis* teenage fanzines. The L2 teacher of adults will be familiar with the situation in which students in the class are superior readers in certain professional or other areas. In such cases, common in LSP situations, the teacher clearly must see their role as that of *facilitator* rather than pedagogue.

This aspect of multiple literacy also throws doubt on the concept of the 'good reader', often referred to in the research literature. Venezky (1990: 12) argues that 'Most readers show differing reading abilities across different types of material', a claim repeated by Urquhart (1996). An implication of this is that, for the L2 reader, we may sometimes need not a single test score but a profile composed of performances on different types of text and task. In Chapter 3 we present evidence from testing to support this view.

What might be viewed as an extreme case of different literacies within the same individual can be seen when the individual moves into a different language area. Venezky draws attention to the immigrant into the USA, illiterate in English but literate in Vietnamese and French; and the reverse, literate Americans who are functionally illiterate when they move to other parts of the world. A large proportion of L2 students in reading classes are already literate in their L1 (but see Wallace, 1988; Williams, 1995). A number of consequences rise from this differential literacy in different languages. The fact that many learners are literate in their L1 but not functionally literate in the L2 is the basis for the notion of 'transfer of reading skills' discussed in Chapter 2. More generally, L1 literacy must be one of the components which readers bring to the task of L2 reading (cf. Bernhardt, 1991b). Bernhardt sees 'literacy' in this sense as consisting of knowledge of texts, etc. However, it must be broader than that, including not just, in many cases, knowledge of script, but also, crucially, knowledge that written text is language, containing messages from other language users.

The scope of the term 'literacy'

When we talked earlier about 'defining literacy', we really meant 'defining levels of literacy'. There is also the question of what precise activities are to be covered by the term. Of recent years, it has been given a wide range of referents. Newman and Beverstock (1990) point out that 'membership of an interpretive community is often referred to as a specific literacy, as when we speak of *computer literacy* . . .'. They later cite 'civic literacy, prison literacy, work-place literacy' (p. 44). Nor is this just rhetoric. As they point out, 'in Michigan, the definition of literacy is being broadened through testing in five areas: written and oral communication, mathematics and related skills, problem, workplace attitude, and job-seeking abilities' (p. 42). They warn that '(while) the old definitions of literacy were too narrow; some of the new definitions may be too broad. The new and humane . . . definitions of literacy are so profuse that we may be loading the word with burdens of meaning that will eventually negate its usefulness as a working term' (p. 43).

Venezky, viewing literacy as a complex of skills, mentions reading, writing, numeracy and document processing as four skill areas lumped under literacy. Venezky argues that 'reading is clearly primary to any definition of literacy, and, in some sense, the others are secondary' (1990: 9). For numeracy, he suggests that it be constrained to 'those basic numeric operations that are critical for ordinary meaning of print' (p. 8). It is a problem which often emerges during reading test construction. On the whole, we tend to think that numeracy should be treated as a separate skills area, as it often is in British educational debate. Venezky seems to see document processing as a separate skill area, dependent on reading. His reason seems to be statistical, based on low correlations found between performance on 'documents' and on 'prose'. There are hints throughout the literacy debate that the texts being used to measure literacy are very traditional – 'stories', etc. There is nothing in the models considered in Chapter 2 to indicate that 'document reading' should differ qualitatively from the reading of prose. We thus have no difficulty in fitting it into what we consider as reading.

Macias (1990) argues against 'multi-literacies': '. . . numeracy and document processing, as well as the uses of literacy (primarily writing), become secondary aspects of literacy study, not parts of the definition of literacy.' With the exception of document processing, we go along with this in practice, though perhaps not in theory. We are concerned in this book with reading, and exclude writing, the second half of the literacy equation. This is in spite of the attractiveness of combining the two activities in realistic tasks. Our reasons are partly pragmatic; it is well known, as is set out in Chapter 3, that using written work to test reading runs the risk of confounding two skills areas. In general, we consider that the two skills areas are distinctive enough to be handled separately, as is conventionally the practice in L2 testing and teaching. Writing is well covered in the comprehensive volume by Grabe and Kaplan (1996). We exclude numeracy, however, because, as is argued in 'Preliminaries' (Chapter 1), we consider that the term *reading* is best kept for the processing of written *language*.

Literacy and power

The introduction of cultural context into literacy studies has led many writers to consider the relationship between literacy and power. Fingeret (1990) cites Goody and Watt (1968) to the effect that 'choices about who reads, what they read, and how they use what they read always have been connected to the distribution of power in a society'. This connection is often seen as negative – one group using literacy to maintain and exercise power over another. Groups accused of doing so include slave owners in nineteenth-century America: slaves in some of the southern states were forbidden to read (Newman and Beverstock, 1990). Missionaries in nineteenth-century Melanesia 'saw literacy practice as a means simply to conversion and to social control, (and thus) they had no interest in providing any more than was necessary for this bare minimum' (Street, 1995: 84). This form of control is nicely dubbed 'domestication' by Mikulecky (1990: 26). The power group in our own culture may be the literate majority, which 'secure in its position of dominance, partially attributes its success to literacy and guards entrance into literate domains' (Fingeret, 1990: 35). Finally it may be the centralised state, through its institutions (Gee, 1990). The antidote to such undesirable aspects of literacy is often seen in 'critical literacy' (cf. Baynam, 1995: 205). Mikulecky cites Kretovics (1985) to the effect that 'the teaching of a "critical literacy" can enable teachers and students to formulate strategies to change the form, content, and social relations of education with an interest in freedom and democracy' (Mikulecky, 1990: 26). This approach, which is closely related to 'critical discourse analysis' (Fairclough, 1995) and 'critical reading' (Wallace, 1992a), stresses not just decoding a text and processing the meaning, but using the text for the reader's purposes, analysing its presuppositions, and how it works on its readers (cf. Freebody and Luke, 1990). Street (1995) comments that 'teaching awareness of . . . the ways in which literacy practices are sites of ideological contest, is itself already a challenge to the dominant autonomous model that disguises such processes' (p. 137).

The motto of the 'critical' group would seem to be '*It's best to be bolshie*' – a position for which we have a certain amount of sympathy. One can, however, give only limited support. It seems to us that Fairclough's argument that the discourse analyst must be aware of the ideological presuppositions contained in a discourse is essentially valid; we would query, however, whether the aims of analyst and reader are necessarily identical. Then it seems a little rich to insist that literacy is primarily a means of socialisation and acculturation, only to add that the reader should be prepared to analyse and possibly reject the power structures inherent in the society or culture. Again, one cannot and should not, in our view, *always* be a critical reader: the first year biology student reading the textbook recommended by the department might do well to adopt a submissive attitude to its contents (see Chapter 2).[3] The nuclear worker reading safety regulations might be wise to restrict any criticism. And if this is true for teaching, it is much more true for testing: the student who rebels against the power structure behind the test is unlikely to obtain a good grade.

There are further problems. Street remarks that 'the student is learning cultural models of identity and personhood, not just how to decode script or to write a particular hand' (1995: 140). We are dubious as to whether the adult students in the L2 classroom are learning 'cultural models of identity', and we are certain that in most instances they are not learning 'models of personhood'. They come into the class bringing their own models of culture, and are often very capable of identifying ideologies in discourses which conflict with their own cultural values.

There is also the problem of the teacher or test writer's own ideological position. Street remarks that the Freireian approach, whereby literacy is accompanied by revolt,

> is vulnerable to such culturally blind manipulation by activists imbued with ideological fervour and believing so strongly that they are 'empowering' 'ignorant' peasants that they fail to see their own cultural and political domination.   (p. 138)

There is, it seems to us, a danger that L2 students in the reading class may be subjected to the ideology of teachers, whether they be radical feminists, environmentalists, vegetarians, atheists, Picts against Fascism or whatever. In fact, teachers would help more to empower students if they were prepared to 'back off', stopped imposing 'correct' interpretations of texts, let students choose their own texts and set their own agenda.

Cognitive v Social

According to Bernhardt (1991b: 6), 'taking a cognitive perspective means examining the reading process as an intrapersonal problem-solving task that takes place within the brain's knowledge structures'. She notes (p. 8) that the critical element in any cognitive view of reading is that it is an individual act. As a social process, she cites Bloome and Greene (1984): 'reading is used to establish, structure, and maintain social relationships between and among peoples'.

Bernhardt doesn't specify the social aspects except to point out that the same individual and the same text can vary:

> the processing of text can be viewed only within a unique cultural context . . . there are basically no generic or generalized readers or reading behaviours . . . there are multiple readers within one person . . . multiple 'texts' within a text.   (pp. 10–11)

There are, however, many more factors than this in the social approach to reading.

No text on reading can ignore the social aspects of the activity. Reading, as the studies of literacy mentioned above have made clear, is a social activity, related always to particular contexts. However, there is no doubt that in comparison to a book like Wallace (1992a) we put more emphasis on the cognitive side. There is more than one reason for this.

1. We consider that the cognitive aspect is primary. Reading without social aspects might be an odd idea, but something like it exists in the experiments of cognitive psychologists, some of whom are mentioned in Chapter 2. Reading without cognitive activity, on the other hand, is simply an impossibility.
2. Wallace remarks, quite correctly, that 'as readers we are frequently addressed in our social roles rather than our personal and individual ones' (1992a: 18) and gives as an example the reader of an advertisement aimed at a social group. We would claim, however, that while this is clearly relevant to an analyst of the text, and certainly relevant to the production of the text, it is not necessarily relevant to readers who probably see themselves as reading the text as individuals. To this extent, reading is always an individual activity. We should not, of course, fall into the trap of equating 'individual' with 'cognitive'; the individuals bring their own societies with them. Nevertheless, there is an element of truth in it – see Bernhardt above.
3. Wallace claims that: 'Classrooms are themselves communities with their own uses of literacy and ascribed roles for teachers and learners.' We agree, but are conscious that the L2 reading class is often a very loose, transitory community, more akin in some ways to the population of an airport lounge. The members have come from different communities and are intending to join different communities. The communities that they plan to join must remain in our consciousness. Again, we see classes as collections of individuals. And if this is true of classrooms, how much more is it true of our other prototypical situation, the examination hall?
4. Finally, in Chapter 4, where we review teaching methods, we try to focus on those areas where empirical evidence exists in support of particular practices. It is our impression that more of such evidence at present exists for those methodologies which have a cognitive, rather than a social focus.

We do, however, try to take the social aspect of reading explicitly into account in our handling of comprehension in Chapter 2, and in the importance we ascribe to authentic tasks and texts in

Chapters 3 and 4. A fuller treatment of the social approach to reading, including activities for the classroom, can be found in Wallace (1992a, 1996).

Organisation of the book

Reading is surprisingly complex to define. Its precise relationship with language in general, and with listening in particular, are a cause of controversy or misunderstanding. So we begin with Chapter 1, 'Preliminaries', in which we attempt to deal with these difficulties.

Chapter 2 is concerned with theoretical issues concerning reading. Here we discuss models of the reading process, including process models, which attempt to model the actual cognitive processes involved in reading, and componential models, which are content to discuss the likely components of the process. In addition, we look at the topics of comprehension, reading skills and strategies.

In Chapters 3 and 4 we proceed to the more applied sections of the book, and examine the testing and teaching of reading. In our accounts of these areas, we have three main aims:

1. To provide a reasonably comprehensive account of the development and current state of the art. We stress the importance of considering expeditious reading strategies (selective, quick and efficient reading activities such as skimming, search reading and scanning) as well as the more conventional careful reading activities.
2. To relate this as far as possible to the theoretical background already discussed. We see this as essentially a two-way issue: one can examine, for example, the justification for testing or teaching practice in terms of theory; conversely, one can examine whether the theory needs to be expanded to take account of some apparently successful or popular practice. Both aspects lead to suggestions for new forms of test and of teaching materials.
3. To provide the reader with guidelines for selecting testing or teaching activities and materials that have some empirical support.

Finally, in the light of our wish to balance theory and practice, we conclude with a chapter on reading research (Chapter 5). Our aim here is to acquaint the reader with some of the methodology and constraints operating in the research area, by suggesting ways in which readers can construct and carry out their own research in the broad areas of theory, testing and teaching.

Notes

1. Rendell, R. (1977) *A Judgement in Stone.*
2. It is perhaps worth noting that, in our own society, highly literate adults will admit without embarrassment to not being able to 'read' music.
3. Wallace (1996) accepts this, suggesting that critical reading is one strategy available to the reader.

1

Preliminaries

What is reading?

We all know what reading is. And many of us have suffered, at some time or another, from the type of bore who stops any argument or discussion with 'Ah, it depends on what you mean by . . .'. So it is with some reluctance that we begin this part with an attempt to define reading, to say what we mean by the term. Our excuse is that people do use the term in different ways, and that while this may be permissible when everyone is conscious of the differences, on other occasions it can cause real confusion and difficulty.

Like Bernhardt (1991b) we approach the problem via dictionary definitions. *The Concise Oxford Dictionary* gives thirteen entries for the word *read*, of which twelve refer to the verb. Below we give, in an abbreviated form, the first three:

1. interpret mentally, declare interpretation or coming development of (*read dream, riddle, omen, men's hearts or thoughts or faces*);
2. (to be able to) convert into the intended words or meaning written or printed or other symbols or things expressed by such symbols . . . ; *reads or can read, hieroglyphics, shorthand, Braille, Morse, music* . . . ;
3. reproduce mentally or . . . vocally, while following their symbols, with eyes or fingers, the words of (author, book, letter, etc.); *read the letter over* . . .

We should say right away that none of these, or in fact any of the entries we mentioned, matches precisely our own definition of reading, which goes some way towards excusing our spending time on such definitions. That apart, for our purposes here, we can from now on reject definition 1 above. It is obviously a legitimate use in the English language of the verb *read*, but we are using the term in relationship to written texts, and so will not include uses like *reading dreams* in our definition. It is worth pointing out, however, that this first entry seems to focus on the use of the verb to mean something like *interpret*, which is an important aspect of text reading. Entry 3 looks as if it is largely confined to the activity often referred to as *decoding*, and will be discussed below. Entry 2 looks the most promising, but even here there is a problem. For reasons which will be discussed shortly, we will consider it appropriate to refer to *reading* hieroglyphics, or shorthand, Braille or Morse. However, we shall not use the term to include the reading of music, or, for example, maps, or mathematical symbols, etc. The reason for this apparently arbitrary decision rests on a prior definition of what is meant by *writing*.

In his book on writing systems, which will be referred to at several points in this chapter, Sampson (1985) finds it necessary to devote several pages to defining 'writing', just as we are having some difficulty defining 'reading'. One of the main difficulties facing Sampson is the fact that there exist written or printed symbols which would not normally be referred to as 'writing'. The international road sign for 'bridges ahead' is one example, as are the symbols distinguishing men's from women's toilets, and so on. Sampson distinguishes between *glottographic* symbols, which represent language, and *semasiographic* symbols, which do not. Thus the printed word *three* is glottographic: it actually represents the English word pronounced [θri:]. The figure *3*, on the other hand, is semasiographic. While it can be 'translated' by the English word three, it can also represent *trois*, or *drei*, or *tatu*, or words all meaning 'three' in any number of languages. Mathematical symbols, in fact, represent a very sophisticated semasiographic system, as does musical notation. Here we follow Sampson in not counting semasiographic systems as writing; hence the interpreting of messages in such systems will be considered as being outside the scope of reading proper. Reading, as used here, will mean dealing with **language messages in written or printed form**. That is why, when discussing the COD entries above, we accepted Braille, hieroglyphics and Morse as messages suitable for reading, but excluded music.

This restriction on the term may strike some of our readers as unduly narrow. From a practical point of view, for example, written messages often include semasiographic symbols, perhaps mathematical figures, or maps, and so on. 'Communicative' reading material often includes maps and time-tables, which the student reader is expected to process along with any written material. Surely it seems pedantic to say that someone *reads* a message until they come across a figure, at which point they stop *reading* and begin another activity? And if we don't *read* bus time-tables, what **do** we do with them?

However, there are good reasons for the restriction. Perhaps the most important, for our purposes, is that reading involves processing language messages, hence knowledge of language. We do not want to become embroiled in the controversy as to whether language competence is separate from, and, in its acquisition, quite different from other areas of competence such as mathematical knowledge. We would, however, consider it fairly uncontroversial that the process of reading, certainly above the level of decoding, makes demands on linguistic competence which are more immediate and more pervasive than appeals to other competence areas.

Secondly, in the classroom, a distinction between reading and other symbol-processing activities is made, even though it may not be made consciously. L1 primary school teachers, or EFL teachers, may incorporate semasiographic material in reading lessons, but they are not likely to think of themselves as teaching students how to *read*, for example, maps. The presence of maps, etc., in reading lessons is incidental to the main teaching focus, which is on how to read language messages. Neither of the present authors can *read* music, but neither found themselves in a remedial reading class, on that account at least.

Finally, our use of the term reading seems to agree with the non-technical, everyday use of the word. Faced with a questionnaire asking about hobbies, the person who gets a thrill out of perusing mathematical formulae is not likely, with that in mind, to respond with 'reading'. That answer is restricted to those who derive pleasure from newspapers, novels, history books, etc.

Before leaving this point, we need to clarify what we mean by *language*. After all, mathematics is often described as being a kind of language; but so is formal logic, and we often talk of computer languages. What we mean, here, however, by the term are languages such as French, Swahili, Mandarin and so on. Sampson refers to them as 'oral languages', but immediately has to qualify this by saying that an 'oral' language is not necessarily 'spoken', which seems rather confusing. We might refer to 'natural' languages, except that this term tends to be used to contrast languages such as French, Japanese, etc., with 'artificial' languages such as Esperanto. From our point of view, Esperanto is a language, just as English is, and can be read as such. Perhaps at this point we just have to rely on our readers' knowledge of the world, and assert that we are using the term 'language' to refer to French, Esperanto, etc., linguistic languages as it were, and not to mathematical or computer languages.

The fact that the information conveyed by a written message is encoded in language obviously has major pedagogical consequences. At the moment, we simply point out that for people learning to read in their native language, it is clearly relevant that they already know the language, or at least a significant part of it. As opposed to the learning of mathematics, that is, the learner does not need to learn both the conceptual system and the conventions of encoding it. And the fact that L1 learners of reading have this advantage is not affected by whether we take the pedagogical decision that 'all' they need to learn is to decode, or whether we decide to make use of previously acquired language knowledge in the process of learning to read.

As far as the L2 situation is concerned, the fact that reading involves processing language should perhaps make us a little sceptical of dichotomies, found in the literature (e.g. Alderson, 1984), as to whether L2 reading difficulties are 'reading' or 'language' problems. It may be difficult to distinguish the two. This question is addressed in more detail in Chapter 5.

Reading and language

The texts which we read, then, are language texts. So reading is involved with language texts. But what is the relationship between reading and language? Roughly speaking, there are two answers to this in the literature. The first defines reading as *decoding*, as Perfetti (1985) glosses it, 'the skill of transforming printed words into spoken words'. This decoding definition offers some good arguments. It delineates a restricted performance and allows a restricted set of processes to be examined. However, as Perfetti points out, it has limited popularity partly because it has limited application to the demands of actual reading. Moreover, it is not really feasible to view decoding as the initial process which is over by the time other cognitive linguistic processes begin. In one of the best-known papers on reading, Goodman (1967) argues that syntactic, semantic and pragmatic knowledge are involved in the decoding process. And this is the position of those advocating an interactive model of the reading process, discussed in Chapter 2.

Finally, a practical, commonsensical view of certain activities should persuade us that decoding cannot be equated with reading. Given the regularity of sound/letter correspondences in the spelling of Spanish, for example, it would be possible, if fairly pointless, to teach an English speaker who knows no Spanish to read aloud from a Spanish text with reasonably good pronunciation, but no comprehension. Few sensible people, however, would describe such an activity – sometimes referred to as 'barking at print' – as reading, even though activities resembling it are carried out under the guise of 'teaching reading' in many parts of the world. (In a seminar conducted by one of the authors, a British teacher remarked thoughtfully, 'I have a boy in my class who's a really good reader. The problem is he doesn't understand anything he reads.') We conclude that decoding must be an important part but not the whole of the reading process.

The second answer defines reading as the whole parcel of cognitive activities carried out by the reader in contact with a text. Thus Nuttall (1982), having considered definitions of reading in terms of reading aloud, or decoding, settles for the extraction of meaning from written messages. Similarly, Widdowson (1979) has defined reading as 'the process of getting linguistic information via print'. And Perfetti, as the alternative to a definition in terms of decoding, suggests that reading can be considered as thinking guided by print, with reading ability as skill at comprehension of text.

Perfetti's second definition, that reading is thinking guided by print, also has problems. Those who have trouble with reasoning or fail to learn from reading will be said to have reading problems. Clearly the difficulty here is one of establishing boundary lines, and being able to say, 'Up to here we have reading problems, beyond . . .'. The problem is present in an ambiguity in Widdowson's definition. One could say that 'linguistic information' was restricted to information about, say, syntax, morphology and lexis. Perhaps we can emend the definition to read 'information carried by linguistic messages via print'. The open-ended nature of what some people mean by reading is what Fries (1963) was commenting on, when he remarked, of 'broadly based' educational approaches to reading:

> But we should certainly confuse the issue if we insist that this use of reading in stimulating and cultivating the techniques of thinking, evaluating and so on, constitutes the reading process.

There is a real difficulty here, one that has resurfaced in recent years in the debate about 'reading skills/strategies' as opposed to 'language skills/strategies'. Here, however, in spite of the difficulties associated with defining reading in such an open-ended way, we consider reading to be a language activity, involving at some time or another all the cognitive processes related to language performance. Thus we consider that any valid account of the reading process must consider such cognitive aspects as reading strategies, inferencing, memory, relating text to background knowledge, as well as decoding, and obvious language aspects as syntax and lexical knowledge. In this respect, at least, we are in agreement with the proponents of 'critical reading', discussed briefly in the Introduction.

This would seem, in practice, to be the position most favoured by teachers and materials writers. Many reading textbooks, for example, contain practice in such cognitive activities as drawing conclusions on the evidence of written messages, making inferences, evaluating texts in terms of truth, persuasiveness, beauty, etc. It would be hard to find an EFL reading textbook which restricted activities to decoding. In fact, it is quite difficult to find one that includes any explicit material on decoding at all.

The same is true in the research area. In an editorial in the *Reading Research Quarterly* in 1980,[1] under the heading 'Why Comprehension?', the editors comment that an emphasis in the 1960s on decoding and early reading attracted much less attention in the 1970s, being replaced by an emphasis on comprehension.

This view can be substantiated by statistics: Figure 1.1 based on data from ERIC,[2] shows the number of articles and other publications, published between 1966 and 1996, which mention the term **reading** in their title, or in ERIC's index or abstract. The graph shows a rapid increase in such papers in the latter part of the 1970s, presumably reflecting a major increase in interest in reading. (It also, of course, shows a gradual decline from that peak, which we are unable to account for, although the very rapid decline after 1994 may have something to do with methods of data collection.)

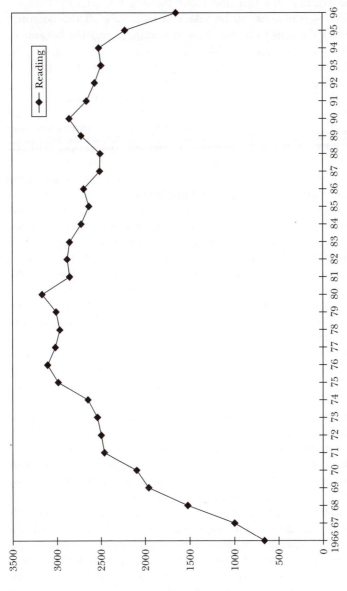

Figure 1.1 Number of articles and other publications published between 1966 and 1996 that mention 'reading' in their title or in ERIC's index or abstract (based on data from ERIC).

The rapid rise after 1966 is paralleled by a rise in interest in **comprehension**, as shown in Figure 1.2. It is likely, as is suggested by the editors, that with the move towards research in 'comprehension' – which has to be taken as including all the cognitive processes thought to be involved in reading – reading became of much wider interest than it had been when decoding was the main interest, becoming attractive to cognitive psychologists and psycholinguists, as well as educationalists.

All this having been said, there are occasions when we may wish to take reading as meaning decoding. When, for example, we say that someone can speak, but not read X language, then we by and large have in mind an inability to decode the script. With L1 learners in mind, Wardhaugh (1969) has justifiably criticised educators who confuse knowledge of the script with knowledge of the language, and make remarks to the effect that, for example, an L1 child does not know the difference between the short and long vowels in English, when in fact what they mean is that the learner does not yet know their spelling in the written language.[3]

This need not be interpreted, however, as meaning that reading is separate from language; rather that, in teaching reading, the teacher should keep in mind that a major component involved in the reading process is already available to the native-speaker and does not need to be taught (though the knowledge may need to be activated).

For the purpose of finalising our definition, we shall return to the Widdowson quotation above, that reading is 'the process of getting linguistic information via print'. While broadly agreeing with this, we want to modify it somewhat. First of all, by talking about 'getting information', Widdowson appears to imply that this is a fairly one-way process from writer or text to reader: 'Here is some information which I am passing on to you. Now take it.' Widdowson would not, of course, want to appear to be implying this, since he has been an important advocate of the view that the reader interprets and contributes to incoming messages. In order to avoid jargon such as 'interacting with written data', we shall settle for 'receiving and interpreting information'. Then there is the problem, already mentioned, of deciding on the limits of the information received. After all, some writers would consider 'linguistic information' to be limited to such items as 'X is the subject of the main clause'. We shall say that the information can be of any kind, but that it is encoded in language. Thus our definition has become:

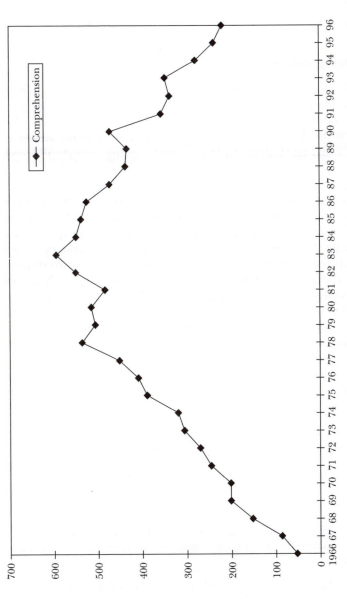

Figure 1.2 Number of articles and other publications published between 1966 and 1996 that mention 'comprehension' in their title or in ERIC's index or abstract (based on data from ERIC).

Reading is the process of receiving and interpreting information encoded in language form via the medium of print.

This may not be very neat but it suits our purposes.

Reading and listening

When, in an earlier section, we discussed decoding, we deliberately omitted one question: If reading consists of decoding, then what do we call the other linguistic processes which presumably follow the decoding stage? From one point of view, the answer to this would be 'Listening'. In this view, reading consists of decoding from written symbols to sounds; after that, presumably, 'normal' listening processes come into play, readers listening to themselves decoding. It is noticeable that Perfetti glosses decoding as 'transforming written words into *spoken* words'. Gough (1972) is another who seems to see the reading process as resulting in speech (see Chapter 2). (The COD definition 3 given above, however, which clearly refers to decoding, refers either to reproducing words mentally or orally, thus allowing for a non-spoken decoding.) Thus reading is seen as parasitic on listening – speech is 'the primary linguistic activity; reading a secondary, language-based skill' (Mattingly and Kavanagh, 1972). 'Language is speech, writing a secondary system – a mnemonic device reminding us of word sounds, intonation, rhythm, etc.' (Lefevre, 1964).

The alternative view, represented by, for example, Sticht (1972), is that speech and writing are alternative manifestations of language. Sticht cites Huey (1968):

> There do not exist two kinds of language comprehension – only one holistic ability to comprehend by language.

And in spite of the fact that, as pointed out earlier, Fries wanted to reserve the term 'reading' for the decoding process, he appears to take a similar view:

> Learning to read is a process of transfer from auditory signals to visual ones. The language signals are the same for both talking and reading.

It should be noted that by this remark, Fries does not mean that the visual signals 'represent' auditory ones, rather that the same set of contrasts is made by both sets of signals.

It is interesting to speculate on what hypotheses follow on from these two contrasting positions. If one adopts View 1, that reading is parasitic on listening, then presumably:

(a) Deaf children would not learn to read. Mattingly and Kavanagh (1972) say they learn very slowly. Rayner and Pollatsek (1989) agree on the whole, but admit that some deaf children do learn to read well. Holcomb and Peyton (1992) claim that most deaf children read at third or fourth grade level. Padden (1990) concedes that deaf children have difficulty learning to read and write, but claims that deaf children from middle-class, educated deaf families perform 'consistently well' in reading and writing. There would thus appear to be a marked social factor in success or failure to read. Attitudes to language also seem to be important. Ramsey (1990) points out that deaf adults 'greatly value ASL (American Sign Language) as a marker of group identity and share a certain proprietary feeling about the mode of signing itself'. We have already mentioned the importance many writers attach to the role of reading in socialisation. Rayner and Pollatsek (1989: 210) note that 'second generation profoundly deaf readers seem to consult their native language (ASL) when reading English'. Cangiano (1992) is one of a number of writers who considers the problem of deaf children learning to read English as an aspect of L2 reading. Clearly the whole area is complex, involving factors in the home, attitudes to the L1 and L2, and aspects of L2 acquisition. It seems clear to us that reports from the area do not support the view that reading is inevitably guided by phonological factors.

(b) At all stages of language learning, both for L1 and L2 speakers, listening would have to precede reading. Menyuk (1984), for example, appears to believe that if a child cannot understand a construction in oral form, then that child will not be able to comprehend it in written form. In EFL contexts, reading instruction would invariably have to follow a course of oral language learning.

(c) All other things being equal, listening would presumably be faster than reading, since reading speed would equal listening speed plus decoding time.

If, on the other hand, one adopts the view that listening and reading are parallel activities, then:

(a) Deaf children might be slow to learn, lacking as they do important sources of data. But once they had learned, their reading might equal or surpass that of non-deaf children. (This seems sometimes to be the case, though rarely; see above.)

(b) For the L1 learner, listening, and learning through listening, would normally precede reading in the early stages, but after reading began, a great deal of language learning – lexis, syntax, rhetorical organisation – would be accomplished via reading. This fits with the commonly expressed view that we acquire a large part of our adult lexicon via the written language. We would suggest that we also acquire much of our knowledge of complex grammatical structure via the written language.

(c) An L2 reading course would not necessarily need to be preceded by an oral course. A 'reading to learn language' stage would precede a 'reading to learn' stage.

(d) It is doubtful whether any hypothesis can be formed about the relative speed of listening and reading (although see below).

It ought to be obvious that this question is not of purely theoretical interest, but is of real practical concern to those engaged in, for example, designing language courses. For this reason, we shall examine the problem further in the following sections.

The primacy of spoken language

There seems little doubt that the position of those who consider reading a secondary process has in the past been reinforced by the assertion, virtually an axiom in linguistics, that spoken language is primary. Spoken language, the textbooks tell us, is primary both *phylogenetically* and *ontogenetically*, i.e. speech preceded writing in the history of the human species, and for the normal individual child, speech also comes first. This is unquestionably true, and no one nowadays would dispute it. But as Sampson points out, linguists adopted this position in a programmatic way; that is, speech was the aspect of language that linguists were *supposed* to study. And one of the reasons for adopting the position was as a reaction against a previously dominant view that written language represented the correct form, as opposed to debased, or 'careless' speech forms. As part of this reaction, written language was held to be derivative, and not worthy of study.

From a strictly theoretical point of view, this attitude is at least unnecessary. De Saussure drew a distinction in language between *form* and *substance*. By *form* he meant the whole structure of relationships, both contrasts and equivalences, inside the language; one of the meanings of *substance* is the medium in which the form is realised. Just as, in de Saussure's well-known analogy with chess, the game can be played with pieces composed of any number of materials or shapes, so language can be 'realised' by different media, in our case by either sounds (spoken language), or shapes (written language). The implication of this argument is that written language can be seen as a realisation of a language parallel to the spoken form. For de Saussure, language was basically **form**; the substance in which the form was realised was immaterial. Based on this distinction, Lyons (1968: 60–1) argues that:

> When we say that [t] is in correspondence with *t*, [e] with *e*, and in general that a particular sound is in correspondence with a particular letter, and *vice versa*, we can interpret this to mean that neither the sounds nor the letters are primary, but that they are both alternative realizations of the same formal units, which of themselves are quite abstract elements, independent of the substance in which they are realized.

Making the same point, Sampson (1980) remarks:

> After all, English is still English whether we realise it as spoken sounds or as ink on paper.

Whether linguists did, in fact, obey the injunction to restrict themselves to spoken language is doubtful. Brown and Yule (1983) remark that the language in descriptive linguistic grammars is often characteristic of the written form. And Lyons (1968) remarks that in a highly literate society, linguists find it difficult to view spoken language objectively.

Apart from this, however, the long-standing linguistic prejudice against written language has recently been eroded. Sampson is one linguist who considers that written language is a proper area of study for linguistics. For him the written and spoken languages are two 'closely related dialects', and the influence of one dialect on the other is not one-way. In an article provocatively titled 'The primacy of writing', Householder (1971) claims that the written language 'has probably been the greatest single cause of phonological change in modern English, both British and American'. It is likely that a considerable amount of the vocabulary, syntax and knowledge of rhetorical structure of a mature native speaker is learned via the written language.

If this was simply a dispute within linguistics, then it would not matter to us here. The study of reading may borrow from linguistics, but does not belong to the area. The linguistic argument as to relative primacy is in one sense irrelevant. From the point of view of a language user at a particular point in time, it is ridiculous to argue that speech is always primary. If we meet a neighbour and exchange greetings, we choose speech; anything else would be strange. On the other hand, when we set out to complete an income tax return, we are more or less obliged to resort to the written language – a failure to complete the form on the basis that written language was secondary would not be treated with much sympathy.

For the purposes of this book, we assume that written and spoken language are parallel realisations of language. This is not to deny that, at least for the native speaker, learning to read will normally involve a transfer from the spoken language to the written language. But we are not bound to believe that the written language, and hence reading, remains parasitical on the spoken form.

We have not, however, answered the question as to whether the reader, when performing, is dependent on spoken language. To some extent, linguists are not well qualified to decide on this question. Linguistics describes language systems. If the systems are different, then linguists are well qualified to describe the difference. However, reading is a process, involving mental activity. Linguists are not professionally equipped to make judgements about such processes, although they are as entitled as anyone else to venture opinions. Thus the view, derived from linguistic theory, that a written language could exist parallel to a spoken language as a separate realisation of the same underlying language system simply allows us to say that such a situation could happen, that is, that users could use written language independently of the oral language. It does not entitle us to claim that users do actually do this, or even that it is practically possible. Thus we are left with the possibility that readers could be 'translating' into the spoken language as they read, as those who push the claims of 'vocalisation' have asserted.

The debate has taken place in terms of a suggested opposition between a direct and a phonological route to word recognition (see Chapter 2). The reader using a direct route is envisaged as going straight from written word to meaning, without an intervening 'spoken' stage. When using a phonological route, the reader is seen as going from the written word to its spoken pronunciation, using phoneme/grapheme correspondences, and finally to meaning. In the pedagogical literature, the distinction can be seen in the difference between the *look and say* method of initial reading and *phonic* approaches.

It might at first seem easy to decide whether readers use direct or phonological routes. One may argue that if the readers can be shown to vocalise while reading, then they are using the phonological route. However, things, as often, are not so simple. Rayner and Pollatsek (1989) distinguish between 'subvocalization' (muscular activity in the speech tract) and 'inner speech' (the 'voice' we hear in our heads while reading). They conclude from the experimental data that subvocalisation is 'a normal part of natural silent reading' (p. 192). However they point out that its function is obscure. They are more interested in the phenomenon of inner speech, but this is a more mysterious entity, and its function is controversial. One might argue that since some L2 readers may not know how to pronounce certain words, they are precluded from phonological access. However, a little thought should show that this is an unjustified conclusion as they may be using a non-native pronunciation.[4] We return to this topic in rather more detail in Chapter 2.

Some light may be thrown on the problem by an examination of different writing systems, both alphabetic and other, which we touch on next. The discussion should be of value in two other respects: statements about reading by European authors often imply the use of an alphabetic system of writing. We need to be warned against such Eurocentrism. Also, the discussion should remind us of a possibly important factor to be taken into account when we discuss the diversity of L2 readers.

Writing systems

The account given here is based on Sampson (1985), and we use his terminology. In particular, we use the term *graph* to refer to any sign in a writing system, e.g. for alphabetic letters and for Chinese 'characters'.

Sampson divides scripts into two major types. In *logographic* scripts, of which his main example is the Chinese writing system, a graph relates to a meaning unit, either a word or morpheme (in Chinese, according to Sampson, the distinction between word and morpheme is not clear, and symbols largely refer to morphemes). It is as if, in English a single symbol, say **C**, represented the word/ morpheme *cat*, and another symbol, say **M**, represented the word/ morpheme *mat*.[5]

Phonographic scripts, on the other hand, rely on analysing language at the sound level. Included under phonographic scripts are *syllabic, consonantal, alphabetic* and *featural* scripts. In syllabic scripts, a graph represents a syllable. In English, *mat* would be spelled with one symbol, but *matted* would require two. Teachers who instruct children that the sequence cat 'spells /kə/, /a/, /tə/ ' could be said to be converting English spelling into a syllabic script. In a system of astonishing complexity, Japanese uses two syllabaries, *hiragana* and *katakana*, to supplement a logographic script, *kanji*, derived from Chinese writing.

In *consonantal* scripts, of which Arabic and Hebrew are two important modern examples, the syllabic sound unit is segmented, but only consonants are systematically represented. It is as if in English, *mftkl* spelled *emphatically*. The system suits Semitic languages such as Arabic, where vowels are largely predictable from the grammar, but would give clear problems in English.

In *alphabetic* systems, such as the ones familiar to readers of English and other European languages, both vowels and consonants are represented. Finally, in what Sampson terms *featural* systems, the symbols represent phonological features. In English, for example, the symbols **k** and **g** represent velar plosives distinguished phonologically by the fact that the first is voiceless and the second voiced. We could move English spelling in the direction of a featural system if, say, we spelled the sounds /k/ and /g/ with one graph, but represented the presence of voicing by underlining. Thus /k/ would be represented by the graph **k**, and /g/ by the graph **k̠**. Similarly **t** could represent the phoneme /t/ and **t̠** represent /d/. Sampson gives two examples of featural systems, Pitman's shorthand, and Han'gul, devised, in a remarkable feat of linguistic analysis, by a fifteenth-century Korean, and used as a national script by both present Korean republics.

For the purposes of the argument here, the most significant point is that logographic scripts do not rely on an analysis of the sounds of words. Thus, according to Sampson, Chinese script was composed originally of graphs which each represented a word/morpheme. At this stage, there was no generalised relationship between graph and sound. The system was extended according to the *rebus* principle, whereby a graph for a word could also be used for another word with the same or similar pronunciation. In English, using this system, a graph representing 'eye' could also be used for the pronoun 'I'. This *does* introduce a phonetic element into the system, though not in any systematic way. The rebus principle, however, has limitations. Chinese contains, by the standards of European languages, an astonishing number of homophones (words with the same pronunciation).[6] It is as if English had, say, twelve words all pronounced the same as 'eye'. In order to reduce ambiguity, the system was again extended to include complex graphs. These are composed of at least two elements, one of which Sampson calls a *phonetic*, and the other a *signific* (other writers use the terms classifier, or radical, for signific). The phonetic hints at pronunciation, the signific at semantic value. If we try to construct an English analogy, we might think of a graph, say M, representing the word *meet*. Then, by the rebus principle, this can be extended to represent both *meat* and the archaic adjective *mete*, which are all homophones. Our graph now represents any of three homophones. We can reduce ambiguity by producing a complex graph. By incorporating a signific f, meaning, say, *food*, we can produce a complex graph M_f which is interpreted as meaning 'sounds like *meet* but has to do with food'. Similarly, having already a graph representing the word *flower*, say F, we can write F_f to indicate 'sounds like *flower* but has to do with food', i.e. *flour*.

So far, it might look as if Chinese graphs were essentially phonographic, but Sampson denies this on two grounds. Firstly, the pronunciation of Chinese has changed radically since the 'spelling' was stabilised; secondly, the sound correspondence between the original phonetic and the secondary complex graph was not always close. To take another example, it is as if in English we had M (= *meet*) plus a signific c indicating *clothing*, giving us the graph M_c for *mitt*. The result is, as Sampson (1985: 157) says,

A Chinese-speaker who learns to read and write essentially has to learn the graphs case by case; both significs and phonetics will give him many hints and clues to help him remember, but the information they supply is far too patchy and unreliable to enable him to predict what the graph for a given spoken word will be, or even which spoken word will correspond to a graph that he encounters for the first time.

It has to be said that Sampson's account has been vehemently criticised by DeFrancis (1984) and by Unger and DeFrancis (1995). They claim that 66 per cent of the graphs used in Mandarin contain enough phonetic indicators to enable a reader to make a good guess at the syllable (this figure being based on an analysis carried out in 1942). They thus claim that Chinese script is basically a rather odd syllabary. They back this up with the claim that learning thousands of logograms would be equivalent to learning thousands of telephone numbers.

To some extent the argument is academic; Sampson does not argue that the system is purely logographic, merely that it is not primarily phonographic. We are, however, rather dubious about some of DeFrancis and Unger's arguments. Any empirical experiment devised to test the phonological readability of graphs would be bafflingly difficult to set up. The subjects would have to be literate readers of Chinese, for which a knowledge of 5000 graphs is often suggested as minimal. On the other hand, the graphs they were shown would have to be unfamiliar to them, otherwise the subjects' evidence would be hopelessly unreliable. Therefore we are justified in doubting the statistics cited by DeFrancis and Unger.[7] As opposed to telephone numbers, Chinese graphs contain a certain amount of iconic information (i.e. some of them are recognisable in picture terms), and semantic information (the significs). Moreover, even if the phonetic information were as important in Chinese reading as Unger and DeFrancis say, it is difficult to see how it would remain important when the same graphs are used to write Japanese, a totally different language. Sampson's main response to earlier criticism by DeFrancis (Sampson, 1994) is that DeFrancis fails to distinguish between the historical origin of a linguistic system and the nature of the system as it exists at the present.

However, we are not in a position to make a real judgement on the issue. It is one of these areas in which empirical evidence is crucial yet seems difficult to collect. We think that there is enough force in Sampson's case to suggest that Chinese and Japanese readers – a large section of the world's literate population – are likely on many occasions to make use of direct access to lexical items. This at least should make us cautious about making Eurocentric generalisations on the nature of reading, based on our experience with an alphabet. As Sampson says (1985: 146):

> The European idea that from a knowledge of the pronunciation of a word one should be able to make at least a good guess at how to write it would seem bizarre to a Chinese.

In fact, what would appear to be the situation in Chinese reading is often very strange, if not bizarre, to a European reader. According to Sampson, because of the differences between the written and spoken languages, a Chinese script can be read aloud but may very well be incomprehensible as a spoken text.

But we can go further than this. Sampson is not the first to argue that, for adult readers of English at least, words are treated as logograms. It has been argued that English orthography is so irregular in its grapheme/phoneme correspondence that it virtually forces readers to use a direct lexical access route. But we should not assume, even if the correspondence is very regular, as in Spanish, that experienced readers will rely on decoding phonologically. It may well be that while this is a useful device for the learner, it becomes increasingly discarded the more advanced the reader becomes.

In this book we shall assume the possibility that both direct and phonological routes may be open to a reader of English, as well as combinations of the two.

Reading versus listening

We have already mentioned the possible relationship between reading and listening. It is obvious that they are likely to be very similar language activities. Once we get past the decoding phase of the reading process, much of what can be said about reading in terms of the reader trying to make sense of the message by relating it to background knowledge, etc., can also be said about listening (and vice versa). Kintsch and van Dijk (1978: 364) consider that their model of reading applies to listening as well.

However, these similarities, while of huge importance, can be overstressed. There are also considerable differences between the two activities, separate from, but related to, the difference in the substance in which the linguistic form is encoded (Rost, 1990).

The most obvious difference between reading and listening is, of course, the fact that the input in the listening situation is sound, whereas that in the reading situation is verbal shapes, writing. Less obviously, the sound is 'raw' data, which has to be structured by the listener. The verbal message which has to be read is linguistically structured; it has already been analysed. Hence the interesting suggestion by Mattingly, among others, that linguistic awareness is a prerequisite for efficient reading.

In addition, there are the linguistic differences between the two dialects mentioned by Sampson. Some of these may not seem to be very important. The fact that *moreover* is more common in writing than it is in speech is not likely to give a competent native speaker much cause for alarm. Differences like this, moreover, are more likely to occur in certain types of text, e.g. academic texts like the present one. A more important difference might seem to be the greater degree of syntactic complexity found in written texts of certain types. Not only is there a whole range of structures which are more common in writing than in speech (and vice versa), but in writing there is likely to be far more embedding than in the comparatively simple structures of conversational English. On the other hand, for the foreign listener, the incomplete structures of spoken English may give at least equal difficulty.

Probably of more importance than any of this, however, are what might be called the contextual, or situational, differences between listening and reading. In listening, intonation patterns are available, as are facial expressions of the speaker. Feedback is immediately available, and the listener can generally ask for clarification (in this respect, as in others, formal lectures are more similar to written texts than to conversation).

The reader, while lacking these props, has available the possibility of stopping the inflow of information at any point desired, while he cogitates or takes notes. He can move forward in the text skimming in order to get an idea of what problems are likely to be encountered, or can 'regress' to reread a point which is either puzzling or perhaps particularly meaningful, or even amusing. (Regression was condemned by specialists in 'faster reading'; however, while it may be bad practice if allowed to become a habit, it is a practice in which we all indulge, probably to our advantage.)

It is true that many of these tactics can be paralleled to some extent by a listener equipped with a tape-recorder. However, fast-forward skimming is not as easy with a tape as it is with printed material. Nor is locating a required passage. And while the average tape-recorder is, of course, capable of repeating part of a message, it cannot easily be slowed down significantly without distortion, while the reading process can be slowed almost infinitely at the control of the reader.

It has often been claimed that reading is potentially much faster than listening, tied as the latter is to the speed of normal speech. Sticht (1984), however, has denied this, using evidence from experimental work using speeded-up but non-distorted speech to argue that there is a maximal speed for both reading and listening, which he estimates as c. 250–300 wpm. However, the number of variables involved in such experiments, the different functions of spoken and written language, and the different tasks they imply, should make us cautious of accepting these results. If valid, they are evidence for the essential sameness of listening and reading.

The L2 reader

Bernhardt (1991b), who distinguishes between already literate and non-literate L2 learners, is one of the few writers who does not treat L2 readers as a homogeneous group. The number of variables to be kept in mind may be very large, including the following:

(a) literacy in the L1: as Bernhardt points out, some readers may be literate in their L1, others may not;

(b) the experience of previously acquired languages (and literacies): some Arabic readers, for example, may approach English as an L2; others may already be highly literate in another language, e.g. French, so that English may become an L3, or L4;

(c) the linguistic relationship between L1 and L2: English and French, for example, are comparatively similar in many respects; English and Turkish are markedly less so;

(d) cultural relationships: readers of English as an L2 from Western Europe are likely to bring far more shared knowledge to English texts than are readers from other cultures;

(e) the script of L1 and L2: English and Swahili are written in the same alphabet; English and Greek are written in different alphabets; Chinese is written in a script which at least tends to the logographic.

If we assume that reading is more or less the 'same' activity in all languages, we shall not pay much attention to such variables. If, however, we consider that reading is a language activity, involving at some levels at least factors specific to a particular language, then these variables, and others, are likely to be given more prominence. Their potential presence should at least make us wary about postulating generalised 'L2 reading processes'.

Summary

In this chapter we have tried to deal with a number of possibly contentious issues. We have argued that reading is a language skill, an aspect of language performance. It follows that level of performance is one aspect of a person's ability to use the language. We have presented the distinction between reading as decoding and reading as message interpretation, and come down conventionally enough on the side of the second view. Somewhat more controversially, we have suggested that reading ability must go beyond 'pure' language skills, and include pragmatic knowledge and skills, whereby the readers interpret the text in terms of their knowledge of the world. Finally, we have pointed out the similarities between reading and listening, both of which are receptive language skills, and taken the position that reading is not necessarily dependent on listening, but may be a parallel mode of language reception, with implications for models of the reading process: activity.

Notes

1. *Reading Research Quarterly*, **XV**, 2.
2. We should like to thank Ted Brandhorst of ERIC for his help in compiling this data.
3. Some years ago *The Guardian* published an article on remedial reading. Discussing her experiences teaching a 10-year-old native speaker, one 'reading expert' remarked: 'So I taught him the word "me".' One would have imagined that most native speakers know the word 'me' by that age; what they don't know is its visual representation.

4. The eastern academic who referred in a lecture to 'ospices deeties' knew perfectly well what he meant. His British audience took some time to work out that the phrase represented 'auspicious deities'.

5. It is arguable that in a language such as English, numerals are logograms rather than semasiograms. That is, the word 'three' is in a one-to-one relationship to the symbol '3', which thus represents a linguistic word rather than a non-linguistic concept. The fact that '3' in French represents a different word, 'trois', is of no relevance to English. However, symbols such as '+' are clearly semasiographic: the string '3+3' could be translated into English as 'three plus three', 'three and three', 'adding three and three' and so on.

6. One of the authors was told that a Chinese student called 'Yang' was due to join a forthcoming course, and that 'yang' in Mandarin meant 'sheep'. When he asked another Chinese student, a university lecturer, whether this translation was accurate, he was surprised to get the answer, 'I don't know'. It emerged that 'yang' has about 10 or 12 meanings, so that without the appropriate Chinese graph, the particular meaning intended cannot be decided on.

7. Sampson (1994) doubts the statistics for another reason, namely that the appropriateness of the phonetic element to a graph's pronunciation cannot be measured statistically.

2

The theory of reading

2.1 MODELS

Reading can clearly be viewed as a cognitive activity; it largely takes place in the mind, and the physical manifestations of the activity, eye movements, subvocalisation, etc., are comparatively superficial. As a cognitive activity, reading has, since the 1960s, been a major interest of cognitive psychologists. In fact, the huge increase in articles cited in ERIC, which took place in the 1960s, is probably brought about to a major extent by psychology research. In this section we begin by looking at some of the psychological work which we consider to be relevant to our main themes.

Cognitive psychologists who are interested in reading construct and test hypothetical models of the reading process as it is thought to take place in the human mind. Some of these models are in outline familiar to many teachers of reading: the bottom-up and top-down models have achieved some fame in the teaching world since the 1970s, as has the later development, the interactive-compensatory model. These will be examined in some detail below. The first two of these models have inspired recognizable methodological approaches; the third has, perhaps, yet to make its mark.

In fact, the contribution of the cognitive psychologists to L2 reading has been a major one, and would in itself be justification for a review in this chapter. In addition, these psychologists provide an admirable example of how to formulate and test empirical hypotheses, activities which have not always been the strong point of L2 reading. In this chapter, there is not enough space to give a full account of the experimental methods involved – a number of which will be examined in Chapter 5. We hope, however, that we have included enough in this part to indicate how hypotheses are tested.

When one sets out to examine a factor possibly involved in reading performance – for example, grammatical knowledge, or knowledge of the world – there are basically two questions to ask. The first is whether it can be shown that the factor does have a measurable effect on reading performance. Once that has been established, one can then ask in what precise way the factor operates. It is our impression that researchers in L2 reading have largely been content with examining the first question, and that for determined attempts to answer the second question we must turn to the psychologists.

That having been said, the psychologists cannot be expected to answer all our problems. They tend to be at their most convincing when reporting work on what are often labelled 'low level' activities, e.g. word recognition, and not to have a great deal of empirical data on 'higher level' activities, such as comprehension of extended text. Then again they have their own professional interests which are not likely to be identical to those of teachers and testers of reading.

An example of the sort of explanation psychologists look for may make this clear. Stanovich (1980), well known for his formulation of the 'interactive-compensatory model', reports that adults and children faced with the task of naming a target word, were faster when the word was preceded by an incomplete sentence congruent with it (so that, presumably, the completed sentence made sense). However, the children's performance was badly affected when the target word was preceded by a non-congruent sentence. Adults, on the other hand, showed no difference in the time they took in this second condition from the time when the word was presented out of context. Stanovich suggests that these results may be explained by a theory which postulates that there are two processes acting, an **automatic activation** process and a **conscious attention** mechanism. Faced with such a discussion, the L2 researcher may be tempted to think that, whatever the validity of the theory, it has little to offer the teacher or tester of L2 reading. Such a reaction may be unwise, but the example should remind us that, however grateful we are to the psychologists, we must constantly assess their work for its relevance.

Classes of reading model

It is useful to distinguish between two different classes of model. In the first type, of which the models of Gough (1972), Just and Carpenter (1987) and Rayner and Pollatsek (1989) are examples, an attempt is made to model the actual process of reading. This sort of model may include descriptions of how words are recognised, how long they are kept in working memory, when syntactic processing begins, and so on. We call these **process** models. In contrast, **componential** models merely describe what components are thought to be involved in the reading process, with little or no attempt to say how they interact, or how the reading process actually develops in time. To return to the distinction mentioned above, componential models limit themselves to arguing that such and such a factor is actually present in the process, whereas process models attempt to describe how the factor operates. It might appear that process models are more desirable; certainly they might seem braver. However, there is an argument that for the reading process as a whole, the design of process models may be premature, and that we should, perhaps, restrict ourselves to componential ones. We think both are valuable.

We begin below with an account of the better-known process models, before moving to an account of componential models.

Process models

Process models may be **sequential**, that is, they model the reading process as a series of stages, each of which is complete before the next stage begins. Alternatively, they are non-sequential, as in the case of Stanovich's interactive-compensatory model, where 'a pattern is synthesised based on information provided *simultaneously* from several sources' (Stanovich, 1980: 35).

The popular view of the development of process models, which turns up in many article introductions and innumerable PhDs, goes roughly as follows. First of all came the bottom-up approach, which was then replaced by the top-down model, which in turn was replaced by interactive models. In fact, the most frequently cited example of a bottom-up model, that of Gough, was published in 1972, whereas the corresponding most frequently cited example of a so-called top-down theory, that of Goodman, was first published in 1967. On the evidence of this paper, Goodman was reacting, not against a psychological model, but against a pedagogical approach to the teaching of initial reading. More seriously, although Goodman is usually cited as a top-down theorist, there is a good argument that his theory is an interactive one. Most serious of all, while the name 'top-down' suggests the reverse of a bottom-up model, no such top-down model exists, nor does it seem likely that it could ever exist. Finally, while we are all interactive theorists now, the general impression given by some is that a bottom-up approach, with some modifications, has won the day, e.g. 'while all reading may not be characterised as a data driven, bottom-up process, fluent reading may best be characterised as just such a process' (Hoover and Tunmer, 1993: 4). It is worth keeping in mind that, while this may well be true of word recognition, and less certainly of syntactic processing, it is certainly not proved to be the case for other aspects of the reading process.

Bottom-up approaches

Bottom-up analyses begin with the stimulus, i.e. the text, or bits of the text. In Gough's (1972) model, the reader begins with letters, which are recognized by a SCANNER. The information thus gained is passed to a DECODER, which converts the string of letters into a string of systematic phonemes. This string is then passed to a LIBRARIAN, where with the help of the LEXICON, it is recognized as a word. The reader then fixates on the next word, and proceeds in the same way until all the words in a sentence have been processed, at which point they proceed to a component called MERLIN, in which syntactic and semantic rules operate to assign a meaning to the sentence. We should point out that this is only part of the model. The final stage is that of the *Vocal System*, where the reader utters orally what has first been accessed through print. Gough's model of the reading process is a model of the **reading aloud** process.

We should note that in a model like Gough's, there are two sets of entities. First there are text units, arranged more or less in order of size – that is, the model envisages the reader dealing with *letters*, *words*, then *sentences*, in that order.[1] This in itself would entitle it to the term 'bottom-up'. In addition, though, there are the processing components, in Gough's case the scanner, decoder, librarian, then 'Merlin', which are brought to bear on the text units. More generally, such knowledge/skills components as letter recognition, lexical access, syntactic parsing, semantic parsing, are frequently ranked in the literature as 'lower' or 'higher' skills – usually, it seems, because of the text components they relate to. In Gough's model, textual and processing components operate in parallel, but this, as we shall see, is not absolutely necessary.

As Rayner and Pollatsek (1989) point out, Gough's model is explicit enough to be tested at various points, with the result that the straightforward bottom-up direction has had to be emended. For example, in the original model, the letters were seen as being fed serially into the scanner for recognition. If this were true, then a word should take longer to recognize than a single letter. But in fact experiments have shown that this is not the case: words can be recognized more quickly than individual letters, and even pseudo-words can be recognized at the same speed as single letters. It appears, then, that at the word-recognition stage, letters are processed in parallel. More importantly for the debate about the direction of processing, readers have been shown to use syntactic information to deal with ambiguous words. And Kolers (1969) found that bilingual readers, reading part French, part English texts aloud, pronounced words as they would be in the 'predominant text language', e.g. 'murs' might be read as 'moors'. Thus it appears that 'higher level' information is being used in word recognition, which conflicts with the unidirectionality of the model.

It is also difficult to see how, as is claimed, one stage of the process is over before the next stage begins. If all the words in a sentence had to be recognised before syntactic processing began, then the model would not appear to have any way of knowing when to stop processing words and move to processing sentences. With words, there seem to be few problems: not only is a word indicated by white space on either side, but it will, if all goes well, be present for recognition in the lexicon. With sentences, however, there is no real equivalent of the lexicon, and it is hard to believe that the reader is entirely dependent on the clues provided by stops and capital letters.[2] On the other hand, if words are accessed one at a time and fed into the syntactic processor once recognised, then recognition and syntactic processing are surely going on at the same time.

Top-down approaches

If, with bottom-up models, it is difficult to see when to stop, with top-down models, the difficulty is seeing where they should begin. Bottom-up models start with the smallest text unit, either letters or letter features. One might expect, then, that top-down models should begin with the largest unit, the whole text. However, it is virtually impossible to see how a reader can begin by dealing with the text as a whole, then proceed to smaller units of the text, say paragraphs, then down to individual sentences, ending with single letters. In fact, the term 'top-down' is deceptive, appearing to offer a neat converse to 'bottom up', a converse which in reality does not exist.

In practice, the term is used to refer to approaches in which the expectations of the reader play a crucial, even dominant, role in the processing of the text. The reader is seen as bringing hypotheses to bear on the text, and using the text data to confirm or deny the hypotheses. The scope of a hypothesis varies considerably. In the account by Goodman (1967), possibly the best-known name associated (perhaps wrongly) with top-down approaches, the hypotheses relate largely to single words. In the applied linguistic and L2 literature, the hypothesis may relate to the whole text, and be generated by reference to supposed schemata. Given the somewhat misleading nature of the term 'top-down', we suggest that the related terms 'text(or data)-driven' and 'reader-driven' are more generally useful when describing the contrast between 'bottom-up' and 'top-down'. In the first, the reader processes the text word for word, accepting the author as the authority. In the second, the reader comes to the text with a previously formed plan, and perhaps omits chunks of the text which seem to be irrelevant to the reader's purpose.

Goodman is often cited as the representative of the top-down approach, though he himself has denied the association, and it is arguable that Frank Smith (1971, 1973) is the more appropriate choice. As is well known, Goodman views reading as a process of hypothesis verification, whereby the readers use selected data from the text to confirm their guesses. Judging by the 1967 paper, it appears that he developed his position as a reaction, not against theorists like Gough, but against a pedagogic tradition, which stressed a fairly strict bottom-up approach to the teaching of reading to young native speakers. Goodman characterizes this approach as viewing reading as 'precise, sequential identification', with the consequence that children should be made to be more careful in their identification first of letters, then of words. From his work with young native speakers (in the 1967 paper, one of the subjects is definitely L1, the other appears to be bilingual), Goodman concluded that this view of reading was wrong, that rather than painstakingly going from letter to letter, word to word, readers in fact sampled the text, employing text redundancy to reduce the amount of data needed and using their language knowledge (syntax and semantics) to guide their guesses. His model of reading, then, sees the reader as (1) scanning a line of text and fixating at a point on the line; (2) picking up graphic cues guided by constraints set up through prior choices, his language knowledge, his cognitive styles, and strategies he has learned (p. 270); (3) forming an image which is 'partly what he sees and partly what he expected to see', then making a tentative choice (presumably as to the identity of the word).

It can be seen from the description above that Goodman's model is top-down, to the extent that readers' expectations are seen as being brought to the text, i.e. the model is reader-driven. Secondly, the reading process is seen as cyclical, the reader moving from hypothesis to text to hypothesis, and so on.

The popularity and influence of Goodman's first paper was probably due to a number of reasons. First, it offered an alternative to what might be seen as the grind of moving from letter to letter, word to word. Learning reading became a more exciting business. Secondly, it fitted what Chomsky (1965) was saying at the time about human language users imposing existing 'rules' or expectations on 'degenerate' data. Finally, it meshed well with, although probably pre-dated, notions which became commonplace about texts always being incomplete and being completed by the readers by referring to their background knowledge.

The importance which Goodman attributes to hypothesis formation and sampling has had a considerable influence on L2 reading theory: see, for example, Hosenfeld's claim that the good reader is a good guesser (e.g. Hosenfeld, 1984). It is also the aspect which has turned out to be most vulnerable. One criticism comes from studies of eye movements; Rayner and Pollatsek (1989) point out that fixations occur on the majority of the words in a text. While this is only indirect evidence of the process of reading, it does not conform easily to Goodman's claims that only part of the text was sampled. But perhaps the most damaging criticism concerns the claim by Goodman, Smith and other writers that good readers guess more, and use the context more than poorer readers. A great deal of work has shown, quite conclusively, that while **all** readers use context, good readers are less dependent on it than poor ones. In fact, it has been shown that what distinguishes good from poor readers, at least among young populations, is the ability of the members of the first group to decode rapidly and accurately.

Goodman found that his young subject read words in a supposedly 'difficult' text which she failed on when she encountered them in a more or less meaningless, phonics-focused text. At other times, he claimed that readers read (i.e. recognized words more accurately) when faced with the words in a real text than when the same words were met in a list. However, when Nicholson (1993a) tested these claims with quite large groups of children, the results did not seem to support Goodman's position. While the results are not always clear cut, it seems that it was the poor and average readers who benefited from contexts; older and better readers seem to have been mainly affected by a practice affect, in that they made fewer errors on the second presentation, whether it was a list or a text (Nicholson is not clear as to how much time was allowed between the two trials). In fact it is virtually accepted in psychology nowadays that, at least at the level of word recognition and lexical access, some form of bottom-up process is followed.

In spite of this, as has been said above, the assertion by some that good readers use a bottom-up approach is only really proven for word recognition. Nicholson, as described above, only partially succeeded in contradicting Goodman's findings, and it is not easy to see how a bottom-up approach can account for Goodman's original data. It is possible that his model is more appropriate for L2 readers at certain stages of development than it is for skilled adult L1 readers. Goodman has also been more careful than some writers in distinguishing between reception and production.

Interactive approaches

Bottom-up models are sequential, in that one stage is completed before another is begun. In interactive models – one of which was first credited to Rumelhart (1977) – such a regular sequence does not occur. As we noted above for Stanovich (perhaps the best-known proponent of interactive models), in interactive models, a pattern is synthesised based on information 'provided *simultaneously* from several sources' (1980: 35). In Rumelhart's model, once a **Feature Extraction Device** has operated on the **Visual Information Store**, it passes the data to a **Pattern Synthesiser** which receives input from **Syntactical, Semantic, Lexical** and **Orthographic Knowledge**, all potentially operating at the same point. If one takes Stanovich's description as defining interactive models, then Goodman's is one such, since, according to him, 'Readers utilize not one, but three kinds of information simultaneously' (Goodman, 1967: 266). The information is orthographic, syntactic, and semantic.[3]

Interactive-compensatory approaches

Stanovich calls his model an 'interactive-compensatory' one. The compensatory refers to the idea, intuitively appealing, that a weakness in one area of knowledge or skill, say in Orthographic Knowledge, can be compensated for by strength in another area, say Syntactical Knowledge. At the risk of labouring a point, we might claim that Goodman's account contains this notion, since he refers to weaknesses in the orthographic area being made up for by the 'strong syntax' of a real text, meaningful to the young reader. The notion of compensation has been alluded to in research in L2 reading, for example in Alderson and Urquhart (1985), where it was hypothesised that background knowledge might make up for inadequate language skills.

Interactive-compensatory models are very attractive and have received a great deal of support. Their main weakness, from the experimental point of view, is that, as Rayner and Pollatsek (1989: 471) point out, they are very good at explaining results but comparatively poor at predicting them in advance. To some extent this is because each reader must be viewed as potentially different, with different strengths and weaknesses. Hence two readers may on one occasion arrive at the same level of performance by utilising different strengths. But this situation, while exasperating for the model-building psychologist, may simply reflect a widely pertaining reality.

Before we leave these models, which all to some extent attempt to mirror the actual process of reading, we shall make some points about such models in general. First, one consequence of the advent of interactive models is that an almost infinite variety of models might seem possible, since one can have all sorts of variations of interactive top-down and interactive bottom-up models. Thus Rayner and Pollatsek consider Just and Carpenter's model to be basically bottom-up, with interactive elements, while they concede that Goodman's model, while basically top-down, also might be said to have interactive aspects.

Secondly, while there does seem to have been a swing towards bottom-up models (see the remark by Hoover and Tunmer earlier), it should be stressed that the empirical evidence in favour of such models is strongest only in the area of word recognition and lexical access. Beyond that stage, there is comparatively little agreement, so all sorts of model may be possible.

Thirdly, the psychologists take as a given what is sometimes referred to as 'normal reading'; Rayner and Pollatsek narrow this down to the careful reading of textbooks. But while such a position may be convenient for experimenters, it is too narrowly defined to be acceptable to those interested in the whole range of reading activities. Once we include other kinds of reading as legitimate, we may then be tempted to take the view that different tasks may require different types of reading and different models of the processes involved. Thus it might seem reasonable to suggest that search reading (see below) is largely reader driven, while the careful reading of new material is likely to be predominantly text driven. And investigations by educational psychologists (e.g. Entwhistle et al., 1979) suggest that either text driven or reader driven may be the preferred styles of particular classes of reader (see Section 2.3). While appreciating the cognitive psychologists' attempts to equip themselves with operational definitions in order to make testable predictions, we must always keep in mind the sheer complexity of the activities grouped under the term 'reading'. Thus Gibson and Levin (1974) deny the possibility of having models of the reading process, precisely because of different styles and different responses to different reading tasks.

Componential models

The models we have looked at above attempt to describe the actual process of reading, a cognitive activity operating in real time. In fact, Rayner and Pollatsek are critical of some models, including those of Goodman and, to a lesser extent, that of Rumelhart, in that they are insufficiently explicit about the process, and hence, in their terms, are not really models at all. The componential descriptions we now look at do not even begin to model the process, consisting as they do simply of areas of skills or knowledge thought to be involved in the process. According to Hoover and Tunmer (1993), such descriptions try to model reading **ability** rather than the reading process. The use of such componential models, again according to Hoover and Tunmer, is 'to understand reading as a set of theoretically distinct and empirically isolable constituents' (1993: 4). Thus one should be able to account for different reading performance in terms of variation in one of the components.

The two-component model

The simplest componential model will consist of two components. In the case of Hoover and Tunmer, who refer to theirs as 'the simple view', the components are **word recognition** and **linguistic comprehension**. They claim that Fries (1963), Venezky and Calfee (1970) and Perfetti (1977) hold the same view.

Clearly, provided that it can account for the observed data, a model with fewer variables is preferable to one with more. So if the simple two-variable model can do this, then it should be chosen. Hoover and Tunmer claim that it can, and adduce evidence of different types in support of their claim (see Chapter 3 for further discussion of the componential issue in relation to testing). The evidence takes two main forms: first, data showing that the two variables are separable. Here we might point to the obvious evidence that L1 illiterates, both young and adult, can generally be assumed to understand language, but cannot read, because of their lack of decoding skills. Then Hoover and Tunmer cite evidence from disabled readers. Dyslexics have normal linguistic competence, but are deficient in decoding skills (1993: 10). Children suffering from hyperlexia, on the other hand, show high levels of decoding skill but poor linguistic comprehension. Finally, longitudinal studies of normal children have shown that, in the early grades, the correlations obtained between decoding and linguistic comprehension are low, but become steadily higher as the children advance through the school.

The other kind of evidence comes from statistical techniques measuring the contribution that different factors make to reading performance. In a typical study by Stanovich et al. (1984), decoding accounted for 38 per cent and linguistic comprehension 13 per cent of the variance in reading comprehension of fifth graders, after the effects of non-verbal intelligence had been removed (p. 12).

However, while this accumulation of evidence is impressive, doubts must remain as to the simplicity of the 'simple' view. Hoover and Tunmer use the terms 'decoding' and 'word recognition'. Definitions of the first vary, they admit, with some limiting the term purely to the ability to replace strings of graphemes (letters) with corresponding strings of phonemes, and others insisting on including full lexical access, i.e. recognising what the word means (Goodman is one of the latter). Hoover and Tunmer use 'decoding' for accessing the lexicon by means of a phonological route (spelling it out) and 'word recognition' for the process of accessing the lexicon 'based on graphic information' (i.e. presumably, without recourse to the phonological route). This doesn't appear to leave any term for the ability to decode pseudo-words which do not appear in the lexicon (although they at one point say that the ability to recognize such 'words' should be taken as evidence of decoding). But if 'word recognition' involves accessing the mental lexicon, isn't this an important part of 'linguistic comprehension'?

The situation becomes more complex when we consider 'linguistic comprehension'. Hoover and Tunmer define this operationally as the ability to answer questions about an oral narrative. There are two objections to this: one, that it is too narrow; the other, that it is too broad. The narrowness relates to the obvious limitation on text-type; the broadness concerns the fact that such an ability may, and almost certainly does, involve far more than linguistic competence. For example, Carroll (1972) tries to distinguish 'pure' or 'simple' comprehension from 'total' comprehension. The second includes processes of inference, deduction and problem solving, the first does not. His description of pure comprehension as that which is linguistically committed to the text, is probably very similar to what Fries had in mind when he limited comprehension to 'a grasp of meaning in the form in which it is presented' (1963: 115). It is clear, however, both from the way in which it is assessed, and from descriptions such as 'the ability to take lexical information (i.e. semantic information at the word level) and derive sentence and discourse interpretations' (Hoover and Tunmer, 1993: 8) that Hoover and Tunmer's view of comprehension is closer to Carroll's 'total' comprehension.

The distinction may seem very academic, but it does have quite immediate consequences, particularly in the L2 area. As we shall see below, attempts to distinguish between 'reading skills' and 'language skills' often rely on a definition of language skills similar to that implied by Carroll, i.e. a competence in the system. Thus they depend on splitting 'language ability' into 'language competence' and 'language use'. And it is of great importance to language teachers to know whether increasing their students' knowledge of part of the linguistic system, e.g. grammar, will help their reading (see Section 5.2 for how this might be investigated). Hence it is important to define one's terms more precisely than Hoover and Tunmer have done. Even with native speakers, it is perfectly feasible that aspects of their L1 language use may develop differentially in different students who all share the same basic competence. Hence one might expect variation in later performance which could not be accounted for in Hoover and Tunmer's simple model.

The simple view and the L2 reader

For all the attractions of the simple view, there are obvious difficulties in using this model to describe L2 readers. Describing as they do young L1 learners, Hoover and Tunmer can make the reasonable assumption that their language knowledge can be tapped by an oral comprehension test. This is unlikely to be a safe assumption to make with L2 learners, who may well perform better on a reading test than on an equivalent oral test. It is not even clear whether it is a safe assumption to make with adult L1 readers.

Faced with this difficulty, the L2 researcher is likely to have to pay more attention to what is meant by language, and may have to subdivide this area into components such as syntax, cohesion, text structure, etc. As has been argued above, this may have the effect of rendering the simple view no longer very simple.

Three-component models

Coady (1979) and Bernhardt (1991b), both describing L2 reading, include three variables: in Coady's case these are **Conceptual Abilities, Process Strategies** and **Background Knowledge**. Bernhardt's model consists of **Language**, **Literacy** and **World Knowledge**. Taking Coady's model first, 'conceptual abilities' are equivalent to intellectual capacity, and Coady (1979: 7) remarks that some 'adult foreign students . . . may fail to achieve the competence necessary for university instruction because they lack intellectual capacity and not totally or necessarily because they cannot learn English'. He adds that there is not much to do about this situation. 'Background knowledge' will be dealt with below. It might be pointed out here, however, that Hoover and Tunmer constructed their experiments to neutralize the possible effect of background knowledge. By 'process strategies', Coady means both a knowledge of the system and the ability to use the knowledge, e.g. 'knowledge of the phonology of a language implies the ability to identify phonemes and use this knowledge for practical purposes such as listening' (p. 7). In other words, Coady's component consists of language use, rather than 'simple' competence.

One can see Coady's model as adding more components to the simple view. Alternatively, one may see it as subdividing Hoover and Tunmer's 'comprehension' into separate components. Given that Coady considers the interaction between his components to result in 'comprehension', the latter is the neater solution. In other words, for Coady, background knowledge is not an addition to comprehension, it is an actual component of comprehension. However, there is one important component in Hoover and Tunmer's model which is lacking in Coady's, namely Word Recognition. The only acknowledgement Coady makes of this is to include phoneme/grapheme correspondences as part of the Process Strategies component. Of course, it could be argued that Coady's is a model of comprehension and not of the reading process. It seems more likely, however, that this is evidence of the predominance in L2 reading of applied linguists, with a tendency to emphasize high-level processes.

Bernhardt's model also lacks a separate word-recognition component. Like Coady, she also proposes a model with three variables, namely World Knowledge, Language and Literacy. World knowledge equals background knowledge; language includes the 'seen' elements of the text, such as word structure, word meaning, syntax and morphology. It must, however, be seen as including language use. Literacy equals operational knowledge: knowing how to approach text, knowing why one approaches it and what to do with it. How would one go about finding empirical support for the separate existence of Bernhardt's literacy component? Presumably by finding students who shared equivalent background knowledge of a topic, and were at the same proficiency level in the language, but differed in performance on texts in a systematic way which could be attributed to self-monitoring etc.

2.2 COMPONENTS IN DETAIL

We now proceed to examine in detail some of the components mentioned, namely word recognition, language (examined in different subcomponents), background/world knowledge and literacy. In other words, the 'model' whose components we are going to discuss is in some ways an amalgam of those of Hoover and Tunmer (1993), Coady (1979) and Bernhardt (1991b). In many cases, the research we touch on involves L1 subjects. However, when L2 data exist, we shall concentrate on that.

Word recognition

We should start by saying that even the definition of the meaning of the term 'word recognition' is disputed. Hoover and Tunmer (1993) mention three interpretations. The most obvious one would be to have the term mean 'recognize an English word in print, be able to pronounce it, and give its meaning'. Some people would dispute the need to include pronunciation (the phonological part). Many of the experiments on word recognition have involved the use of pseudo-words, such as 'mard'. So we might have to extend the term to mean 'recognition of pronounceable strings of letters which are not actual words in English'. But some of the experiments involve recognition of 'unpronounceable' pseudo-words. So we might have to add 'recognition of any letter string with space boundaries on either side'.

Then the processes of word recognition appear to be extremely complicated, and not well understood. So we will content ourselves here with stating what is generally agreed, what facts any theory has to account for, and the immediate implications for a reader of a foreign language. In our account we rely mainly on Rayner and Pollatsek (1989), keeping in mind that most of what they have to say concerns skilled adult readers.

First, as we reported earlier, letters are not processed serially. If they were, then the time taken to recognize a word would be longer than the time needed to recognise a single letter, and the longer a word, the longer it would take to recognise. Within reason, this does not seem to be the case. Furthermore, subjects are more accurate in reporting letters in words, e.g. the 'd' in 'word', than they were in recognizing 'd' by itself.

On the other hand, it cannot be the case that words are recognised as templates or pictures. In the experiments mentioned above subjects were as quick to report letters in pseudo-words like 'orwd' as they were to report the single letter, although it is inconceivable that they had a template for such pseudo-words. And as Rayner and Pollatsek point out, the notion of templates cannot account for subjects' ability to read in a number of different fonts.

So Rayner and Pollatsek settle on a modified version of a model by Paap et al. (1982), in which the visual input goes first to FEATURE DETECTORS, then to LETTER DETECTORS, and finally to WORD DETECTORS. Since on their own admission the evidence for the viability of the model is too complex to present in their book, we shall content ourselves with mentioning it.

Given that in normal reading the purpose of word recognition is to access the lexicon, it is generally recognised that there are two routes to this. The first, known as the **direct** route, goes straight from the visual input to meaning without recourse to sound; the other, known as the **phonemic** or **phonological** route, goes from visual input to sound to meaning. Evidence that readers of English use a direct route comes from consideration of the writing system; the system notoriously contains too many irregularities to allow total reliance on the phonological route. However, use of the direct route alone cannot explain subjects' ability to handle pseudo-words like 'mand', or 'birn', which are not likely to be present, and hence accessible, in the reader's lexicon. Other evidence for a phonological route comes from phonological influence on word recognition: recognition of words like 'touch' have been shown to be slowed down when they are preceded by, in this case, the word 'couch'. Also recognition of pseudo-homophones (nonwords which share the same pronunciation as real words, e.g. 'phocks') have been shown to be slower than recognition of other pseudo-words. Here, presumably, the activation of the pronunciation collides with the real word in the lexical entry, thus causing confusion.

Finally, Rayner and Pollatsek cite as evidence for two routes the fact that so-called surface dyslexics can pronounce most words, but regularize irregular ones, while phonemic dyslexics pronounce most words correctly but cannot pronounce non-words. This can be explained by arguing that the first group are limited to the phonological route, and the second group to the direct route.

Thus Rayner and Pollatsek (1989: 109) conclude that 'the common ground for all positions is that direct visual access is important and that sound encoding plays some part'.

Two other aspects of word recognition seem to be relevant here. Most of the research appears to have been done with single morpheme words, such as 'touch' and 'word'. It seems, to say the least, somewhat odd to suggest that there is a separate lexical entry for, say, not only 'expect' but also 'expects', 'expected', 'expecting', 'expectation', 'unexpected', etc. Rayner and Pollatsek report evidence that, in such cases, the root morpheme is accessed first, together with some evidence that 'content' words are stored separately from 'function' words, so that, for example, 'expect' would appear in a different lexicon from, say, 'the'. Function words would seem, anyway, to pose problems for the 'phonological route only' school: it seems, frankly, incredible that a skilled reader, reading fast, will distinguish between different phonologically conditioned pronunciations of 'the'.

Word recognition in L2

Randall and Meara (1988) remark that most L2 reading research 'has been centred on the relatively higher-order skills of discourse organization and the interpretation of continuous text', and say that this is 'for obvious reasons'. Perhaps one obvious reason is that many of the potential subjects are presumed to be past the 'simple' stage of word recognition by the time they become available to researchers, though such an assumption is by no means certain. A further reason is that many L2 researchers have a training in applied linguistics, which has tended to ignore this area.

Whatever the reasons for the neglect, it is clear that word recognition poses intriguing problems for L2 reading researchers. Take, for example, the question of phonological access to the lexicon, which presupposes that for a word to be accessed in reading, the lexical entry must contain a phonological component, i.e. it must contain information as to how the word is pronounced. In most cases, skilled adult L1 readers can be assumed to have this information, while most difficulties for young L1 learners can be avoided by careful control of vocabulary. But these assumptions cannot be made with respect to many L2 readers; in a huge number of cases they are going to come across words which they have not heard pronounced. Does this mean they are unable to access them? Then there is the question of the script with which the L2 learners are familiar when they begin to read the L2. If the learners come from a different orthographic tradition, is this likely to affect their reading in the L2?

Phonological versus direct access

Koda (1987) cites experimental findings which show that English readers took longer and made more errors judging homophone sentences than Chinese readers. The claim is that Chinese readers, brought up on a logographic script, will access words directly. Suarez and Meara (1989) argued that as Spanish readers are used to a 'regular' script – i.e. one in which there is a regular correspondence between phoneme and grapheme – they may, when faced with English, behave differently from English readers. One hypothesis was that they might rely entirely on the phonological route, and hence make a disproportionally large number of errors on 'irregular' words. Suarez and Meara used a method devised by Glushko (1979), whereby the subjects were exposed to (a) regular words (e.g. 'bleed'), (b) regular pseudo-words (e.g. 'dreed'), (c) irregular words (e.g. 'blood') and (d) irregular pseudo-words (e.g. 'drood'). The authors consider that their results were inconclusive, though the pattern of errors seemed to be similar to that of English-speaking surface dyslexics. We are somewhat dubious in this case as to the validity of the experimental method, in particular the status of 'irregular pseudo-words', and, more generally, of 'regular' words in the context of L2 research. We deal with these doubts in Chapter 5.

The effect of script type

Randall and Meara (1988) tested Arabic speakers to see if they processed letter strings in the same way as English speakers (Arabic, of course, is written from right to left). Studies of English speakers had shown that, given a target shape, then presented with a verification task of locating the target among an array of five shapes, English speakers displayed a 'ᴗ' pattern of response, i.e. they took longest if the target was either at the beginning or end of the array. On the other hand, when faced with an array of five letters or digits, the pattern they displayed resembled a tilted 'M' shape; in other words, they located the target quickest if it was located at the beginning or end of the array, and rather quicker if it occurred at position 3 than at position 2 or 4. The argument is that this reflects reading patterns, and that English readers are used to paying attention to the beginning and end of words (an argument which seems a little tenuous to us). Arabic readers responded in a similar way with target shapes, displaying a 'ᴗ' response pattern. However they also showed this response pattern when confronted with arrays of English letters. Moreover, their responses seemed to show that they were processing the words from right to left. The study was repeated over a period, during which the right-to-left processing disappeared, but the same 'ᴗ' pattern persisted. Randall and Meara point out that they are not predicting any direct consequences of this difference in response, but presumably some consequence may be possible.

The effect of morphological differences

Ryan and Meara (1991) noticed in a pilot experiment that Arabic speakers, when presented with incomplete words like 'presrve' and asked to complete them, were more likely than other L2 subjects to produce different words, e.g. 'pressure'. In their main experiment, Arabic speakers, when given an identification task involving either identical or slightly altered words, e.g. 'department/dpartment', made far more errors than either L1 or other L2 subjects. Ryan and Meara tentatively suggest that this is the result partly of the structure of Arabic, in which the 'root' of a family of words is composed of a sequence of three consonants, and partly of the Arabic orthography, which largely omits vowels (see Chapter 1). This combination of factors may dispose Arabic speakers, when reading English, to identify words on the basis of their consonants, while not paying sufficient attention to vowel letters.

Learning unknown words

Cognitive psychologists investigating the reading behaviour of skilled adult L1 readers can assume, on the whole, that words encountered will be in the subject's lexicon; hence, with the exception of pseudo-words, what they are studying is word recognition. In the case of L2 learners, however, such an assumption cannot be made, so that, in addition to word recognition, there is also a major area of concern involving the initial handling and learning of unfamiliar words.

Pitts et al. (1989) showed that L2 readers were able to acquire a number of unfamiliar lexicon items when reading chapters from *The Clockwork Orange*. The words were 'nadsat' words, Russian lexical items used as slang in the book, and hence were presumably unknown to the readers on first encounter. Day et al. (1991) found that Japanese readers were again able to acquire previously unknown vocabulary, this time English, from reading an English text. Both studies showed that readers had correctly assigned meaning to the items; in neither case did the investigators enquire whether they had also assigned phonological readings to the words. The English words used by Day et al. were on the whole orthographically regular, e.g. 'fire', 'clear', 'stare', so a phonological reading could have been carried out. Unfortunately Pitts et al. do not list the 'nadsat' words used.

Koda (1987) tested Japanese students reading an English text in which a number of previously encountered pseudo-words had been inserted. Some of the words were 'pronounceable', some 'unpronounceable'. The aim was not, in fact, to examine word recognition; previous studies had shown that phonological recoding appears to be important in short-term memory syntactic processing (see below) and Koda wanted to see if Japanese readers, used to a logographic *kanji* script, would be affected in this respect. The subjects reading unpronounceable words, contrary to expectations, and in contrast to the behaviour of L1 readers, read the text faster than those reading the text with pronounceable words. However, later self-monitoring reports by subjects showed that they had adopted a range of avoidance strategies, e.g. renaming the pseudo-words, so the experiment tells us little about how unknown words are used. In addition, we are dubious about the general acceptance, in the psychological literature, of 'unpronounceable' words (see Chapter 5, Section 5.1).

In general, the whole topic of the recognition and learning of lexis in reading seems to us to be one of major importance in L2 reading, and one to which L2 researchers are in a position to make a valuable contribution.

Language

It has already been pointed out that the distinction between language and word recognition, drawn by Hoover and Tunmer, is not a clear one, since the lexicon is clearly part of our linguistic competence. However, we are keeping the distinction here for convenience. We need, however, to break the topic down into more manageable subtopics. Hence, below, we discuss syntax, then cohesion, and larger aspects of text structure.

Inner speech

Before we consider syntax, we should look briefly at the notion of inner speech. This is the 'voice in the head' which many of us are aware of while we are reading. Rayner and Pollatsek (1989), who devote considerable space to the issue, try to distinguish inner speech from subvocalisation. The latter, which involves actual physical activity in the speech tract, used to attract the attention of reading teachers, who taught that it should be suppressed. However, electromyographic recording shows that subvocalisation is a normal part of silent reading.

Inner speech is more interesting. There is considerable evidence that the sounds of words influence the speed or accuracy of silent reading. Rayner and Pollatsek report that readers find strings like

> *Crude rude Jude stewed food*

difficult to read **silently**. They suggest that the effect of inner speech is post-lexical, i.e. occurs after lexical access, and that its function is to hold material in the working memory until it is processed. Perfetti and McCutchen (1982) claim that inner speech is not a complete representation of every word in the text, but is biased towards the beginning of words. They suggest that function words may not require as elaborate a phonetic representation as content words.

As far as we know, nothing is known about the effect of the presence or absence or form of inner speech in L2 readers. Koda's experiment, reported above, was directed towards this area, but produced no convincing results. Rayner and Pollatsek (p. 211) report that inner speech 'may be somewhat less important in Chinese than in English'. With reference to deaf L1 readers, they report that 'the comprehension and memory advantages provided by one's primary language weigh heavily in the choice of a recoding system' (p. 210). One would speculate that if the L1 reader of English relied on a phonological rendering of the message to assist in processing syntactic units, then the L2 reader is likely to be doubly handicapped, being uncertain of both the syntax and the phonology. It is just possible that the finding by Dhaif (1990) that Arab students' comprehension of written English was significantly improved by the teacher reading aloud while they read silently in parallel has some relationship to inner speech.

Syntax

In addition to words being recognised, the significance of the relationships between them (e.g. the syntax) needs to be extracted by the reader. It would be reasonable that, given the vast amount of work which has been done in linguistics in the area of syntax, we would be well informed as to how readers operate. This, however, is not the case (the reader may remember that the syntactic and semantic component in Gough's model was called 'Merlin'). Rayner and Pollatsek mention a number of approaches, none of which seems to have attracted anything like the attention in psychology as have problems of word recognition or eye movements. They single out for special mention two approaches. The first, they refer to as the 'Clausal' model of processing, developed in the 1970s. This 'model' consisted of a number of pragmatic strategies, e.g. 'take the first clause to be the main clause unless there is a subordinating conjunction'. Rayner and Pollatsek are fairly dismissive of this approach, claiming that such pragmatic rules would form 'an unsatisfactory hodgepodge' (p. 246). However, it seems to us that L2 readers may well build up such a set of strategies, partly derived from their L1, partly constructed to deal specifically with the L2.

The approach Rayner and Pollatsek favour is the so-called 'garden path' approach. This contains two main principles. According to the first, known as 'minimal attachment', the reader structures data to try to minimize the number of grammatical nodes required. Thus, a sentence like 'The girl knew the answer by heart' is likely to cause fewer processing difficulties than the sentence 'The girl knew the answer was wrong' since the latter, in terms of Phrase Structure Grammar, requires a subordinate sentence node not required for the former sentence. The second principle, known as 'late closure', claims that, when grammatically possible, readers will attach new items to preceding items rather than subsequent ones. Hence, given the two sentences

Since Jay always jogs a mile this seems like a short distance to him.
Since Jay always jogs a mile seems like a long distance to him.

readers are predicted to have fewer problems with the first, since in both cases they will initially attach 'a mile' to 'jogs' – a move which works with the first sentence but has to be revised in the case of the second.

Rayner and Pollatsek claim that experiments using observation of readers' eye movements support the existence of both principles. However, on the examples they produce, it is not clear to us that there are, in fact, two principles involved. In both sets of sentences quoted above, the readers' difficulties might be attributed to taking 'knew' and 'jogs' as transitive verbs requiring an NP object, then assuming that the first possible NP, 'the answer' and 'a mile', completes the Verb Phrase; in other words, a version of 'late closure'. In fact, one is tempted to agree with Ridgway (1997) that an approach based on 'dependency' grammar would be fruitful. Such grammars, however, have the disadvantage of being relatively underdeveloped.

Syntax in L2 reading

When we turn to grammar in L2 reading, we find again a dearth of data. There are probably at least two factors involved here. Some years ago it was not uncommon to find EFL books containing 'reading passages' which seemed to have been included mainly to supply fodder for grammar teaching. If one considers written text in this way, then it is not likely that one will investigate the effect of one on the other. After this, the 'communicative' approach tended to stress language use, and hence disparage attention being paid to 'knowledge' areas such as syntax. Finally, as commented on by Randall and Meara (1988), a concentration on 'high-level' factors such as background knowledge, skills and strategies, led to the comparative neglect of lower-level factors such as syntax.

We have been taking the conventional position that syntactic parsing of some kind was necessary in order to impose meaning on the words recognised. This apparently commonsensical position has been contradicted by findings of Ulijn and his associates. In Ulijn and Kempen (1976), Dutch and French speakers read a text about finding their way around an imaginary town, Beausite. The text, which was in French, existed in two versions. In one version, French syntactic structures not found in Dutch were included. In the other, such structures were avoided. However, there was no difference in either the Dutch or the French readers' responses to the text. Ulijn and Kempen conclude that: 'under normal conditions reading comprehension is little dependent on a syntactic analysis of the text's sentences.'

In later experiments (Strother and Ulijn, 1987) students from different linguistic backgrounds – English and others – read a text on an aspect of computer science. One version of the text was the original; in the other, ten 'passages' (i.e. sentences) had been 'simplified' in certain specific syntactic ways, e.g. passives were replaced by active equivalents, nominalisations by expanded Noun–Verb constructions. Again no significant differences were found between responses to the original and simplified text. Strother and Ulijn conclude that readers use a 'conceptual strategy', consisting largely of knowledge of word meanings together with knowledge of the text's subject area. Thus, in the model, a syntactic element could be eliminated.

As far as simplification of text for L2 readers is concerned, there may well be a case for an emphasis on lexis, as Strother and Ulijn argue, though whether results based on the 'simplification' of ten sentences of a text of unspecified length is good evidence for this is debatable. To claim, however, as Ulijn seems to do at times, that syntactic processing is not necessary, is frankly unbelievable. This is easily demonstrated. The following string represents an English sentence from which most (not all) function words and all inflectional morphemes have been deleted. Moreover, since ordering plays a major part in English syntax, the order of the remaining words has been jumbled.

begin several it recogniser module machine digital pass record speech

We challenge anyone, whether expert in the content area (artificial language) or not, to process this string. Things begin to be a bit better if we restore the original ordering:

Machine begin digital record speech pass it several recogniser module

However, it is only when we restore function words and inflections that the message becomes easy to extract:

The machine begins by digitally recording the speech and passing it to several recogniser modules.

The subjects used by Ulijn and his associates were comparatively expert in the L2: for example, the Chinese students used by Strother had TOEFL scores of 550+ and had been in the USA for nine months. Ulijn's Dutch students had studied English at secondary school for six years and had had 'considerable exposure to English' (Ulijn and Kempen, 1976: 94). It can be assumed, therefore, that the subjects' syntax was sufficient to cope with whatever was given them. It might, of course, be reasonably concluded that, at their level, extra syntactic tuition would give smaller returns than an emphasis on vocabulary building. But that is a very different thing from claiming that 'reading comprehension is little dependent on a syntactic analysis'.

One point of interest that can be retrieved from the work of Ulijn and his associates can be found in the remark that 'a *thorough* syntactic analysis is unnecessary' (our italics). It has sometimes been claimed that the amount of syntactic knowledge necessary for reading is less than that required for writing or speaking. Thus, given that the readers had enough background knowledge, they might make quite reasonable sense of, say,

machine begin by digitally record speech and pass it to several recogniser module.

In other words, a successful processing of this text might not depend on a detailed knowledge of the determiner system, morphological marking of plurals, etc. Thus it might be possible to distinguish between a **receptive** and a **productive** syntactic processor (see Section 5.2).

Alderson (1993) has produced evidence of a strong connection between grammar and reading. During the preparation of the IELTS test, item writers were instructed to produce a test of grammar which could be used along with tests of reading, listening and writing in the total test. After tests had been trialled in both the UK and Australia, it was found that very high correlations held between the grammar test and different tests of reading. For example, the correlation between the grammar test and the science and technology reading test was 0.80. This was in spite of the fact that the grammar test was designed as a test of grammar in general, rather than of structures found in the reading tests, and that the reading tests did not include any specifically grammatical item.

While we have some doubts about details of the tests used (see Part 5), there seems little doubt that Alderson is correct in concluding that 'it must be the case that, in some intuitive sense, a reader must process the grammar in a text in order to understand it', and that '. . . the evidence certainly does not support any claim that one can successfully understand text without grammatical abilities' (p. 219).

However, this is more or less where the case rests. We don't know how L2 readers process texts syntactically, though, as mentioned above, we may suspect that they apply a collection of pragmatic strategies, e.g. in English, the first NP is likely to be the Subject. These strategies are likely to be influenced by their experiences with reading in their L1, as Cowan (1976) has posited. It is quite likely that more breakdowns occur in processing than are obvious on the surface; one of the authors discovered that Indonesian students seemed not to be able to assign Subject or Object roles to nouns in relative clauses. But little is known of this area.

Background knowledge

Both Coady's and Bernhardt's models contain a component called 'background knowledge' (in Coady's model) or 'world knowledge' (in Bernhardt's model). Hoover and Tunmer also mention background knowledge but only to attempt to exclude it. They are interested in reading ability, rather than reading performance; presumably also one's background knowledge can be assumed to be constant whether one is reading or listening, and therefore cannot be used to distinguish between the two activities. In L2 reading, however, and in particular in the area of LSP, the concern is more to predict performance on particular reading tasks, and for this, the background or world knowledge of L2 readers may well need to be taken into account.

The theoretical justification for including background knowledge as a component of our reading model can be seen as deriving from two different sources. First, it is part of the theory of comprehension associated with the notion of 'schemata' (see below) that text is never complete, and that the reader (or listener) must supply additional material derived from their existing knowledge of the world. From this point of view, background knowledge is inevitably present in all kinds of reading, both L1 and L2. The second source is interactive models of the reading process. Although not by any means constructed with L2 readers in mind, such theories are good at predicting that L2 readers, with significant defects in their knowledge of the language, may sometimes perform as well as L1 readers. The theory will predict that, assuming they have the required background knowledge, L2 readers may use this knowledge to compensate for linguistic shortcomings. The possibility of such an outcome is of practical importance in deciding, for example, whether an L2 student is capable of proceeding to an academic course of study involving reading in their own speciality. Thus background knowledge has been of particular interest to those involved in testing and teaching LSP (see Chapter 3).

There is a considerable amount of experimental evidence in L2 reading that background knowledge can play the part envisioned for it in the theory. Bernhardt (1991b) gives an extensive list of studies, to which we refer the reader. The majority of studies she cites were successful in showing that readers' familiarity with content had a significant effect on their performance. However, in a number of cases no such effect has been found (e.g. Clapham, 1990, who found that 'subject area had no significant effect on scores'). Because of this, we shall focus on the conditions required before the effect of background knowledge becomes evident.

We shall begin by examining two studies – one by Mohammed and Swales (1984) and one by Alderson and Urquhart (1985) – which will serve to illustrate some of the relevant factors. Both these studies belong to the same group in Bernhardt's classification, being concerned with background knowledge of topic rather than cultural background. However, if we accept the claim by Widdowson (1978), that science constitutes a culture, this division becomes somewhat arbitrary.

Mohammed and Swales gave twelve postgraduate students the tasks of using an instructional pamphlet to (a) set the current time on a digital clock and (b) set the alarm for a specific time the next day. Performance was measured in time required to accomplish the tasks. The subjects were categorized as (a) Native speaker scientists (NS), (b) Native speaker arts (NA), (c) Non-native speaker scientists (NNS), (d) Non-native speaker arts (NNA). The linguistic proficiency of the non-native speakers was arrived at using teachers' estimates of the subjects' potential band scores on the IELTS test: General and Reading modules.

The subjects were video-taped during the tasks, to investigate their overall behaviour (reading different parts of the instructions, manipulation of controls, etc.). While this record is irrelevant here, such data are clearly important for studies of different reading behaviours and different reading models.

The main measure of performance was the time subjects took to complete the tasks. They did so in the following order of proficiency: (1) NS, (2) NNS, (3) NA, (4) NNA. Thus the non-native speaker scientists performed better than the native speaker arts subjects, in spite of the fact that their average band score was 5.4, while the native speakers were assumed to have a band score level of 9. Moreover, the NNS group also outperformed the NNA group, in spite of the fact that the latter group had an average band score of 7.9. Mohammed and Swales (1984) ascribe the difference between groups to 'either *field-familiarity* or, more likely, familiarity with the genre of technical instructions' (p. 211), and express surprise at the strength of the influence of technical experience, and the 'apparent unimportance of general English proficiency above a presumed threshold level' (p. 216).

Alderson and Urquhart (1984) carried out a series of three studies using subject-related groups of L2 postgraduate students, namely Engineers (ENG), Science and Maths (SM), Development Administration and Finance/Economics (DAFE) and Liberal Arts (LA). In Studies 1 and 2 there were three groups of texts, aimed primarily at the ENG, DAFE and LA groups. The tasks were gap-filling (Studies 1 and 2), and gap-filling plus short-form answers (Study 2). In Study 3, three modules of the ELTS test, Technology, Social Sciences, and General Academic were used.

The results were inconsistent. In Study 1, ENG outperformed DAFE on the engineering texts, as predicted, while DAFE outperformed ENG on the DAFE texts. However, in Study 2, while the DAFE group outperformed ENG on the DAFE texts, there was no difference between the two groups on the ENG texts. In Study 3, in contrast, the SM–ENG group (ENG and SM combined) outperformed the DAFE group on the Technology module, while on the Social Science module, the two groups did not differ significantly. Alderson and Urquhart concluded that in the case of the Engineering texts, the background knowledge of the engineering students was compensating for their comparative low level of language proficiency.

Thus while the studies provided evidence of an effect of background knowledge, this effect was not consistent throughout. There was also evidence of a factor related to language proficiency (the LA groups, which were all through more proficient on measurements of proficiency than the other groups, in virtually all the tests either equalled or surpassed the other groups). There was in addition evidence of both text effect (some texts proving consistently easier than others, though on a Fog Readability Index they were equivalent) and of method effects.

In spite of such inconclusive evidence, it seems to us undeniable that background knowledge has an effect on reading. While this is probably true for *all* texts, it is most easily comprehended in relation to what, for some people, are highly specialised texts. Given such a text on nuclear physics, for example, taken from a professional journal, it seems undeniable that a professional physicist will read it differently from most of the readers of this book (as well as the authors). We can state this in relativistic terms, and say, as do Harri-Augstein and Thomas (1984), that our comprehensions will be different, or we can be more absolute and claim that the physicist's reading is likely to be better. We think most people, after comparatively little reflection, will be inclined to agree with this.

If, however, we accept that background knowledge is involved in all normal reading, then we are obliged to account for the fact that studies have not always been able to detect a significance difference brought on by apparent differences in knowledge brought to the task by experimental subjects. There are at least three factors to be discussed, and we shall now discuss this factor by factor, referring to the two studies described above.

Texts

If our aim is to show, as it was in Alderson and Urquhart, that two or more groups of readers will perform differently as a result of differences in background knowledge, then it seems obvious that the texts used should be as specialised as possible. Clearly, a text which is equally accessible to both groups in terms of the knowledge required will not show any difference between the groups. Clapham's remark that it is only with highly specific texts that background knowledge has an effect on student test performance seems almost too obvious to make (Clapham, 1996a). In the first two studies by Alderson and Urquhart, the Engineering texts were chosen with the help and advice of an academic engineer. Even so, on the whole they failed to discriminate between engineers, on the one hand, and science and maths students on the other, presumably because of being insufficiently specialised in the direction of the engineers. If one uses parts of existing tests aimed at a wide range of testees, as was the case in Study 3 of Alderson and Urquhart, and also in Clapham (1990), then there is a danger of the texts being insufficiently specialised, having been filtered by test constructors and editing committees. This was certainly the case for the IELTS tests used by Clapham. The focus of the research then shifts to the question of whether, in cases like IELTS, having 'specialised' ESP modules is justified. This is a worthwhile question to ask, but tells us little or nothing about the effect of background knowledge.

In fact, some of the conflicting findings in the literature may be traceable back to a difference in focus on the part of the researchers, leading to a difference in text selection. In the first two studies by Alderson and Urquhart, the focus was on possible differences caused by differing background knowledge. In their third study, and in some at least of Clapham's work, the focus changes to whether the texts (and possibly tasks) of existing ESP tests are successful in discriminating between different groups, and are therefore worth using. It is perfectly possible to consider that background knowledge is an important factor in reading performance while at the same time being of the opinion that broad-based ESP tests are probably not worth having.

In view of what has been said above, the text used in Mohammed and Swales – instructions for setting a digital clock – seems slightly anomalous. After all, it was not presumably aimed at a specialised audience: digital clocks are widely used by non-scientists. Presumably we have here a case of a sender of a message who has not taken sufficient account of the skills of their audience.

Subjects

It follows from what has been said above that if we are to find significant differences between groups, the groups should be as different as possible from each other in terms of the relevant knowledge each group possesses. This is fine in theory but often difficult in practice. Suppose we try to use two groups, one of postgraduate management students, the other of engineers. One often finds (generally after the experiment) that some members of the management group have prior training as engineers. Mohammed and Swales operated with two groups, scientists and arts students. Yet the distinction is a very rough and ready one. Many linguists would wish to describe themselves as scientists, but Mohammed and Swales classified students of applied linguistics as arts students.

Tasks

The test tasks used by Alderson and Urquhart in Studies 1 and 2 were of the form of gap-filling and short-form answers. Such tasks have the advantage that they are easily designed and administered. They have the disadvantage that they are not particularly appropriate in terms of reading either to the texts or to the readers. Hence, if no difference is found, suspicion may fall on the tasks. Bernhardt (1991b), for example, has suggested that the frequent use of cloze procedure may be a factor in obscuring the effect of background knowledge. An alternative is to use tasks which are functionally appropriate both to the text and to the readers. Preferably, they should be composed by members of the discourse community which uses the text. That is, if the text relates to, say, architecture, then the task should ideally be devised by architects. Without having to go through all the difficulties this is likely to entail, Mohammed and Swales score highly in this respect, since, as they point out, the appropriate task relating to instructions is for the readers to carry out these instructions. Otherwise what we are likely to get is either cloze tasks, which Bernhardt has characterised as 'a syntactic/productive measure of clausal knowledge', or 'comprehension' tasks devised by item writers with a training in EFL or applied linguistics, which may be fine for describing what a typical EFL teacher may extract from a text, but hardly suitable to map out what a specialist may learn from it.

Language level

Many of the studies in this area refer to the language proficiency level of the students. In Alderson and Urquhart's studies, for example, though a language factor was not built into the design of the experiments, it was noted that, according to earlier proficiency tests, liberal arts students were more proficient than development and finance students, who were in turn superior to the engineers. In Mohammed and Swales' design, language (or general reading proficiency) was integrated more closely into the design, though the method of ascertaining it, by asking teachers to estimate ELTS reading scores, was to say the least subjective. Ridgway (1997) argues that the level of language proficiency is crucial, and differences in level may have masked the background knowledge effect in some cases. Certainly, Alderson and Urquhart's LA group equalled the engineers on engineering texts in two out of three studies, presumably because of their higher language proficiency. Ridgway, like Mohammed and Swales, argues for a threshold linguistic level, below which any relevant background knowledge cannot be brought into play, and this seems reasonable (see below for threshold effects). We have less sympathy with his claim that there is also an upper threshold level beyond which the readers' language ability is sufficient to allow them to read any text with equal success. This, we feel, runs counter to our experience of subject-specialised texts.

Schema theory

Finally, we should touch on the vexed issue of background knowledge itself and what it consists of. Fairclough (1995) has criticised some discourse analysis because of the assumption that background presuppositions are 'neutral', or in accord with some kind of objective reality. Instead, he points out that such presuppositions may represent the views of ideological groups. While he seems to us to make a good case for his position, the criticism cannot be applied in much of the area we are discussing. This is not because advocates of the role of background knowledge are not vulnerable to criticisms of the type Fairclough raises. It is rather that background knowledge is often not specified in sufficient detail to enable the presuppositions to be examined.

Carrell (1983b) distinguishes between formal and content sche-mata, i.e. knowledge about (a) the rhetorical structure of texts and (b) the content. Both have been shown to have an effect at times on reading performance. Mohammed and Swales (1984), for example, are inclined to attribute their results to 'familiarity with the genre of technical instructions' (p. 211), more or less equivalent to Carrell's formal schemata. We, however, prefer to discuss this aspect of background knowledge under the heading of 'Literacy' (below). Bernhardt, as we mentioned above, divides studies into those concerned with cultural knowledge, subject-specific content, and information supplied to readers shortly before reading. In terms of the individual, we see no harm in grouping the first two types of knowledge together. We suspect, however, that information supplied to readers shortly before they read a text is likely to play a different part in reading from that played by longer established knowledge. We would like, then, to consider this under teaching methodology, and concentrate on well-established knowledge.

There are two related problems here: (a) to define in some way what it means to say, for example, that someone 'knows' chem-istry; and (b) to test the person's knowledge. Clearly the answer to (a) must be more than just a collection of facts: it must include relationships between 'facts', some idea of the purpose of the pursuit, possibly of the history of the subject, and future applica-tions. Equally obviously it cannot be determined in terms of vocabu-lary. As far as (b) is concerned, some form of test, such as the free-association tests used by Langer (1984), might be considered. However, while tests might successfully establish whether or not a reader was already well informed about limited topics such as cricket or baseball, it is difficult to imagine an easily adminis-tered test of an adult's knowledge of, say, production engineering. Given this problem, one tends to fall back on the sometimes naive assumption that if readers have already completed several years' study of an academic subject, then they will possess a store of background knowledge about it. This is the assumption made by Alderson and Urquhart. Given the uncertainty of a lack of ability to define the crucial variable, it is hardly surprising that some experiments fail to come up with positive results.

In spite of all this, however, there is enough evidence in the literature to support the theory that background knowledge plays a crucial part in the reading process.

Studies of the effect of background knowledge, when they find a positive effect, provide evidence that such knowledge can legitimately be considered a component of reading. They tell us nothing of the process, i.e. what is going on to produce this effect. For any sort of answer to this, we are usually referred to schema theory. This theory has been extensively described in the reading literature; in fact it sometimes seems to be obligatory for anyone writing a thesis on reading to begin with a lengthy description of the theory, beginning with Kant (1781), moving to Bartlett (1932), then to Rumelhart (1980). Bartlett found that English subjects, given a North American folk tale, were unable to comprehend or remember parts of it. This was in spite of the fact that none of the words or sentences was linguistically unfamiliar or senseless. It appeared that for comprehension and remembering to take place, the linguistic input needed to match existing mental configurations or concepts. Input which did not match the configuration was not remembered, even though it presented no actual linguistic difficulty.

While the notion of such configurations, or schemata, seems very attractive, there are huge problems attached. Sadoski et al. (1991: 466) quote Bartlett as saying:

> I strongly dislike the term 'schema.' It is at once too definite and too sketchy.

Below are some reasons for believing that schemata are not very useful in reading research (or possibly, by the ease with which they can be invoked in any number of situations, too useful):

1. Schemata are often described as being 'structures' or 'templates', and are often seen as being hierarchical (e.g. Collins and Quillian, 1969). Rumelhart (1980), on the other hand, sees schemata as being fluid and constantly capable of adapting to fresh information. Bartlett, also, in the excerpt referred to by Sadoski et al., refers to the need to invoke 'active, developing patterns'. But a constantly changing template is not likely to be a very useful instrument. In fact, the need for schemata to be structured in advance, yet adaptable to text-driven alterations, has been a problem for schema theorists from the beginning.
2. It has been argued that the term 'schema', as commonly used, is virtually synonymous with 'background knowledge', and hence is useless (cf. Sadoski et al., 1991).

3. Related to this is the odd fact that, at least in the L2 research literature, while schemata are frequently appealed to, they are seldom described in any detail. Compare the more rigorous experimental investigations of prototype theory, particularly the work on the cognitive representations of semantic categories by psychologists such as Rosch (1975) and Rosch et al. (1976). Thus L2 researchers invoke experimental subjects' possession, or lack of possession, of schemata related to weddings, Christmas, etc., without ever giving a description of what is contained in such schemata. Given that schemata are simultaneously described as 'structures', this is very odd indeed. It is not always the case that such description is missing. In the theoretical literature we find some illuminating descriptions of hierarchical structures, either of single vocabulary items, e.g. for the item 'canary' in Collins and Quillian (1969), or for an event such as a 'ship christening' in Anderson and Pearson (1988). But such fairly detailed structures, while admirable and capable of being tested, raise suspicions immediately. For example, the 'canary' schema has, attached to the 'bird' node, the fact that a bird 'has wings', 'can fly' and 'has feathers', but not that it has a beak or builds nests. The 'ship christening' schema, which is a very loose 'structure', and basically in fact is just a set of unordered components, contains the information that the christening takes place 'in dry dock'. But how many readers are likely to know this?

4. In addition to such lack of explicit description, L2 researchers entertain remarkably loose notions of the whole concept, so that schemata can be 'activated' or even 'acquired' at the drop, so to speak, of a short passage of introductory reading. But if the term is to have any use at all, then surely it must describe mental constructs of some stability, developed over some time by a sizeable portion of a population.

In the reading literature, different types of schemata have been suggested. We have already referred to Carrell's distinction between: 'content schema(ta)', relating to the content of a text read; 'formal schemata', relating to the rhetorical structure of the text; and 'cultural schemata', more general aspects of cultural knowledge shared by large sections of a cultural population. Carrell (1988a) has also added 'linguistic schemata'. Whether it is in reality useful to apply the same term to notions as different as, say, our knowledge of the passive voice, of behaviour at a wedding, of birds, of the meaning and purpose of life, or of newspaper articles, is questionable. Here we prefer to use the term 'background knowledge' for content or cultural schema. Formal schemata we prefer to deal with under Bernhardt's 'literacy' component, and linguistic schemata under different areas of language. For a detailed treatment of schemata, the reader is referred to the work of Cavalcanti (1983).

Threshold levels

Mohammed and Swales found that one of their NNS/Science subjects, whose estimated proficiency in English was low, was unable to perform the tasks, although presumably the subject had the necessary background knowledge. They put this down to the existence of a **threshold level**, which in this instance they locate at about Band 5 of the IELTS scale. In terms of an interactive model, what this amounts to is a claim that there is a level below which a deficit in one component cannot be compensated for by a corresponding strength in another. The term was first used by Clarke (1979) to account for aspects of data gathered from Spanish speakers reading English. Clarke hypothesized that some of his subjects, who were good readers in Spanish, were unable to transfer those reading skills because of inadequate mastery of the L2. Recently Ridgway (1997) has again invoked the threshold effect, this time, like Mohammed and Swales, to explain why a group of Turkish readers were unable to utilize background knowledge in reading English. Thus the threshold level has been used to explain why either background knowledge, or 'reading skills' (possibly equatable with Bernhardt's 'literacy' component) are unable to compensate for a lack of linguistic proficiency (Bernhardt, 1991b).

The notion of a threshold level seems commonsensical: no matter how good our reading skills are in the L1, or how expert we are in the content area, we are not likely to make much of a text in a language which is totally unknown to us. The mistake is to imply or infer that there is a general linguistic threshold level, valid for all tasks and all subjects. In fact, it seems obvious that some tasks will require a higher threshold level than others. It is probably also true that some subjects are able to make more of their limited linguistic proficiency than others. Thus the threshold level must be 'reset' for each subject or group of subjects, and each set of tasks. Given this limitation, it is a constraint which experimenters (and teachers) should keep in mind.

Literacy

Our final component is again taken from Bernhardt. By 'literacy', she means operational knowledge: knowing how to approach text, knowing why one approaches it and what to do with it. It includes the reader's preferred level of understanding, goal setting and comprehension monitoring.

Under this heading, we include both 'cohesion' and 'text structure'. Both decisions may seem slightly controversial: Halliday and Hasan (1976) would clearly class cohesion as a part of language knowledge. And Alderson (1993) is not unusual in deciding to including cohesive items in a test of grammar. De Beaugrande (1980), however, criticises an exclusive focus on the linguistic elements because of the lack of consideration paid to 'the underlying connectivity of text-knowledge and world-knowledge that makes these (cohesive) devices possible and useful' (p. 132). The relationship between cohesive elements and text knowledge seems a good argument for including cohesion under 'Literacy'.[4]

As far as text structure is concerned, Carrell's labelling of knowledge of such structures as 'formal schemata' might suggest that this topic should be included under the general heading of 'background knowledge'. However, to return to Bernhardt's formulation of literacy, 'knowing how to approach a text' must surely include knowledge of what kind of text it is, and hence how it is likely to be structured.

It would also be in line with Bernhardt's description to place in this section an account of readers' *strategies*. However, for various reasons, we have chosen to discuss these in Section 2.3. We should like the reader to note, however, that strategies clearly, in our opinion, form part of the literacy component.

Decisions as to where to place various elements are not just part of authorial housekeeping. We argue below that some of the discussion of reading skills versus language skills has been vitiated by vagueness as to what 'reading skills' actually consist of. It seems to us that Bernhardt's 'literacy' component is the best place to look for distinctively reading skills. Hence, what we decide to include in this component becomes crucial in an interesting and important area of research.

Cohesion

For de Beaugrande (1980), 'cohesion subsumes procedures whereby surface elements appear as progressive occurrences such that their sequential connectivity is maintained and made recoverable' (p. 19). In the 1970s and early 1980s, there was considerable interest in the effect of cohesion on L2 reading, and many books designed for classroom use, such as the Focus series (e.g. Glendinning, 1974), contained exercises designed to train readers in responding to cohesive devices in texts. Teachers, in our experience, have not always been convinced of the usefulness of such exercises. There is, moreover, comparatively little good research in this area. The topic, in fact, is rather more difficult and obscure than is sometimes recognised.

There is a hint in de Beaugrande's definition that 'cohesion' is a cover term, and this introduces a problem for the researcher. Different cohesive procedures may have radically different functions. The most obvious difference is that between Conjunction,[5] whereby a cohesive device indicates the pragmatic relationship between two text utterances or blocks, and devices such as Reference, Substitution, and Ellipsis, where the cohesive item replaces previously occurring parts of the text. The skills employed in handling these two groups are likely to be very different, raising the question as to whether it is desirable to investigate the effect of 'cohesion' seen as a homogeneous entity. The actual function played in texts by the different elements is not obvious, and it might be useful to distinguish between writer functions and reader functions. It might seem that the function of conjunction is not difficult to account for: by making the relationships between text units more transparent, the presence of conjunctive items might be expected to make texts more transparent for the reader, and hence easier to read. It is true that both Meyer (1975) and Urquhart (1976) found that, in the case of native speakers, marking the relationships did not seem to effect recall of a text. On the other hand, Cohen et al. (1979) found that with a reasonably extended text, native speakers of English structured their understanding in part by depending on conjunctives, whereas the nonnative readers failed to appreciate the relationships signalled by the conjunctives.

As various writers have pointed out, however, a sequence of text units may be coherent without the conjunctive item formally signalling the relationship. Thus the importance of conjunction on any particular occasion is open to question, varying as it is likely to do between readers. Steffensen (1988) argued that if cohesion was weakly related to coherence, recall of 'native' texts, i.e. relating to the culture of the reader, being more coherent, should contain more cohesive items than recall of corresponding 'foreign' texts. The hypothesis was not confirmed and Steffensen concludes that the formal teaching of cohesive devices in L2 reading should be treated with caution. We would argue, however, that her data suggest that the use of conjunction here is writer-focused, the writers using conjunctions to try to make sense of the text they are producing.

Urquhart (1976) found that academically gifted L1 teenagers introduced conjunctives when recalling texts which had not originally contained them. This, and Steffensen's results, then, serve to remind us that cohesion may be at least as important for the writing class.

The textual function of the other main group of cohesive devices, Pronominal Reference, Ellipsis and Substitution, and its relationship to reading, is perhaps even more problematic. Different writers have suggested different functions: continuity (Halliday and Hasan, 1976); economy (de Beaugrande, 1980); foregrounding (Chafe, 1972). We find it easier to describe such functions from the writer's point of view: 'Use pronouns to be economical and avoid repetition', etc. From the point of view of the reader, the effect of such cohesion is more difficult to define. With respect to economy, de Beaugrande refers to the trade-off between compactness and rapid access, i.e. pronominal reference is compact but ambiguities in reference may confuse and delay access. The final effect on readers may depend on individual skills, language proficiency, and knowledge of the world. The effect of foregrounding might seem to be even more difficult to assess.

In some cases, the effect of cohesive items may be very much on the surface. Cohen et al. (1979) report that in some cases their subjects simply did not know the meaning of conjunctives such as 'thus'. Some similar lack of surface familiarity may have been responsible for the situation, reported by Berman (1984), that L2 readers preferred texts in which pronominals and substitution items had been replaced by their lexical equivalents. The readers may just not have been familiar with the use of the cohesive items.

As far as the question of **how** readers handle cohesion is concerned, psychological research in the L1 area has concentrated on the relative difficulty of identifying antecedents. One hypothesis is that the distance between antecedent and pronoun will cause processing difficulty (this hypothesis is implicit in Halliday and Hasan's description, with its taking account of 'distance' in terms of number of sentences, and 'mediated ties' (sequences of pronouns all with the same antecedent). Rayner and Pollatsek (1989: 273), reviewing the evidence, conclude that 'pronoun reference . . . is governed not only by linguistic rules but by a looser set of discourse guidelines . . . based on the type of verb, parallelism of form, and whether the noun is still the topic of the discourse'.

Kintsch and van Dijk's model of reading (see below) relies heavily on repetition to establish overlap and hence coherence between propositions (Kintsch and van Dijk, 1978). Depending on how one defined it, repetition could include, in Haliday and Hasan's terms, '*lexical reiteration*', '*collocation*', major aspects of *grammatical reference* and *substitution*. We are a little cautious about such a seemingly crude approach to coherence, but there seems little doubt that repetition must be involved in readers' perception that the writer is continuing to talk about 'the same thing'.

It would thus seem very likely that cohesive procedures on the part of the reader have effects on reading performance. In both L1 and L2, however, the investigation of these effects would seem to require more subtlety than has been evident up to now. The importance of the teaching of cohesive procedures in the *writing* class should perhaps be emphasised.

Text structure

Brown and Yule (1983) point out that some of the coherence of a text derives not so much from the presence or absence of surface cohesive features such as conjunctives, but from underlying text relationships to which the conjunctives are pointers. From the 1970s onwards, several models have been available which attempt to map underlying coherence in text. Meyer (1975) points to a distinction between models which take into account the author's organization of the text being analysed, and those which impose another type of organization. Meyer has in mind analysts like Crothers (1972) who impose a form of logical structure on texts. Davies also ignores the author's organization, basing the analysis on types of information found in texts, so that, for example, 'physical structure' texts contain information about *part, location, property* and *function* (Davies and Greene, 1980; Davies, 1983; Johns and Davies, 1983). In the discussion below, we shall concentrate on models of the first type. We have selected descriptions which are (a) similar enough to each other to make for, hopefully, a coherent discussion and (b) dissimilar enough to make comparison interesting. Of the three selected, the models used by Meyer (1975) and Kintsch and van Dijk (1978) have been used in reading experiments; the 'composite' model formed by the work of Hoey (1983) and Winter (1994) has been offered as 'pure' text analysis, independent of reading.

Our models typically consist of (a) some form of 'unit' out of which the larger structure is constructed, (b) a set of relationships between such units and (c) a larger, global structure, to which the more local structures are in some way related.

Thus in the work of Winter (e.g. Winter 1994) and Hoey (1983) the units are natural language *clauses*, and the local relationships include Generalisation/Exemplification, and Denial/Correction. In addition to these 'clause relations', Winter and Hoey refer to basic *text structures*, such as Situation/Problem/Solution. As far as the relations between clause and text structures are concerned, Winter is not very explicit. Hoey (1983: 57) provides suggestions for mapping clause relations on text structure, along the lines of:

> If a Cause/Consequence relation consists of *a* and *b*, and *a* is identified as a Problem, then if *b* contains the role of agent, *b* is Response.

We don't know whether such mapping rules have ever been systematically tried on extended texts.

Meyer's (1975) model is taken from the linguist Grimes (1975). The basic unit is the *proposition*, consisting of a *predicate* and one or more *arguments*. There are two kinds of proposition: *lexical* and *rhetorical*. In the first, arguments are related to their predicates by semantic roles such as agent, patient, range, etc. (cf. Fillmore, 1968). The second kind are *rhetorical* propositions.

> Their main function could be thought of as that of organizing the content of discourse. They join lexical propositions together, and they join other rhetorical propositions together.
>
> (Grimes, 1975: 207)

One might reach the conclusion that lexical propositions operated up to clause level, while rhetorical propositions took over to link clauses or sentences. This is not strictly true, since rhetorical predicates can occur within clauses: 'the rhetorical predicates attribution, specific, collection and equivalence are frequently found in simple sentences' (Meyer, 1975: 45). They do, however, tend to be superordinate in text structure. According to Grimes (p. 207)

> In a tree that represents the underlying structure of a discourse
> . . . most of the propositions near the root are likely to be rhetorical,
> while most of the propositions near the leaves are likely to be lexical.

Rhetorical propositions are divided into three types: *paratactic, hypotactic* and *neutral*. In paratactic propositions, both arguments are at the same 'level'; a typical paratactic predicate is *collection*, of the sort '[there is] A and B and C', in which A, B and C are equal in rhetorical level. In a hypotactic proposition, one argument is superordinate to another. Thus in the *Evidence* predicate, the evidence argument is subordinate to the argument for which it supplies evidence. Neutral predicates can be either paratactic or hypotactic.

Since hypotactic predicates have the effect of subordinating one argument to another, and, more generally, since an argument can consist of a proposition which can include arguments which . . . etc., the result of the analysis of a text is a 'hierarchically arranged tree structure' called a '*content structure*'.

There are some quite close resemblances between Meyer's analysis and that of Winter and Hoey. Relationships such as 'Cause/consequence', 'General/specific', occur in both, though with different terminology. 'Problem/solution' again is present in both analyses. However, in Meyer, it is a rhetorical predicate, capable of appearing at different levels of the content structure; in Hoey it is a basic text structure, seemingly different from clause relations In general, in the 1975 account, Meyer does not distinguish between local and global relations. Meyer and Rice (1984: 326) refer to three levels, with micropropositions at sentence level, macropropositions at paragraph level, where 'the concern is with the relationship among ideas represented in complexes of ideas or paragraphs', and the third level is 'the overall organising principle' of the text, e.g. causality, problem/solution, etc. (p. 327).

Before beginning our account of our third model, that of Kintsch and van Dijk (1978), we should point out that it is much more than a description of text organization. In fact, it sets out to model a large part of the process of reading and remembering an extended text. As such, it contains a considerable amount of discussion about how the reader proceeds to take in a certain amount of information at a time, and operate on this information while it is in working memory before proceeding to the next chunk of information. It also deals, in rather less detail, with how the reader, simultaneous with processing the clauses and sentences of the text into a coherent whole, the text base, also proceeds to build up an account of the gist of the text, the macrostructure, or rather, given the constraints of memory and the cyclical nature of the processing model, a sequence of macrostructures. To the extent that Meyer also tested her model empirically, this constitutes a similarity between her and Kintsch and van Dijk, and a major difference between these writers, on the one hand, and Winter and Hoey on the other.

As with Meyer, the basic unit of analysis for Kintsch and van Dijk is the proposition, consisting of a predicate and arguments. Predicates 'may be realized in the surface structure as verbs, adjectives, adverbs, and sentence connectives' (Kintsch and van Dijk, 1978: 367). Thus the distinction drawn by Grimes and Meyer between lexical and rhetorical predicates is not observed. Propositions are expressed in the form (BETWEEN, ENCOUNTER, POLICE, BLACK PANTHER), which represents the text 'encounters between police and Black Panther Party members' (p. 377). The system incorporates a set of semantic role relationships similar to those described by Grimes, but in the 1978 article, these are not indicated, 'to keep the notation simple', and in fact, Kintsch and van Dijk's trees are much easier to read than Meyer's.[6]

These *micropropositions* are built up into a structure referred to as a *text base*, or *microstructure*, which can be depicted as a *coherence graph*. Such graphs are very similar to Meyer's *content structure*. Coherence is maintained largely by referential coherence, depicted in the graph as overlap of arguments. Thus the two propositions 'ABC' and 'XDC' achieve coherence by the presence in both of the argument 'C'. Sometimes coherence cannot be detected in this way, and then the reader may need to generate *inferences* to maintain coherence. Thus the total list of propositions may be longer than that contained in the text. Propositions are also arranged in terms of 'level', i.e. some propositions are superordinate to others. This ordering is done partly in terms of the simplicity of the resulting graph structure, and partly in terms of coherence relations. If, for example, proposition 17 has been nominated as superordinate, and propositions 15, 10 and 13 relate cohesively to 17, then they are all considered as subordinate to 17. If, then, propositions 20 and 23 relate cohesively to 13, they are in turn subordinate to it.

The other main organizational component in Kintsch and van Dijk's model is the *macrostructure*. If the microstructure is 'the local level of the discourse, that is, the structure of the individual propositions and their relations', the macrostructure is 'of a more global nature, characterising the discourse as a whole' (p. 365). Thus Kintsch and van Dijk, like Winter and Hoey, have two separate, though connected levels of organization. Kintsch and van Dijk see the macrostructure as being built up at the same time as the microstructure; in other words, the former is not a summary of the latter. The macrostructure is formed partly by the application of *macrorules*, which operate on the microstructure, for example deleting irrelevant propositions, or substituting generalisations for sequences of detailed propositions. The propositions so derived are organised by a *schema*, which is brought by the reader into contact with the microstructure.

On the whole, Kintsch and van Dijk deal with schemata as 'conventional schematic structures of discourse' (p. 366), equivalent to Carrell's 'formal schemata'. However, they do make allowances for a different form of schema.

> The reader's goals in reading control the application of the macro-operators. The formal representation of these goals is the schema.
>
> (p. 373)

In other words, the schema is produced in accordance with the reader's goals in reading. Given this view of schema, Kintsch and van Dijk (1978) envisage three situations. In the first, 'a reader's goals are vague, and the text that he or she reads lacks a conventional structure' (p. 373). In this case, the schema invoked and the macrostructure would be unpredictable. This is the form of reading which we shall later be discussing under the term '*browsing*' (p. 103). In the second situation, the text type is highly conventional, and this in turn sets clear goals. In the third situation, the goals are again clear, but are set by the reader who has a special purpose in mind, which may override the text structure. Such a reader is discussed below as a 'dominant' reader.

Empirical validation of the text structure models

Various aspects of the models above have received some measure of experimental validation. Kintsch and Keenan (1973) found that sentences became more difficult to read and understand in relation to the number of propositions they contained: the more propositions, the more difficulty (see also Weaver and Kintsch, 1991). Meyer (1975) used her model to investigate the type of information recalled by subjects after reading an extended prose text. Information which the model showed to be at a higher level in the text was recalled better than lower level information. At the overall organization level, Stanley (1984) found that both natives and non-natives preferred summaries organised according to a Problem/Solution model, as opposed to texts of the same length and linguistic difficulty which deviated from the model. Carrell's findings (Carrell, 1984) that familiar rhetorical organisation appeared to help readers, can be added here. Rayner and Pollatsek (1989) again cite evidence that readers' recall of the gist of texts tended to resemble the macrostructure.

Conclusion

Clearly an organized text is more than a string of clauses or sentences or propositions. Equally clearly, this fact is likely to be relevant to the reading process. All the descriptions of text structure above seem to us to have something to contribute in this area and the most useful will be discussed further in Part 3 in relation to choice of texts for testing. However, before we leave the topic, some criticisms remain to be dealt with.

The use of propositional analysis by Kintsch (1974) and van Dijk (1977) has been criticised by Brown and Yule (1983) on the grounds that, in spite of its appearance of formalism and objectivity, it is fundamentally subjective. While this is probably true, it does not seem to us to be exceptional. Most interesting analysis of natural language rests on consensus; the most formalized generative grammar is supposed to be constructed on the basis of native speakers agreeing on whether such and such a sentence is acceptable or not. The fact that they are seldom consulted is beside the point. It is fairly easy to check the extent to which two or more analysts agree.

Brown and Yule also criticize such analyses for concentrating on content, and for being unable to deal with staging. This again is probably true; Meyer (1975) comments on the inability of Grimes' analysis to incorporate staging successfully. From our point of view, given that our main focus is on students' learning from texts, it is possible that staging is of minor importance in comparison with conventional text structure. This would not be surprising: we have already noted how another linguistic aspect of writing, namely signalling, seems to have comparatively little effect on the reader.

Rayner and Pollatsek query whether the elaborate apparatus used by Kintsch and van Dijk is justifiable, or whether it could be replaced by something less formal, available to the 'intelligent lay reader'. This certainly seems to be a valid criticism of an analysis such as Meyer's, which is difficult to read, made scoring of subjects' recall scripts, on her own admission, an 'extremely tedious' task (p. 101), and which is made complex by the inclusion of case roles which could not be correlated with any effects in the recalls. The complex formality is particularly dubious, given the comparatively crude description of how to arrive at the analysis, e.g.

> The topic sentence of the third paragraph of this passage states that the breeder reactor is the solution to the previously stated problems.   (p. 54)

In Section 5.3 (pp. 275–7), we put forward less formal ways of analysing texts for our particular purposes.

Finally, we should like to make a comment on specific patterns of organization in texts, referred to and to some extent critical for all the analyses above. The question is: How finite are these different patterns of organization? We have seen that Kintsch and van Dijk's macrostructures seem in part to depend on what they refer to as 'highly conventionalized text types'. Such text types unquestionably occur. It is our experience, however, based on teaching the analysis of written texts, either that the number of such text types is very large indeed, or that a number of the texts encountered are indeterminate as to overall text structure. Hoey (1983: 34) argues that 'the number of discourse patterns that can be built out of a finite set of relations signalled in a finite number of ways is indefinitely large'. Whether the first part of this claim is true (Hoey appears to be rather coy about listing interclausal relations), we tend to agree with the second part.

Text types

Text types have been referred to above in relation to Kintsch and van Dijk's model. With their reference to 'highly conventionalised text types', it seems that these authors have in mind something like Swales' genres (Swales, 1990). Just because they are so specific, Swales' genres seem to us more useful in accounts of writing. In our discussion here, we concentrate on an older tradition of describing rather generalised types which, in our opinion, are of more general relevance for reading.

De Beaugrande (1981: 307) asserts that '... reading models will have to find control points in the reading process where text-type priorities can be inserted and respected'. The implication is that the different textual and communicative demands of different text types will affect reading performance, and further that some readers may be limited with regard to the types they can handle.

De Beaugrande mentions *Narrative, Descriptive* and *Argumentative* types. Calfee and Curley (1984) have *Object, Sequence* and *Idea*, in which *Sequence* relates to *Narrative, Idea* to *Argument*, and *Object* is loosely related to *Description*. Moore (1980) adds *Exposition* and *Enquiry*, and Brooks and Warren (1952) have *Exposition, Narrative, Description* and *Argument* as the four 'basic types of writing'.

An examination of these writers suggests that there are at least four criteria involved in defining text types.

- **Communicative intent**. Thus Brooks and Warren define *Argument* as 'the kind of discourse used to make the audience . . . think or act as the arguer desires'.
- **Content**. Calfee and Curley's *Object* category is defined as 'discussions of things, persons and even ideas'.
- **Structure**. Calfee and Curley define *Sequence* as 'to do with any account in which progression is the key to the structure'.
- **Status of the information**. Moore argues that *Exposition* 'presents knowledge already established', while *Enquiry* is concerned 'to raise questions, . . . and express doubts and possibilities'.

There is an interesting attempt at a taxonomy using communicative intent, status of information, and expected response from reader in Baten and Cornu (1984). A development of their taxonomy relating to Expository texts is presented in Urquhart (1996).

There appears to be little work done on the possible differential effects of text types on readers. However, individuals often report that they prefer fiction (imaginary narrative) or are poor at reading instructions. McCormick (1992) hypothesized that narratives should be easier than expository texts. This was not confirmed but she considers that background knowledge is more important in the case of expository texts. Reading tests, such as that contained in IELTS, use a fairly informal categorisation of text types. A combination of different text types with tasks suitably tailored for particular types (Narrative would seem to invoke a different set of responses from Exposition) has been put forward by Urquhart (1996) as a potentially rewarding area of research (cf. Kobayashi, 1995). We shall revisit the issue of text types in Chapter 3 when it will be considered as a performance condition in testing activities.

Having examined in some detail the components of the various models we need to explore how they might be operationalised by readers interacting with text(s) for different purposes. As well as a concern with the nature of text readers may engage with, we need to look in more detail at the process and product involved in and resulting from such interactions.

2.3   COMPREHENSION, SKILLS, STRATEGIES AND STYLES

The concepts that we discuss in this section are rather more disparate than might appear at first sight. *Comprehension* is frequently mentioned in cognitive and educational psychology, as well as, of course, the pedagogical literature. There is often an assumption in the literature that it is the goal of the reading process. As such, it does not appear in the models discussed above. On the other hand, much of what has been said about the components of models could be translated into terms of *skills*: decoding is a skill, accessing the lexicon is a skill, parsing syntactic structures is a skill, and so on. The focus on Skills can be seen historically partly as a development of interest in comprehension, an attempt to break down that rather vague and undifferentiated concept into more accessible chunks. Educationally it may be seen, at least in part, as an attempt to give teachers a structure for both syllabuses and for materials. *Strategies* appear to have come into Reading

Research via psychology, where they were used to describe how an organism sought to attain its goals. In both reading research and practice, a focus on strategies has had the effect of making the whole operation more learner-centred. Finally, what we are calling here *Styles*, also known as Strategies, have for some time been an important topic in Educational Psychology. All four terms relate, in different ways, to reading activities and outcomes. The first three, in particular, have been important foci of attention in pedagogically related studies of reading, while the fourth is likely to become of greater importance in future research.

Comprehension

As noted in Chapter 1 (Preliminaries), the focus of attention among people concerned with reading in education was 'decoding', whereas in the 1970s the focus moved to 'comprehension'. This can be seen clearly in Figure 1.2 above, based on ERIC data, which shows comprehension studies taking off from 1966 onwards.

The switch of attention from decoding to comprehension must have been very liberating for teachers and researchers, since, although we have stressed the importance of decoding, there seems little doubt that a focus on the information being communicated by texts has more potential for interest. A focus on comprehension is in line with our feeling that this is what reading is 'about', i.e. getting information from written texts. And there is no doubt that our monitoring of our own reading comprehension is of major importance. A judgement that we have not understood a text may well leave us unsatisfied, or lead us to re-read it, or perhaps reject it in disgust.

In spite of this, however, comprehension in some areas remains a somewhat elusive entity. Rayner and Pollatsek (1989), for example, give neither definition nor description of comprehension itself, though, according to their index, the larger part of the chapter dealing with 'Representation of Discourse' is concerned with 'comprehension processes'. From the first part of their chapter, one might gather that, for them, comprehension equals ' "the meaning of the text" that is being read' (p. 264).

It is, in fact, our contention that in the teaching and testing of reading, 'comprehension', as generally defined, has been either not very helpful or positively dangerous. Urquhart (1987) summarises common assumptions behind the pedagogical view of comprehension as follows:

Assumption 1. There is such a thing as 'total' or 'perfect' comprehension of a text.

Assumption 2. Careful reading, which aims to extract perfect comprehension, is superior to any other kind of reading, e.g. skimming, and is, in fact, the only kind of reading which deserves the name.

Evidence of the existence of these assumptions is pervasive. As evidence for Assumption 1 we may quote Fry (1963) as saying that 100 per cent on his comprehension exercises equals 'perfect comprehension'; Sticht (1984) argues that claims for the possibility of reading much faster than listening rest on a confusion between skimming and scanning on the one hand and reading on the other. Hence skimming and scanning, which can accept lower levels of comprehension, are not really 'reading' at all.

Whether or not 'perfect comprehension' is a feasible goal, we should reject the assertion by Fry and others that it is equivalent to a 100 per cent score on comprehension questions. Even with a short text, it is usually possible to devise a large number of questions. The conventional ten questions, often multiple-choice, which pass as a comprehension test, represent at best a sampling of information gained by reading. As Lunzer et al. (1979: 66) put it,

> How a student completes a test is an INDEX of his capacity to comprehend; it is not the capacity itself and still less is it the comprehension itself.

We have said that the typical pedagogical view is 'dangerous'. Firstly, by largely insisting on the superiority of one type of reading at the expense of all others, it has the effect of disparaging perfectly normal types of reading behaviour. This does not just apply to reading types such as skimming and scanning (see Section 2.4 below), where the view allows a drop in comprehension in return for an increase in speed. By giving preference to what we call 'careful' reading – i.e. the type normally associated with study – it also effectively downgrades the value of the type of reading behaviour many people will adopt when reading, say, detective novels for enjoyment, where the reader's monitor is likely to accept lower standards of comprehension. Classroom reading becomes almost exclusively 'intensive' reading (see Chapter 4), and if classroom tasks have any influence on students' behaviour outside the classroom, this may well result in slow, laborious reading when this is not, in fact, necessary.

The other danger lies in the assumption that a text contains a finite amount of information, accessible to all readers. The information is, in other words, 'on the page'. This clashes with the currently widely accepted view that the reader interacts with the text in order to obtain a message, e.g.

> Thus, contrary to conventional wisdom, which states that comprehension is the process of getting meaning from a page, comprehension is ... the process of bringing meaning to a text.
>
> (Samuels and Kamil, 1988: 206)

This view has serious consequences both for the teaching and testing of reading. If each reader brings meaning to a text, then each comprehension is likely to be different. The notion of a 'right' answer has now to be treated with care. Variations in comprehension are likely to come from different background knowledge brought to the text (though this is not the only possible source). In a classroom where teacher and students share the same culture, such variations may not be very large. In EFL or ESP classrooms in the English-speaking world, however, where teacher and students may come from a wide range of backgrounds and cultures, the possibility of varying comprehensions may become a major problem. And if this is true for the classroom, it is even more true for international EFL reading tests.

Urquhart (1987) distinguishes between 'comprehensions', referring to differences brought about by readers setting themselves different levels of acceptable comprehension (i.e. between reading a book for an examination and reading it for light amusement), and 'interpretations', referring to differences resulting either from different readers bringing different information to a text, or the same reader at different times, bringing a different mind-set. While the terms may not be perfectly chosen for keeping the different factors apart, the distinction should serve as a reminder of the number of variables likely to be present in many teaching or testing situations (discussed in Chapters 3 and 4 below).

We should mention here the notion that the 'ideal' comprehension consists of the recovery of 'author's meaning'. We do not think that it can be doubted that readers often strive to do this; it is an important aspect of careful reading, and, since it involves close attention to textual features such as use of conjuncts ('however', etc.), headings, the ordering of information, and so on, it is something that can partly be taught. We have only two doubts about it being used as the 'ideal' comprehension. First, it can never be fully achieved. We can never be sure that we have totally entered the writer's mind. It could be said, however, that it is in the nature of all good ideals never to be achieved. Secondly, a careful attempt to recover author's meaning is not characteristic of all reading; the reader engaged in scanning, for example, may pay little attention to author's intentions. Such attention is, in fact, characteristic of careful reading, particularly where this is submissive (see below). As such, it is important, but cannot be a definition of comprehension in general.

We have just argued that 'author's meaning' can never be recaptured in its entirety. It can be argued, however, that just recapturing author's meaning is not enough. Advocates of 'critical reading' (cf. Fairclough, 1995; Wallace, 1992a&b) point out that texts are dependent on presuppositions stemming from their authors' own particular world view, their 'ideology'. It then becomes the duty of the critical reader, by spotting such ideological presuppositions, to evaluate a text in its cultural context.

It is clear that *comprehension* cannot be viewed simply as the product of any reading activity. Rather, in any reading situation, comprehension will vary according to the reader's background knowledge, goals, interaction with the writer, etc. *Comprehension* is a useful term to contrast with *decoding*; otherwise it is best perhaps taken as the product resulting from a particular reading task, and evaluated as such.

Skills

A reading skill can be described roughly as a cognitive ability which a person is able to use when interacting with written texts. Thus, unlike comprehension, which can be viewed as the product of reading a particular text, skills are seen as part of the generalized reading process.

Skills have been a major area of reading research over recent years, as can be seen in Figure 2.1, based on data from ERIC.

Skills have been recommended by Lunzer et al. (1979) and Vincent (1985) as a means of structuring reading syllabi, and are

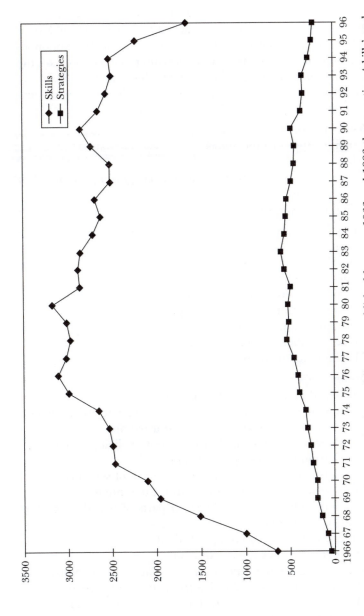

Figure 2.1 Number of articles and other publications published between 1966 and 1996 that mention 'skills' and 'strategies' in their title or in ERIC's index or abstract (based on data from ERIC).

probably still the best framework for doing this. They have also been used for test construction, notably in the ELTS test and TEAP (Weir 1983a, 1990). Useful as the concept of skills has been, there are considerable problems attached to it. Williams and Moran (1989: 223) point out that while a number of skills taxonomies exist, there is little consensus concerning the content of the taxonomies or in the terminology used to describe them. Below we give a selection of fairly typical taxonomies, which serve, incidentally, to justify Williams and Moran's comment.

1. Davis (1968):
   - Identifying word meanings.
   - Drawing inferences.
   - Identifying writer's technique and recognising the mood of the passage.
   - Finding answers to questions.

2. Lunzer et al. (1979):
   - Word meaning.
   - Words in context.
   - Literal comprehension.
   - Drawing inferences from single strings.
   - Drawing inferences from multiple strings.
   - Interpretation of metaphor.
   - Finding salient or main ideas.
   - Forming judgements.

3. Munby (1978):
   - Recognising the script of a language.
   - Deducing the meaning and use of unfamiliar lexical items.
   - Understanding explicitly stated information.
   - Understanding information when not explicitly stated.
   - Understanding conceptual meaning.
   - Understanding the communicative value of sentences.
   - Understanding the relations within the sentence.
   - Understanding relations between parts of text through lexical cohesion devices.
   - Interpreting text by going outside it.
   - Recognising indicators in discourse.
   - Identifying the main point of information in discourse.
   - Distinguishing the main idea from supporting detail.
   - Extracting salient points to summarise (the text, an idea)
   - Selective extraction of relevant points from a text.

- Basic reference skills.
- Skimming.
- Scanning to locate specifically required information.
- Transcoding information to diagrammatic display.

4. Grabe (1991: 377):
   - Automatic recognition skills.
   - Vocabulary and structural knowledge.
   - Formal discourse structure knowledge.
   - Content/world background knowledge.
   - Synthesis and evaluation skills/strategies.
   - Metacognitive knowledge and skills monitoring.

It is comparatively easy to criticise some of these taxonomies, even at first sight. Davis's 'Finding the answers to questions' seems to include all the others, and prompts the query: 'Which questions?' It is hard to believe that the assignment of separate status to 'Drawing inferences from single strings', and 'Drawing inferences from multiple strings' in Lunzer et al.'s taxonomy is really justified. There are, however, wider questions to ask about the taxonomies.

How inclusive is a skill? Clearly, in the taxonomies above, some skills seem more inclusive than others; Grabe's taxonomy, for example, uses very general categories, virtually equivalent to knowledge areas. Rayner and Pollatsek (1989) begin their preface, 'Reading is a highly complex skill . . .' (p. ix). Clearly, if reading itself is a skill, it must be possible to break this down into different levels of component skills categories. Williams and Moran (1989) suggest a rough distinction between 'language related' skills and 'reason related' skills.

Various attempts have been made to arrange skills into hierarchies. Of the taxonomies above, that of Lunzer et al. is so arranged, with the 'lowest level' skill at the top. Munby's taxonomy was not intended to be hierarchically arranged, though in his review of the work Mead (1982) argued that it should have been, on the grounds that some skills seem to presuppose the learning of other skills. Some possible criteria for ranking skills are as follows:

(a) *Logical implication.* One component in the system can logically be considered to presuppose all components below it. This is the criterion used by Bloom et al. (1956, 1974).

(b) *Pragmatic implication.* A reader displaying one skill in the system can be assumed to possess all the 'lower' skills.

(c) *Difficulty.* The components are arranged in order of increasing difficulty.

(d) *Developmental.* Some skills are acquired earlier than others. Some syllabi, rather unwisely, in our view, assume that readers pass through a period of comprehending 'explicitly stated' information before they arrive at the stage of inferencing.

(e) *Discourse level.* A skill is ordered with respect to the size or level of the discourse unit it relates to. We have not found explicit mention of this criterion in the literature, but suspect it is commonly used by teachers and applied linguists. It would explain a tendency to rate 'thematic' questions, aimed at the whole of a text, as being 'high level'.

There have been various attempts to investigate the psychological reality (or separateness) of different skills. On the basis of tests based on the taxonomy given above, Lunzer and Gardner (1979) concluded that there was no evidence for the separate existence of the skills, and that:

> reading comprehension should not be thought of in terms of a multiplicity of specialized aptitudes. To all intents and purposes such differences reflect only one general aptitude: this being the pupil's ability and willingness to reflect on whatever it is he is reading.
>
> (p. 64)

This is the so-called 'Unitary Hypothesis', as opposed to the 'Multi-divisible Hypothesis'. Lunzer et al. also investigated the pragmatic validity of their hierarchy of skills, testing the hypothesis that:

> there exists an identifiable group of pupils whose performance on higher-level tasks is defective to a degree which would not be predicted on the basis of their performance on lower-level tasks.
>
> (p. 61)

Again they found no evidence for this, although they did find some evidence of a difficulty hierarchy. Further research in these areas is discussed in Part 3 in relation to testing.

Before we leave the topic of *skills*, we can make the following general comments:

1. The possession of a specialised comprehension skill, if we hypothesise such a thing, does not guarantee success in completing

a particular task. We are all capable of making mistakes. This argues for the need for a longitudinal study into the reality or otherwise of such skills.

2. The conclusions by Lunzer et al., cited above, can only apply to **comprehension**. Virtually everyone concedes that decoding is a separate component/skill, since, as pointed out earlier, normal young children can comprehend, without being able to decode, while some disabled individuals can decode without comprehending. Hence we have to accept at least a twin-skills model (this discussion is taken further in Section 3.2 (p. 120).

3. Pragmatic validation is not the only form of justification for skills taxonomies. Difficulty has been mentioned as a criterion for a hierarchy, and most of us would presumably agree that, on average, 'Understanding the relations within the sentence' is an easier skill than 'Extracting salient points to summarise (the text, an idea)'. The L2 learner, forced back to an earlier developmental stage by the difficulties of unfamiliar syntax or lexis, may well have to wait before being able to summarise a text.

Finally, as said before, skills are useful tools for the development of both teaching materials and tests. In spite of the doubts that have been raised, we shall continue to make use of the taxonomies.

Transfer of reading skills

During the 1980s, there was considerable debate about the amount of transfer of reading skills from reading in one language to reading in another. The focus of the debate is encapsulated in the title of Alderson's article, 'Reading in a foreign language: a reading problem or a language problem?' (Alderson, 1984). Since we are taking the view here that reading can be defined as the receptive handling of a language in written form, the dichotomy implied by Alderson's title does not really exist. Moreover, much of the discussion was poorly focused, since the 'reading skills' which were supposed to be transferred across languages were seldom well defined. This is discussed further in Section 5.2. In the light of the discussion above, however, it would appear that 'reading skills' are best seen as Bernhardt's 'literacy' component. The extent to which the 'literacy' skills that she describes are transferable remains to be examined. Perhaps the single most important literacy skill, surely likely to be transferred, is the ability to view a printed text as a piece of language discourse, to be viewed in a similar way as an oral discourse.

Strategies

Reference to Figure 2.1 shows that strategy research is a later development than skills research, only becoming popular in the 1980s. The research methodology is very different from that associated with skills. In much skills research, the investigator begins with a taxonomy of skills, arrived at, perhaps, by means of text analysis. The psychological validity of this taxonomy may then be empirically checked. In strategies research, on the other hand, the researcher begins by having subjects (often divided into 'good' and 'poor' readers) read a text and, either retrospectively at the end of reading or at points during reading, report on what they are doing. The strategies revealed by these reports are then categorized. If a prior division of subjects has been made, an attempt is often made to equate some aspect of strategy use to the 'good' or to the 'poor' group.

Because of the time-consuming methodology, the number of subjects tends to be small, and there is an emphasis on qualitative rather than quantitative results. However, it should be noted that the uncovering of strategies is pragmatic; hence, unlike skills, their psychological validity does not need to be investigated.

Two fairly representative examples of strategy research are the investigations of Olshavsky (1977), who did her work with English-speaking readers, and Sarig (1987), who worked with bilingual Hebrew- and English-speaking subjects. Since the focus here is on the actual strategies used by readers, together with definitions of what constitutes a strategy, no details are given as to the hypotheses examined, or the discussion of strategy use.

The strategies detected and categorised by Olshavsky were as follows:

- *Word related*: Use of context to define a word, synonym substitution, stated failure to understand a word.
- *Clause related*: Re-reading, inferences, addition of information, personal identification, hypothesis, stated failure to understand a clause.
- *Story related*: Use of information in story to solve a problem.

Sarig used a similar technique to investigate the behaviour of Hebrew-speaking students reading in English and in Hebrew. Again a 'think-aloud-when-reading' technique was use, though it is not clear from Sarig's account precisely when they verbalised. Sarig refers to responses to any particular problem as 'moves', and strategies as being combinations of moves. To avoid confusion, however, her 'moves' will be referred to as strategies. The strategies she uncovered and categorised were as follows:

- *Technical aid*: Skimming, scanning, skipping.
- *Coherence detecting*: Identification of macroframe, use of content schemata, identification of key information in text, etc.
- *Clarification and simplification monitoring*: Syntactic simplification; using synonyms, circumlocutions, etc. Change of planning, mistake correction, ongoing self-evaluation, controlled skipping, repeated reading.

Even given the ten years between the two papers, it is striking just how different are the two lists of strategies. While, as claimed above, it can be argued that the detection of strategies, unlike that of skills, is pragmatic, there is clearly an element of subjectivity both in identifying and in categorising them. This subjectivity may be reduced if we can agree on a definition of strategies.

Definitions

Both Olshavsky and Sarig view reading as 'a problem-solving process'. Admittedly there may be some problems defining 'problem', but, in commonsense terms, we can regard strategies as ways of getting round difficulties encountered while reading. Thus, initially at least, strategies can be seen as responses to local problems in a text. We should also include in our definition a reference to the fact that the response must be a conscious one. Olshavsky claims that a strategy is 'a *purposeful* means of comprehending the author's message' (p. 656; our emphasis). Pritchard (1990: 275) defines a strategy as 'a deliberate action that readers take voluntarily to develop an understanding of what they read'. Cohen (1998: 5) points out that the question is controversial but comes down firmly on the side of conscious choice:

> In my view, the element of consciousness is what distinguishes strategies from those processes that are not strategic.

Given a definition along the lines we have indicated above, it is hard to accept some of Olshavsky's strategies as such; in particular, '*stated failure to understand a word*' or '*stated failure to understand a clause*' as strategies. Olshavsky emends this by dividing her strategies into 'problem identification' (i.e. monitoring), and 'problem solving'. Another of her 'strategies' involves the reader substituting synonyms during recall. But this is a general feature of readers' recall of text (cf. Steffensen and Joag-Dev, 1984).

Strategies and skills

There is a fair amount of confusion in the literature as to what distinguishes a skill from a strategy. Some writers (e.g. Nuttall, Grabe) refer to 'skills/strategies' as if the two were interchangeable. Table 2.1 illustrates the amount of overlap. Admittedly, some of this apparent confusion may be due simply to the fact that the skills proponents did not attempt to separate skills from strategies (we have already noted the practice of referring to 'skills/strategies' as if the two were interchangeable). However, it would be satisfying, for the sake of clarity, to arrive at some generally accepted distinction. The following are possible differences:

- Strategies are reader-oriented, skills are text-oriented. It is certainly true that skills taxonomies tend to focus on text. Munby's taxonomy of skills is overwhelmingly text based. In the list of 19 reading skills cited by Criper and Davies (1988), only 7 can be said unambiguously to take the reader into account, e.g.

    Interpreting text by going outside it.
    Selective extraction of relevant points from a text.

    The other 12 are text based, e.g.

    Understanding conceptual meaning.
    Understanding the communicative value of sentences.
    Understanding the relations within the sentence.
    Understanding relations between parts of text through lexical cohesion devices.

In fact, Munby's skills represent a passive reader, typical verbs used being 'understand', 'recognise'. Anything which the reader actively contributes to the text, such as Olshavsky's 'Personal identification', or any behaviour which the reader, as an individual,

Table 2.1 Distinguishing features between 'skills' and 'strategies'

STRATEGIES		SKILLS
Olshavsky	Sarig	Munby, Nuttall, Lunzer et al.
Use of context to define a word or synonym		Deducing the meaning and use of familiar lexis
Synonym substitution	Synonyms	
Stated failure to understand a word	Ongoing self-evaluation; mistake correction	
Re-reading	Repeated reading	Repeating reading
		Skimming or scanning
Inference	Paraphrasing	Understanding information in the text, not explicitly stated
Addition of information	Extra-textual content	Interpreting text by going outside it
Stated failure to understand a clause	Deserting a hopeless utterance	
	Flexibility of reading rate	Variations in reading rate

manifests towards the text, e.g. skipping, are likely not to appear on Munby's list. Obviously, since monitoring is a reader-directed activity, many of its manifestations will not appear, e.g. self-evaluation in general, admitting failure to understand part of the text, are again unlikely to appear. The fact that some such activities do appear – e.g. scanning and skimming – may be an indication that Munby's 'skills' do, in fact, include a number of 'strategies'.

- Strategies represent conscious decisions taken by the reader, skills are deployed unconsciously. Another way of phrasing this is that skills have reached the level of automaticity. Certainly many of Munby's skills, such as lexical recognition and syntactic parsing, can be assumed to have reached automatic levels in L1 or advanced L2 readers, and hence would not be reported in strategy research. There are difficulties associated with this criterion; all the descriptions detailed above include 're-reading'. The regressions reported from eye-movement research could be considered a type of re-reading, and it might be difficult to decide just how conscious readers were of regressing. However, the criterion of 'conscious v automatic' seems a good one to us.

- Strategies, unlike skills, represent a response to a problem, e.g. failure to understand a word or the significance of a proposition, failure to find the information one was looking for, etc. This criterion is closely related to our first one: at a local level, something only becomes a problem if one becomes aware of it. It is true that the term 'problem' poses some difficulties in itself. We have been using the term to refer to local difficulties encountered when reading a text. However, in Newell and Simon's theory, used by Olshavsky, a problem may be anything in the task environment which stands between the organism and its goal. In this wider sense, if we decide to read a book for information on a particular subject, the whole text of the book becomes a problem. We discuss what we call 'global' strategies in the next section.

On the whole, however, we agree with the distinction drawn by Williams and Moran (1989: 223):

> A skill is an ability which has been automatised and operates largely subconsciously, whereas a strategy is a conscious procedure carried out in order to solve a problem.

Strategies and styles

A rather different approach to strategy research can be found in the work of Pask (1976) and Entwhistle et al. (1979) in Britain, and Marton (1976), Saljo (1975) and Fransson (1984) in Sweden. Widdowson (1984) should be included in this group, as should Hartman (1992) in the USA. These researchers are usually concerned with effective learning, rather than reading as such, but since their subjects are usually students in tertiary education, much of whose learning is achieved through reading, their work is relevant here.

Table 2.2   Different reading styles

Pask	**Holistic**: Characterised by the attempt to relate text content to what is already known or to current concerns. The reader uses personal analogies, illustrations, and concrete examples which, while formally incorrect, serve as temporary pegs on which to hang partially understood abstract concepts.	**Serialist**: Learners attempt to build understanding out of the component details, logical steps and operations taken strictly in a linear sequence. Relationships are sought entirely within the context of the task.
Marton, Saljo, Fransson	**Deep processors**: Aim at a thorough understanding of the author's main message or argument (Marton); relate ideas of the text to their own personal experience (Fransson).	**Surface processors**: Attempt rote learning of important pieces of information on which questions might subsequently be asked (Marton); direct their learning toward learning the text itself (Fransson).
Hartman	**Logocentric**: The reader is buried in a passage, his or her 'textual world' being largely defined by the author's meaning.	**Resistant**: The reader tries to absent the author's meaning by asserting his or her own.
Widdowson	**Dominant**: The reader asserts the primacy of his or her conceptual pattern, fitting textual information into it directly and short-circuiting the discourse process (p. 223).	**Submissive**: The reader adjusts in a submissive manner to the writer's scheme, following the discourse development the writer has plotted.

The different reading strategies suggested by these authors, and the oppositions between them may be roughly summarised in Table 2.2.

There are clear similarities between some of the global strategies given in Table 2.2. Pask's 'holistic' reader resembles Fransson's 'deep processor', while both have resemblances to Hartman's 'logocentric' reader. Hartman's 'resistant' reader seems to be an extreme example of Widdowson's 'dominant' reader. However, the parallels must not be pushed too hard. Both the 'holistic' and 'serialist' readers are being submissive with respect to the author's message, just employing different local strategies to achieve their aims. The 'surface processors', as described, are different in responding, not so much to what they perceive as the author's message as to the task.

As to which is the 'best' global strategy, the Swedes appear to be most prescriptive, in favouring deep processing at all times. Fransson, in fact, cites Dewey to the effect that everyone is a deep processor when not inhibited by nervousness, task demands, etc. Widdowson, on the other hand, along with Pask, sees the different strategies as being appropriate to different reading contexts. Pask, in fact, refers to an exclusive reliance on one strategy as a 'pathology'.

Global strategies, as we have been calling them, are important for a number of reasons, in spite of differences in the descriptions. They can be related to different contexts and outcomes; in practical terms, it is difficult to see how anyone doing a test can be anything but a submissive reader, but teachers should keep in mind that students should be given the opportunity to be dominant in appropriate contexts. Finally, the definition provided by Entwhistle et al., that a strategy is 'a description of the way a student chooses to tackle a specific learning task in the light of its perceived demands', makes it possible for us to incorporate different reading types such as skimming, search reading and scanning, as strategies.

2.4   DIFFERENT KINDS OF READING

All the models of reading that have been looked at so far have been designed with careful reading in mind. Hoover and Tunmer (1993), for example, consider that their notion of the simple view 'assumes careful comprehension: comprehension that is intended to extract complete meanings from presented material as opposed to comprehension aimed at only extracting main ideas, skimming, or searching for particular details' (p. 8). In fact many of the models of reading that have surfaced in the literature to date have been mainly concerned with careful reading; Rayner and Pollatsek

(1989: 439) state that for most of their account of the reading process they are focusing on the skilled, adult reader reading material of the textbook variety. They point out that careful reading models have little to tell us about how skilled readers can cope with other types of reading such as skimming for gist (Rayner and Pollatsek, 1989: 477–8).

However, while such a restriction of focus is perfectly legitimate for psychologists attempting to establish precise experimental data about the reading process, it is a luxury which we cannot allow ourselves, since the reading needs of students, and hence the teaching and testing of reading, requires a wider range of reading behaviours. Thus, if possible, we must expand the model in order to accommodate this wider range.

The overriding attention paid to careful reading in the theoretical literature has meant that, in Britain at least (see Section 3.1 below), we have somewhat ignored expeditious reading behaviours such as skimming, search reading and scanning in both L1 and L2 teaching of reading. We have theories of careful reading but very little on how readers process texts quickly and selectively, i.e. *expeditiously*, to extract important information in line with intended purpose(s). Given the value of these types of reading to the work forces of states in the northern hemisphere, let alone those of emerging nations, it is time more attention was paid to them in the professional and 'academic' literature.

In addition, because of the focus on the local level, e.g. word recognition or syntactic parsing, the psychological literature has paid only limited attention to careful reading at the global level, i.e. comprehension of the main ideas in a text or of the discourse topic; the macropropositional as against the micropropositional level of text.

We feel, therefore, that in addition to careful reading at the local level, it is important to discuss a further five kinds of reading: **Search reading, Skimming, Scanning, Careful reading (at the global level)** and **Browsing**. We choose these as our main illustrations, with no assumption that the list is exhaustive, or even that it includes all the most important kinds of reading (irrespective of how one would set about judging that). We do know, however, that the first four are the kinds of reading that appeared most frequently in our analysis of textbooks for the teaching of reading and in published and available tests of reading, and that they will be familiar to teachers of L2 reading at least.

One problem which confronts us immediately is that, while at least the first five terms for different types of reading are often used in the literature, they often appear to be used in different ways. For example, in the remark by Hoover and Tunmer cited above, they appear to distinguish between 'extracting main ideas' and 'skimming', although many people would consider these two to represent the same behaviour. The IRA dictionary of reading terms (Harris and Hodges, 1981) defines *scanning* as 'to read something quickly but selectively', but then equates it with skimming. As examples of scanning, they give 'to scan an article for the general idea, scan a directory for a telephone number'. Many people would consider that reading 'for the general idea' constituted skimming. Under *skimming*, they say that the term 'shares only the first of two primary meanings of "scan", to read rapidly and selectively, but purposely, rather than to read carefully'. It is difficult to justify the apparent contrast between reading 'selectively' and 'purposely'.

In Appendix 1 (pp. 297–304) we try to make clear the distinction between the different types of reading by providing an example of a specification produced by the Testing and Evaluation Unit at CALS, University of Reading, in collaboration with colleagues in Shanghai Jiatong University, PRC, for use in the development of the Advanced English Reading Test (AERT). These types of reading are used for different purposes. The specification sets out a number of reading behaviours categorized along the two axes of (a) Local v Global, and (b) Careful v Expeditious. To help clarify the distinctions between the different types, we take each type and examine it in terms of *Purpose, Operationalisations, Comprehension Focus, Text Coverage, Rate of Reading, Direction of Processing* and *Relationship with Underlying Process*.

In Chapter 3, on the testing of reading, and in Chapter 4, on the teaching of reading, we will use this taxonomy as a basis for discussion as we feel it provides a simple but coherent route through the vast literature in this area. It should help teachers and researchers make sense of a difficult and often overcomplex field. In Chapter 3 we will examine these reading types (operations) more fully and also discuss the performance conditions that affect them, such as length of text, topic, etc. For the moment we put forward the following rough working definitions:

Skimming: Reading for gist. The reader asks: What is this text as a whole about?, while avoiding anything which looks like detail.

Reading schemes like SQ3R recommend starting the reading to learn process with skimming, so that the reader has a framework to accommodate the whole text. While Hoover and Tunmer appear to distinguish skimming and 'reading for main ideas', these appear to us to be the same thing. The defining characteristics are (a) the reading is selective, with sections of the text either omitted or given very little attention; (b) an attempt is made to build up a macrostructure (the gist) on the basis of as few details from the text as possible.

Search reading: Locating information on predetermined topics. The reader wants information to answer set questions or to provide data, for example, in completing assignments. It differs from skimming in that the search for information is guided by predetermined topics so the reader does not necessarily have to establish a macropropositional structure for the whole of the text.

Scanning: Reading selectively, to achieve very specific reading goals, e.g. finding the number in a directory, finding the capital of Bavaria. The main feature of scanning is that any part of the text which does not contain the preselected symbol(s) is dismissed. It may involve looking for specific words/phrases, figures/percentages, names, dates of particular events or specific items in an index.

Careful reading: This is the kind of reading favoured by many educationalists and psychologists to the exclusion of all other types. It is associated with reading to learn, hence with the reading of textbooks. The defining features are (a) that the reader attempts to handle the majority of information in the text, that is, the process is not selective; (b) that the reader adopts a submissive role (see Section 2.3 above), and accepts the writer's organization, including what the writer appears to consider the important parts; and (c) that the reader attempts to build up a macrostructure on the basis of the majority of the information in the text.

Browsing: We have to say that we do not know what 'normal' reading consists of; there are far too many reading behaviours to allow us to be confident about selecting any of them as predominant. 'Careful reading' may be the preferred mode among students faced with textbooks, and hence may be of particular concern to us here, but it is not something that the majority of people are likely to engage in for a large part of the time. So we have added a type 'browsing' to describe the sort of reading where goals are not well defined, parts of a text may be skipped fairly randomly, and there is little attempt to integrate the information into a macrostructure, except, perhaps, for a topic structure like 'This text seems to be about . . .'. As noted above, Kintsch and van Dijk (1978) refer to the cases where 'people read loosely structured texts with no clear goals in mind. The outcome of such comprehension processes, as far as the resulting macrostructure is concerned, is indeterminate.' This is what we are referring to as 'browsing'. We should add, however, that it is not a requirement for browsing that the text be 'loosely structured'; we can 'browse' through virtually any text, given only that it consists of more than a few words.

Note

We can expand this to point out that there is no necessary correlation between a particular reading behaviour and a particular genre of text. We might assume that people are more likely to apply their 'careful reading' processes to a study text, but textbooks can be read for amusement, not learning, while texts taken from tabloid newspapers may be scrutinised with great care. We should also point out that readers are under no obligation to maintain a particular reading behaviour throughout the length of a text; they may switch from careful reading to skimming to search reading to scanning and back to careful reading over a small number of pages.

We can now compare and contrast the five provisional types, in order to examine the factors which are involved in differentiating them.

1. Skimming, search reading, scanning and careful reading are distinguished from browsing by the presence in the first four of a **clearly defined goal**. The goals, of course, differ widely, but in all four cases, the reader can be assumed to know before reading what it is they want from the text.
2. Search reading, scanning, skimming, and possibly browsing are distinguished from careful reading by the factor of **selectivity**. In the last type, all the text can be presumed to be examined; in at least the first two types, and probably the third, the reader will deliberately either avoid, or pay minimum attention to some parts of the text. In scanning, the parts ignored may constitute a majority of the text.

3. In careful reading, and in skimming, the reader makes a conscious effort to construct a **macrostructure**, the gist of the text. In careful reading, this is likely to be done by reference to the whole text, in skimming from parts of the text. In scanning, there is no attempt to construct a macrostructure; in browsing, some vague notion of the topic may be built up, but without any attempt to retain it; in search reading it is probable that only certain key ideas in the macrostructure will be sought.

Expanding a model

We shall now try to illustrate this by referring our descriptions to a generalised representation of aspects of the reading process. Figure 2.2 is derived from Just and Carpenter (1980, 1987) with additions from Kintsch and van Dijk (1978). However, we should stress that it is for discussion purposes only and not intended to be taken seriously as a model of the reading process.

Since the discussion concerns a number of different reading behaviours, we have included in the figure a *Goalsetter*, which, by deciding on the overall goal of the reading, also selects the type of reading which is likely to achieve that goal, and a *Monitor*, which provides the reader with feedback about the success of the particular reading process. The monitor is controlled by the goalsetter, since, as will be seen, the monitoring procedure depends crucially on the type of reading.

Comparisons we have recently made with the 'blueprint for the speaker' developed by Levelt (1989) are encouraging. He portrays talking as an intentional activity and his 'conceptualizer' involves both message generation and monitoring:

> Talking as an intentional activity involves conceiving of an intention, selecting the relevant information to be expressed for the realization of this purpose, . . . These activities require the speaker's constant attention. The speaker will, moreover, attend to his own productions, monitoring what he is saying and how . . .   (p. 9)

In our 'blueprint' for reading, skills presumably should be seen as automatised aspects of the long-term memory. Local strategies emerge in response to the monitor, which alerts the reader that a problem has emerged, and sets the reader to choosing and employing a suitable strategy. Global strategies can be seen as being

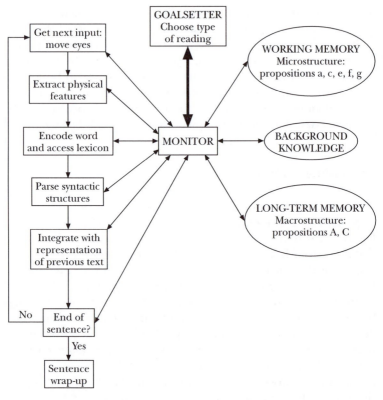

Figure 2.2   A development of Just and Carpenter's model of
the reading process.

activated by the goalsetter. The reader may choose to scan, skim,
search read, or read carefully, all in response to the perceived
demands of the learning task.

We shall begin with **Careful Global Reading**, since it shows
all components of the model in use. The reader decides to read
the text carefully, presumably for study or some similar purpose.
In terms of the figure, the goalsetter is set to careful reading. This
in turn gives the monitor its instructions. The reader begins
each sentence at the beginning and continues through to the
end, following the processes detailed, i.e. extracting features,
encoding words, parsing, etc. If we are to follow Kintsch and van
Dijk's account, microstructures are processed, converted into
semantic propositions, and stored in the working memory, while

the coherence between them is established. As the process moves on, a macrostructure has begun to be built up. Background knowledge, actually stored in long-term memory, is utilised to supply an appropriate schema for the macrostructure, as well as to aid coherence detection in the construction of the microstructure.

While all this is going on, the monitor is at a high level of attention, checking, among other matters, whether meanings accessed from the lexicon are appropriate, whether parsing results in an acceptable sentence structure, whether the micropropositions appear to cohere, whether an appropriate provisional schema has been located, and so on.

Compare this now with **Scanning**. Here far fewer components of the model are involved. Suppose at the lowest level, the goal has been set as scanning a text to find a name. We don't know what processes go on when the goalsetter is set to 'scan'. Presumably, however, little or no syntactic processing needs to be involved, no checking of coherence, and no attempt to build up a macrostructure. In fact, it is arguable that only a limited amount of lexical access is required; the reader might scan by decoding alone, without accessing the meaning and phonological representation of the words. Whatever is the case, the monitor can be envisaged as set at a simple Yes/No level, checking only to see if the word or words being scanned fitted the search description or not. If it did, then the search would be over; if not, the word would be rejected, and the search continued. There is no need to complete the reading of the sentence, or to integrate the word into the structure of preceding text. Checking the coherence of micropropositions would seem to be redundant, and there seems little use for any sort of macrostructure to be built up.

Skimming is more complex. Like Scanning, it is selective, but we are unsure how much data the reader decides to process at any point. They may access words, and possibly process entire sentences. However, since the process **is** selective, some material must be skipped. Presumably, here, as with scanning, the monitor checks as to whether the material surveyed is appropriate or not; however, in this case, the amount processed may be quite substantial. If skimming is equivalent to gist extraction, then presumably propositions are committed to the long-term memory on the hypothesis that they represent the macrostructure. That is, the process of debating whether a proposition is part of the macrostructure or not, which is assumed to take place during careful reading, is here replaced by a guess that it is. The macrostructure will then have more components contributed by the reader, making skimming a more reader-driven activity.

Search reading seems at different points to share affinities with both scanning and skimming. The search will primarily involve keeping alert for words in the same or related semantic field and operationalisations such as using titles, subtitles and other discourse clues will be employed (see van Dijk 1977: 79). The reader may contribute formal knowledge of text structure to assist in this search for information on prespecified macropropositions. As with skimming, where selected text is identified as being important, it will be read more carefully and the process identified above for careful reading will kick in.

Finally, we come to **Browsing**. This is the least well defined of our reading types. The goals are vague, the monitor operates at low attention, and the macrostructure, if built up in any sense, is probably at a level of 'topic'. We will pay little further attention to this reading type as, given the difficulty of defining its purpose, it is difficult to operationalise for teaching and testing purposes.

Most of what has been said above is speculative, and quite possibly wildly inaccurate. The important point is that in our view future models will have to be able to explain at least five types of reading: *reading carefully at the local level; reading carefully at the global level; skimming; search reading;* and *scanning.*

In Chapters 3 and 4 we shall explore the extent to which these types of reading can be tested and taught. In this way we hope to make a contribution to the development of a framework of reading that goes beyond decoding and the microlinguistic level to take account of reading for different purposes.

Notes

1. Gough's 'decoder' converts letters into phonemes. This is in line with his apparent assumption that the end-product of reading is a spoken sentence. Since we don't share that assumption, the decoder has been left out.
2. We do not know of experiments testing the effect of lack of punctuation on reading. However, in Britain at least, the fact that teachers can read students' essays seems to be evidence that it is possible.
3. Rayner and Pollatsek admit that Goodman's account can be viewed as interactive, but consider it as basically top-down because 'bottom-up

processing plays such a minor role' and there are 'so little constraints on the interactions'. In a sense, though, this is a repetition of their criticism that his account lacks precision, a criticism earlier made by Gibson and Levin (1974).

4. De Beaugrande's reference to background knowledge here should remind us of the crucial role of such knowledge in, for example, identifying pronominal reference. This role suggests that cohesion tests may be a useful way of assessing the effect of background knowledge on reading.

5. We are using the terms found in Halliday and Hasan (1976). Other writers on cohesion, e.g. de Beaugrande, and Quirk et al. (1973) use similar though not identical terminology.

6. It should be remembered that Kintsch and van Dijk's model sets out to describe the actual reading process, in which propositions are processed in cycles, generally about 4 at a time, with selected propositions being carried over to the following cycle.

3

Testing reading comprehension(s)

3.1 INTRODUCTION: THE LIMITS OF TESTING

We begin this chapter on the testing of reading with the question as to whether reading can be tested. This may seem a strange procedure; however, it is important to address this issue because we need to be aware of the parameters we can work within. We need to be sure that we can actually test what we want to test (validity) and that we can depend on the results our tests provide us with (reliability).

Measuring types of reading

Conventional testing involves measuring subjects' performance against an agreed standard. For any reading test, this means that there must be a consensus as to what constitutes good reading in the context established by the test. Given this, if the purpose of reading is for amusement, entertainment, aesthetic satisfaction, to gain a general background in an area, or merely browsing, then it is difficult to see how reading performance can meaningfully be tested. For example, enjoyment derived from reading a novel may be investigated, even measured, but since we do not have explicit standards of enjoyment, we cannot test it. We can certainly test retention of a plot, or of details, or of characterisation, etc., but this is quite different.

However, many language tests do not set out to measure students' aesthetic reactions to texts, pleasure and so on, so it might be argued that the above remarks are irrelevant. EAP reading tests, it might be claimed, measure learning in the sense of adding to our knowledge base, and this can be tested. However, even with EAP reading we need to be careful about the statements we make on the basis of our tests. While the claim for addition to our knowledge is to some extent true, a closer examination of this claim also leaves it in some doubt. Neville and Pugh (1982) comment that: 'The output of reading is ... difficult to capture, since what is achieved from (real life) reading with comprehension is often a modification of the conceptual system.' Furthermore, the reading modules of EAP tests cannot normally be said to measure learning *per se*; rather they measure behaviour that we hope is associated with successful learning.

As we argue in Chapter 2 and Section 5.2, it is imperative that we specify as clearly as possible what it is we are attempting to test, teach or research. The more explicit we can be, the more we are likely to understand the nature of reading or, more precisely, the limits of such understanding.

Comprehensions and interpretations

A further limitation arises when we consider the interaction between readers and texts that makes up the reading process. As we noted in Chapter 2, there has been for some time a consensus in the field of reading theory about the general outlines of the relationship between reader, text and 'comprehension', though, of course, details vary. Thus there is agreement among reading theorists that every text is incomplete, and has to be converted into meaningful discourse by the reader. Candlin (1984: x) remarks:

> Texts do not have unitary meanings potentially accessible to all, they rather allow for variety in interpretation by different readers, governed by factors such as purpose, background knowledge, and the relationship established in the act of reading between the reader and the writer.

This in turn entails the likelihood, in fact necessity, of different readings of the same text.

As we noted in Section 2.1, Urquhart (1987) sees the variation in product as operating in two dimensions. Readings may differ in the case of readers from different cultures, either ethnic or professional, or in the case of the same reader at different times, with different knowledge or different preoccupations. Such differing readings, which are generally not under control of the readers, Urquhart terms '*interpretations*'.

The reading product may also vary according to a dimension controlled by readers' purposes, As Candlin points out (op. cit.), the reader 'may decide to glimpse at the text, extracting "gist", or work conscientiously through it, satisfying himself that he has made sense of all of it'. In Urquhart (1987) such variations are labelled '*comprehensions*'.[1] Books teaching reading, and many reading tests, tend to assign special importance to 'deep' or 'intensive' careful reading, but there is no particular justification for this and, as we argued in Chapter 2, expeditious reading skills may be just as important.

On the whole, variations in the comprehension dimension should not cause testers much difficulty, once the validity of different purposes for and different types of reading is accepted. In testing terms, different purposes can be translated into responses to different tasks. Pugh (1978: 78) argues:

> comprehension is best regarded as a state of achievement, rather than as an activity or a skill which is applied to texts. By stressing the different strategies and styles of reading which are appropriate for achieving various goals, one breaks away from the apparent impasse into which many of the discussions of comprehension lead.

'*Interpretations*', on the other hand – variations brought about in the reading product on account of different schemata – are a major problem for conventional testing. In fact, this is perhaps the greatest area of potential dispute between theories of reading and reading tests. It is of crucial importance, yet it is seldom discussed. The theory insists that the good reader makes sense of the text by supplying knowledge based on his or her own unique experience. The testers, on the other hand, are obliged to look for 'correct' answers. Candlin (1984: xi–xii) remarks that conclusions regarding different readings

> put at question . . . how we make use of tests to assess reading skill; the viability of much product-oriented testing must be in doubt, especially if the results of such tests are deemed to be revelatory of reader strategy.

We have claimed that there is a consensus among people concerned with the theory of reading about the all-pervasive

importance of background knowledge and of different interpretations of the same text. However, outside the circle of reading
theorists, it is by no means the case that this importance is either
fully accepted (although it may be paid lip-service) or accepted
at all. This lack of appreciation may take two forms. In the first,
background knowledge is seen as a resource available to readers
when, as it were, the going gets tough. Some taxonomies of reading strategies (see discussion in Chapter 2, and, for example,
Pritchard, 1990) mention recourse to background knowledge as
an appropriate means of overcoming a reading difficulty.

As is often the case, however, strategy research, by concentrating on readers consciously problem-solving, tends to deal with the
tip of the iceberg. It must be stressed that if the theory is correct,
then background knowledge is not just an extra resource, it is, as
it were, a filter through which we view all texts.

Secondly, the importance, or even possibility of differing interpretations is simply not considered. For example, when studying
adult native speakers' confidence in their answers to 'thematic'
questions on 'challenging' texts, Pressley et al. (1990) conclude
that their subjects suffered from 'gross comprehension problems' (p. 247) and showed 'high confidence in the majority of the
incorrect answers' (p. 245). The authors put this down to poor
monitoring, and do not seem to have considered the possibility
that the readers' interpretations may have had at least as much
validity as their own (cf. McCormick, 1992).

Beyond the editing stage, questions aimed at inferential processing which often seem to produce a scattering of responses between
different multiple-choice options are often dropped as 'poor' items.
Yet it is possible that the responses reflect differing, but possibly
legitimate, responses on the part of different testees relating the
item to different backgrounds.

Of greater concern in testing reading proficiency is emerging
empirical evidence (Perkins and Brutten, 1988) that inference
questions are poor discriminators and perhaps should be avoided
for that reason alone in testing. If good students (as defined by
overall performance) are getting items wrong and poor students
such items right, this does not appear to be telling us much of use.

It is likely that conventional tests simply cannot make allow-
ance for individual interpretations. This is not sufficient reason
to abandon reading tests, but it is a necessary caution against
extrapolating too much from them. We cannot emphasise too

much the need to be explicit about exactly what it is reading tests can tell us. We may never be able to detail precisely the complexity of individual differences in reading ability (Spiro and Myers, 1984). However, we will argue that by selecting appropriate texts, tasks and formats we can still generate useful performance test data on a person's ability to read for certain purposes under certain performance conditions.

Focusing on comprehensions

Despite the limitations discussed in the previous section we are still left with the need to make statements about reading proficiency for many areas of human activity, e.g. for academic study, business or technological purposes. As Farr et al. (1986: 135) point out: 'tests . . . are, above all, a political reality. They are a constant with which all students, teachers, and administrators know they will have to contend.'

As we have indicated above, we do not believe that it is possible to incorporate '*interpretations*' into testing as it is practised at the moment. The answer must be to concentrate on '*comprehensions*', that is, variations resulting from different and consciously adopted purposes. This does not mean, of course, that we can eliminate different interpretations from testees' performance; it means that we cannot formally take account of them in awarding grades.

One of the main causes of differing interpretations is background knowledge, and the elimination of this variable would seem an obvious step.[2] For most practical purposes, however, this is likely to be an impossibility; the theory would suggest that background knowledge is always present. All we can do is attempt to minimise the effect of the variable. As Farr et al. (1986: 140) point out:

> Factoring background knowledge out of reading assessment is next to impossible; yet background knowledge must be controlled so that it will not account for an indeterminate amount of assessment results . . . to factor reader background out of assessment . . . is to assess something other than reading comprehension.

Two methods for minimising the effect of background knowledge suggest themselves, one involving the choice of text, the other the choice of task. As far as texts are concerned, three solutions are suggested in the literature. First, we might employ a variety of short texts, covering a wide range of topics. This appears to be the method chosen by the TOEFL examination. Disadvantages include the large chance factor, if the hope is that all testees will find some texts familiar and others not. Also, the method appears to involve the use of short texts, which may be considered undesirable (see below). Secondly, texts might be selected which are unfamiliar to all the candidates so that, as Roller (1990) argues, text variables rather than background knowledge have the most influence. This was the policy adopted by the Joint Matriculation Board in the UK in its Test in English for Overseas Students where deliberately obscure texts were chosen so as to be equally unfamiliar to all candidates.[3] Thirdly, an appropriate level of familiarity with the topic of the text across the test population might be established in advance through group interview or controlled questionnaire survey (see discussion of background knowledge in the section on performance conditions below).

The other main method of minimising the effect of background knowledge is through the tasks demanded. Ideally we would want to test only what is retrievable from within the text itself irrespective of differing states of background knowledge relating to the focus of information retrieval. This attempt has a fairly long history. For example, Carroll attempted to distinguish what was 'committed' to the text, the retrieval of which constituted 'adequate comprehension' (see discussion in Section 5.3 of ways of establishing this empirically), from what could be built up from the test as a whole together with background knowledge, retrieval of which constituted 'total comprehension' (Carroll, 1972). Others have attempted to distinguish between what Chikalanga (1992) refers to as 'propositional inferences', which are text-based, and 'pragmatic inferences', which are based on information outside the text (see Section 4.2 for a discussion of these in teaching). Similar distinctions can be found in Crothers (1978), Farr et al. (1986), Hughes (1993), Weaver and Kintsch (1991) and Pearson and Johnson (1978). An example should make the distinction clear. Chikalanga used a text in which a violent father asks his wife to confirm one of his stories. She gives an evasive answer, 'flashing her bony hand under her chin' (1993: 946). Students were asked to supply a pragmatic inference as an answer to the question: 'Why, do you think, did Jojo's mother flash her hand under her chin?' Clearly such questions must be answered on the basis of information outside the text.

We must admit, however, that the distinction, while valuable, can only be pushed so far. Given a text like:

> He woke up feeling depressed. He still had not finished editing the testing chapter.

and asked the question, 'Why did he feel depressed?', we can answer by relating two parts of the text. But the relationship is a pragmatic one, and the location of an appropriate answer depends, unless the testee is trusting to luck, on background knowledge.

In general, however, the principle is a useful one; we exclude from testing, though not from teaching (see Section 4.2), items which depend solely on information supplied from outside the text, and include items which, though still depending on the reader supplying background knowledge, can be made to relate to each other in the text. The extent to which such items can be reliable testing items is a matter for empirical research.

What is there to comprehend?

With this in mind we need to examine in more detail what comprehension of a text might involve. When constructing test tasks, testers need to operate with a consensus as to what information readers may be expected to extract from a text, given the constraints of the kind of reading required, e.g. careful or expeditious reading. As we saw in Chapter 2, most attention has been paid by theorists to decoding carefully at the word level. We noted that in contrast Kintsch and van Dijk (1978) offered a model which concentrates on comprehension above word level. As Samuels and Kamil (1988: 188) say, Kintsch and van Dijk:

> have built a model emphasising comprehension to the exclusion of word identification (most other models including Rumelhart's, seem to have a bias for explaining word identification).[4]

A focus on comprehension is important in the real world where we have to develop tests and teaching exercises to account for global comprehension as well as local. If we focus on a text as a whole, for the purpose of, say, careful reading, or possibly skimming, we can use Kintsch and van Dijk's model to describe the elements and relationships which can be taken as constituting comprehension, at least as far as careful reading is concerned. Such research into global theories of text comprehension (Kintsch and van Dijk, 1978; Just and Carpenter, 1980; Meyer, 1975; Meyer and Rice, 1984; Perfetti, 1985; van Dijk and Kintsch, 1983) offer us some hope that we can develop test tasks for expository text comprehension, i.e. measure the extent to which information communicated by the writer is understood at both micropropositional and macropropositional levels.

We noted in Chapter 2 that micropropositions refer to propositions which are the smallest units of text that can logically be proven false (Kintsch and van Dijk, 1978; van Dijk, 1980). McNamara et al. (1991: 491) similarly define propositions as: 'the smallest units of knowledge that can stand as separate assertions; the smallest units that can be true or false'. According to Kintsch and van Dijk, micropropositions may be linked meaningfully to each other either structurally, in sentences, or by cohesion or inferences between sentences. The microstructure consists of a structured network of all the propositions in a text, shown at different levels of importance, thus representing the common view that some propositions (main ideas) are more important than others. Finally, certain of the most important, highest level propositions are mapped onto a schema, e.g. a problem/solution structure, to form the macrostructure.

In the discussion of what to test in terms of skills and strategies (Section 3.2 below) we shall return to the distinction between micro- and macropropositions. It is useful in distinguishing between decoding at the local and comprehension at the global level. An item which tests skimming might be seen as an attempt to expeditiously establish a superordinate macroproposition; a discourse topic for a text. Global careful and global expeditious reading (including both skimming and search reading strategies) could be seen as the means of establishing the macropropositions in a text (i.e. main ideas comprehension; cf. Aulls, 1986). Tests such as scanning for specific detail or gap filling and cloze could be seen as expeditious and careful reading strategies and skills that focus on the micropropositional local level (decoding).

Armed with such a structured description of the content of a text, test developers are in a better position to construct valid items aimed at different types or different levels of information in a text. An understanding of the relationship between micro- and macropropositions is important to the test developer because the level of focus of items may have important consequences for our estimates of candidates' abilities in our tests (see Section 3.2 below for a discussion of this critical issue).

A full analysis of a text, as demanded by models such as those of Kintsch and van Dijk or Meyer (1975), is probably too complex and time-consuming for use in test construction. Harri-Augstein and Thomas (1984) suggest more rule-of-thumb apparatus for arriving at a consensus on, say, main as opposed to minor ideas in a text and the relationship between them. In Appendix 2 below (pp. 305–6), we propose a form of text-mapping, designed to serve the same purpose.

In constructing tests it is important to include texts and activities which mirror as closely as possible those which students have been exposed to and/or are likely to meet in their future target situations. In our view tests should, as far as possible, attempt to activate real-life reading operations performed under appropriate performance conditions. We cannot, admittedly, fully replicate reality in language tests, for the reasons discussed in the opening remarks in this chapter of the book. Full genuineness of text or authenticity of task is unlikely to be attainable in the tests we write (see Lewkowicz, 1997). However, we are still left with the need to make our tests as valid as possible if we are to measure anything of value and generalise beyond the test situation to a candidate's ability to perform specified operations under certain conditions to a certain level in real life (Weir, 1993). Our tests must be valid if we are to relate test performance to real-life reading ability (Bronfenbrenner, 1976: 5–15; McNamara, 1996; Venezky, 1984: 27; Weir, 1990 and 1993). The solution must lie in our ability to select appropriate texts, to be read for valid purposes, from which the reader is able to select an agreed level of meaning under certain conditions.

The purposes for reading in the test should, wherever possible, match the purpose(s) for reading those texts in real life. Farr et al. (1986: 141) point out that 'A reader's purpose determines whether and how a reader interacts with a particular text'. The purposes for reading in test tasks should be as appropriate as we can make them (Davies, 1995: 133–4; Grabe, 1991: 378; Weir, 1993). In Section 3.2 we examine in detail the nature of the strategies and skills we might wish to include in our reading tests. It is important that such activities are premised on a strong theoretical basis, validated as far as possible by systematic empirical research.

We need also to implement faithfully any important performance conditions in developing a reading test. Ensuring that these conditions are taken account of in text selection will help us to generalise more directly to performance in the real world on the basis of data provided by reading tests. We need to consider what performance conditions – i.e. contextual features – we need to embody in our reading tests. Weir (1990, 1993) provides an initial taxonomy of such features and these are developed further in Section 3.3 (see also Bachman, 1990).

In choosing texts, and in developing activities for readers to perform on those texts, we need to be as explicit as possible about our criteria for selection. Such explicitness will help establish a descriptive framework for generalisations that can be made on the basis of test performance. Such tests will not tell us everything about a candidate's reading ability but they should provide us with a certain amount of useful, usable information. The value of such information to the people who use it will be the ultimate validation of such tests. This approach to testing might be termed *utilisation focused*.

The discussion of tasks, texts and formats below will draw upon the theoretical discussion in Chapters 1 and 2 and is of obvious relevance to the teaching of reading discussed in Chapter 4.

3.2 TASK-BASED FACTORS

We have already discussed tasks in Chapter 2. At this point we need merely repeat that testing, as we know it, is all about tasks. As pointed out in Section 3.1, we have to reject whole areas of reading as being outside the scope of testing, either because no consensus in general exists as to relevant tasks or what constitutes 'successful' performance on tasks (as in, e.g., reading for enjoyment), or because readers' performance on tasks is so unpredictable that the reliability of items becomes suspect (as with questions aimed at pragmatic inferences).

Testing components

Until the early 1980s the major concern in the testing of reading was with the issue of methodology. However, in the 1980s one noted a switch in concern away from **how** to test reading towards a concern with **what** we were trying to test; a concern with the nature of the reading construct itself – in broad terms, a move away from a focus on method to a focus on the content of reading tests. The next section examines the componentiality of reading and the implications of this for the testing of reading.

The issue of how to test, i.e. deciding which are the most suitable test formats, is still a key decision and we will return to this in Section 3.4. Once test developers have a clear idea of the performance conditions that need to be built into a test (see Section 3.3 below) and the reading skills and strategies that are to be tested, only then can they make decisions on formats. In the past the methods' tail has often wagged the testing dog and formats have been chosen without sufficient thought *a priori* to what is being tested.

Deciding on skills and strategies

To satisfy the need for information on an individual's or a group's reading ability, the language tester would normally try to reduce the possibility of muddied measurement. This might be achieved by eliminating the influence of reading-irrelevant factors associated with the test method, and by focusing on a maximally clear characterisation of the construct of reading *per se*. The tester might therefore avoid tasks such as selective summary based on prior reading of texts – where the extended writing involved in task completion might interfere with extrapolations we might wish to make concerning candidates' reading abilities alone.

However, in certain contexts, such as academic study, such integration might on the contrary be considered desirable (see Weir, 1983a). Additionally, if reading was the major focus the actual writing could be marked at a low level of expertise with the emphasis on successful extraction of content. Whatever decision is taken with regard to reading and writing, first and foremost, the tester is obliged to be as explicit as possible concerning the nature of the ability about which the test is designed to be providing information.

As was seen in Chapter 2, the current consensus is that reading is an interactive process involving both bottom-up and top-down processes. The strength of the interactive model lies in its comprehensiveness (particularly with regard to careful reading) and its applicability to different readers in different reading contexts. In the operationalisation of such models in teaching and testing materials there is an attempt to give students the opportunity to practise across the range of skills and strategies (see Appendix 1 for details of the specification used for an Advanced English Reading Test in China).

Williams and Moran (1989: 224) refer to an apparent current consensus among writers of teaching materials on the nature of reading comprehension, stating that:

> While materials writers may disagree on the emphasis to be devoted to any particular skill, there seems to be substantial agreement on the importance of such skills as guessing the meaning of unknown words, identifying anaphoric reference, identifying the main idea, and inference.

In a less pedagogically oriented discussion, Grabe (1991: 379–82) may also be seen as representative of current views. He comments on the importance of automaticity in reading, particularly in word identification, and also identifies as components of skilled reading: syntactic knowledge; knowledge of formal discourse structure (formal schemata); content and background knowledge (content schemata); and metacognitive knowledge and skill monitoring, e.g. recognising the more important information in a text, skimming, and searching for specific information. Grabe (1991: 382) concludes:

> A 'reading components' perspective is an appropriate research direction to the extent that such an approach leads to important insights into the reading process. In this respect, it . . . is indeed a useful approach.

Carr and Levy (1990: 5) comment: 'this approach attempts to understand reading as the product of a complex but decomposable information processing system'. They argue that the mental operations are distinguishable and empirically separable from each other (see also Chapter 2 for an extensive discussion of these components).

Such a focus would seem to accept that reading can be broken down into underlying skills and strategies for the purposes of teaching and testing – a view shared by many language teachers and testers, though opposed by others. A wealth of taxonomies is available in the literature (see Section 2.3 above). Here, for purposes of reference, and to help move the discussion forward, we provide in Table 3.1 a recent four-level version of such a breakdown based on Weir (1993) and Pugh (1978).

Table 3.1 Matrix of reading types

	Global	Local
Expeditious	A. Skimming quickly to establish discourse topic and main ideas. Search reading to locate quickly and understand information relevant to predetermined needs.	B. Scanning to locate specific information; symbol or group of symbols; names, dates, figures or words.
Careful	C. Reading carefully to establish accurate comprehension of the explicitly stated main ideas the author wishes to convey; propositional inferencing.	D. Understanding syntactic structure of sentence and clause. Understanding lexical and/or grammatical cohesion. Understanding lexis/ deducing meaning of lexical items from morphology and context.

The reader will note that Williams and Moran (1989) and Grabe (1991) identify reading components from all four levels A, B, C and D in Table 3.1. Their inclusion of word-level components relating to more specifically linguistic comprehension is indicative that this is seen by many people as an important part of reading, not as something separate. The contribution of the latter to tests of reading ability is an important issue that will be taken up below.

Global comprehension, which can be related to Kintsch and van Dijk's macrostructure (Kintsch and van Dijk, 1978) normally refers to comprehension beyond the level of micropropositions – from macropropositions to discourse topic. Local comprehension refers to the decoding of micropropositions and the relations between them.[5]

The evidence for a multidivisible view

It is held by many teachers, textbook writers, and the constructors of language tests that reading is made up of different skill and strategy components, and that students may exhibit differences in level of proficiency across these. It is moreover often claimed by practitioners that sets of reading components provide useful frameworks on which to base course design, teaching, and test and materials development (see Lumley, 1993).

There is research evidence in the literature, albeit limited, that reading is not simply a general factor dating back to Gates (1926) (see also Carnine and Silbert, 1979; Davis, 1968, 1972; Hillocks and Ludlow, 1984.)

Dubin et al. (1986: 163) argue that:

> interactive models (of the reading process) suggest a need to test skills at many levels, since all these skills are assumed to play a significant role in the reading process. They include everything from rapid identification of vocabulary and syntactic structures, to the interpretation of larger discourse patterns, the making of inferences etc.

Thus processing at the level of word recognition and lexical access as well as at the level of integration of textual information and resolution of ambiguity are seen as important. The focus of both linear and interactive models discussed in Chapter 2 was largely on decoding rather than on comprehension and they do not in themselves account for higher level text comprehension. As we noted earlier, Kintsch and van Dijk (1978) are among the few researchers who focus on comprehension and offer a theory of text structure (see also Just and Carpenter, 1987).

Perhaps as a result of the lack of any clear-cut theoretical model, it is widespread practice among test developers to focus on these reading components, either singly or in combination, when constructing test items relating to a text, even though the sum of these parts – the answers to these test items – might not necessarily equate fully with what the reader would normally take away from the text. Indeed, whatever theoretical position the test developer takes, the need to construct individual test items will exert strong pressure to attempt to measure individual reading components and strategies, or combinations of them. If specific components or strategies could be clearly identified as making an important contribution to the reading process, then it would of course be at least possible, if not necessary, to test these and to use the composite results for reporting on the reading proficiency revealed. It would moreover be necessary, once hypothesised skill components and strategies were substantiated, to determine the nature and strength of interactions between them. It is, however, as yet too early to explore such interactions; thus far we can have but little idea whether any components may be superordinate to others, or the extent to which 'higher order' operations within reading depend on 'lower order' operations.

Casting doubt on multidivisibility

Despite the widespread influence of a multidivisible view of reading on current practice, caution needs to be exercised. Acceptance of such a view by practitioners tends to be anecdotal, and based on pedagogical 'experience'. Fyfe and Mitchell (1985: 4) comment:

> no analysis of reading skills or the reading process has yet achieved general acceptance. There is agreement that word recognition can be distinguished from reading comprehension, although the distinction is funny at the boundary, but there has been argument for decades over the existence of different comprehension skills.

In opposition to a multidivisible view of reading, a substantial number of studies have found that it is not possible to differentiate between reading components, either through empirical demonstration of the separate functioning of such components when these are operationalised in language test items, or through the judgement of experts on what the focus of such test items actually is (see, e.g., Alderson, 1990a; Alderson and Lukmani, 1989; Carver, 1992; Rosenshine, 1980; Rost, 1993).

This, however, seems at odds with the componential views of reading (see Sections 2.1 and 2.2 above) that are suggested in the theoretical literature. The two- or three-component models we mapped out in Chapter 2 conflict with a unidimensional view of reading. First we shall examine in detail further evidence from language testing that, at the very least, there are two components in L2 reading which we might characterise broadly as global and local. We then consider recent test data that suggest a further distinction between expeditious and careful reading, which is connected to the third component of literacy discussed in Section 2.2 above. As we emphasise later in Section 5.3, language testing is the methodological procedure that is most likely to provide valid and reliable information on this issue.

Quantitative research

A number of empirical test-based studies, typically using factor analysis, have cast doubt on the multidivisible nature of reading (e.g. Lunzer et al., 1979; Rosenshine, 1980; Rost, 1993). Factor analysis is a statistical procedure for extracting the extent to which putatively different variables – in our case the so-called 'skills and strategies' in reading; reading types – in fact function in a similar manner. If a number of putatively different skills and strategies function in a very similar manner it is said that they 'load on the same factor' and we have at least to entertain the possibility that they are not different at all, only a single construct in different guises. If all conceivably different skills and strategies load on a single factor, we have to consider the strong possibility that there are in fact no skills and strategies at all, only a single undifferentiated ability: reading. If some putative skills and strategies function in a statistically similar manner and load fairly heavily on one factor, while other putative skills and strategies function statistically in another manner and load on a second factor, then this is evidence that reading is at least bi-divisible.

For example, the work of Lunzer et al. (1979) is often cited by reading specialists as evidence that it is not possible through test data to differentiate between the so-called subskills and strategies in reading. This study is said to show that reading (at least as defined by completing their reading tests) is a single undifferentiated ability. However, it is interesting to note that while only one principal factor – presumably undifferentiated reading – is identified in this study through factor analysis, there does appear to be some doubt (Lunzer et al., 1979: 55–7) concerning the strength of the loading of test items testing word-meaning on that principal factor.

The reader must also remember that Lunzer et al.'s study (as with many of those finding no evidence of multidivisibility) was conducted on native speakers of English; in fact primary school pupils, presumably still largely free of the specific linguistic problems experienced by some non-native speakers. Our particular concern in this book is different from that of Lunzer et al. in that we are primarily interested in testing adult L2 readers who will tend to be spread out across the language ability range.

The most recent investigation conducted by Rost (1993), again on native speakers, found strong evidence of unidimensionality, leading Rost to warn against differential skill component interpretation for all available reading comprehension tests (1993: 88). However, once again, it is important to note that, in the reported factor analysis, a second factor that Rost believes to be vocabulary did emerge when the factors were rotated. Rost (1993: 80) indeed cites earlier research where 'two factors of reading comprehension, namely "vocabulary" or "literal reading" on the one hand, and "general reading comprehension" or "inferential reading" on the other' emerged from the data (Johnson and Reynolds, 1941; Stoker and Kropp, 1960; Vernon, 1962; Pettit and Cockriel, 1974; Steinert, 1978).

There is further evidence in the literature that the phenomenon of vocabulary loading on a separate factor is not uncommon. Davis (1944) identified two important separate factors in reading as 'memory for word meanings' and 'reasoning in reading' (a combination of weaving ideas together and drawing inferences from them). Similarly, in a later study (Davis, 1968) a recognition vocabulary test accounted uniquely for a sizeable proportion (32 per cent) of the non-error variance. There is also evidence in Spearritt's reanalysis (1972) of Davis's earlier data that vocabulary tests are differentiable from the single basic ability 'reasoning in reading' measured by other labelled reading components in the reading comprehension tests used in the study. Spearritt (1972: 110) concluded:

> Vocabulary is the best differentiated, as in both the Davis and Thorndike analyses . . . it could not in fact be subsumed under one general factor with the other three skills.

Similarly, Rosenshine (1980: 543) admits to the fact that in three out of the four analyses done on Davis's data the one unique factor that emerged as separate from the others was vocabulary ('remembering word meanings'), the only exception being Thorndike's (1973) analysis which he categorises as being less sophisticated than Spearitt's later study. Rosenshine cites data from Berg in support of the non-divisibility position, but in four out of the five studies summarised by Berg (see Rosenshine, 1980: 544) lexical competence appears as a separate factor. Farr (1968) found two factors – one clearly vocabulary, which loaded heavily on the three vocabulary measures, and one that could be labelled as comprehension.

Though the quantitative studies reported above seem to suggest that it may not be consistently possible to identify multiple, separate reading components, there does seem to be a strong case for considering vocabulary as a component separate from reading comprehension in general. Given that most factor analyses in the studies reported above produced more than one factor, it would be difficult to maintain that reading is a unitary ability. Furthermore, even if the components which load more heavily on a second factor also load on the first general reading factor, it might be appropriate only to select test items which load heavily on the first factor when developing a measure of general reading ability. Alternatively, if vocabulary is considered to be part of reading, a bi-divisible view of reading would seem to be more appropriate.

Qualitative research

As part of a new wave of qualitative investigation in language testing studies, Alderson (1990a; see also Alderson and Lukmani, 1989) investigated the reading component question through the judgement of experts on what reading test items actually test. In this study, groups of experts – usually students on MA courses – were presented with a long list of posited reading components, and asked to identify cold ('heuristically') what items in a pilot version of an EAP reading test were measuring in terms of the list. The resulting lack of agreement on assigning particular 'skills and strategies' to particular test items, i.e. on agreeing what an item was testing, and even whether an item was testing a 'higher level' or 'lower level' component, could be taken as evidence of the indivisibility of the reading 'skill', or at the very least could be seen as casting doubt on the feasibility of distinguishing reading components. Nevertheless, these conclusions need to be subjected to scrutiny.

The authors of the reading test items used in the Alderson (1990a) study were aware of the possible overlap between components tested by individual items. At the time, Weir (1983a: 346) had summarised the approach to the design of the reading component in the TEEP as follows (for 'skills' in this quotation, read 'skill components'):

> ... we aimed to cover as many of the enabling skills in each of the reading subtests ... as was feasible ... we indicate opposite each item in the reading subtests what the Project Working Party and

other experts in the field considered to be the major focus of that item. We were aware that though an item might be seen to be dependent on a particular enabling skill for successful completion, other skills and strategies might be contributing to getting the answer right. We realised that the skills and strategies we were sampling were not necessarily discrete.

Thus any conclusions regarding the feasibility of distinguishing separate components, based on the inability of judges in the Alderson (1990a) study to agree on what single component was tested by individual items, must necessarily be open to question. (For a discussion of further weaknesses in this study, see Weir et al., 1990 and Matthews, 1990). Furthermore, any similar investigations in this area should ensure that the experts involved share a common understanding of the categories of description employed in the study. Lumley (1993) emphasises the need for clear definitions and a common understanding of the terms employed, in particular 'higher level' and 'lower level' components, if the attempt to assign components to test items is to be meaningful.

In contrast to Alderson's findings, there is an alternative literature which suggests that it is possible with clear specification of terms and appropriate methodology for testers to reach closer agreement on what skills and strategies are being tested (Anderson et al., 1991; Brutten et al., 1991; Kobayashi, 1995; Lumley, 1993; Weakley, 1993; Weir et al., 1990).

Casting doubt on unidimensionality

It is important to note that, despite the variability in teachers' judgements in Alderson's study, Alderson (1990b: 465) describes how 'there was more or less agreement' when an item was concerned with deducing the meaning and use of unfamiliar lexical items, or involved understanding relations between parts of a text through cohesion devices. If we reanalyse Alderson's data in terms of our broader categories listed in Table 3.1 above, in particular, types C (careful global) and D (careful local), it turns out that there is a majority agreement among the judges on which of these types the items would fall in nine out of the ten cases selected by Alderson (1990b: 466). If one were to discount the scanning felt necessary to locate one of the items, then there would also be agreement that this item would fall into D-type operations.

It therefore seems likely that even untrained judges are able to determine when an item is dependent upon specifically linguistic knowledge (D-type operations) as against focusing on more global comprehension (A- and C-type operations). Alderson himself would seem to make this distinction when he classifies without demur gap-filling items in the TEEP battery as focusing on local D-type reading (Alderson 1990a: 433).

So, perhaps not too surprisingly, it does appear that judges are able to distinguish items which focus upon specifically linguistic knowledge at the word level. Additionally, there is the quantitative evidence from a number of the empirical studies referred to earlier which seems to suggest that these items may well load on a factor separate from that on which other more global items load in reading comprehension tests. Here are two sets of evidence which seem to suggest a bi-divisible view of reading, at least as far as word meanings and reading comprehension in general are concerned. There is thus both qualitative and quantitative evidence for considering specifically linguistic elements as potentially separable from global comprehension. This is a long way from multidivisibility, however.

The status of expeditious reading

There has for a long time been evidence from survey data that L2 readers found particular difficulty in reading quickly and efficiently in the target language (Weir, 1983a). Slow careful reading also poses problems but the difference between L1 and L2 readers is most marked in expeditious reading. For reasons which are difficult to explain, dedicated tests of the latter ability have not featured in examinations with the notable exception of the *Test for English Majors* in the People's Republic of China which has had a separate section on this since 1990. Data from this test support the view that candidates perform differentially in this section as against the careful reading section (see Shen et al., 1998).

There is further empirical evidence emerging of differences in performance on level A operations (reading expeditiously for global comprehension) and level C operations (reading carefully for global comprehension) in the new *Advanced English Reading Test* being developed for undergraduates also in the PRC (see also Carver, 1992; Guthrie and Kirsch, 1987; Weir, 1983a).

Why have such differences not emerged in almost fifty years of research on this issue? The answer is depressingly obvious. Given that the research instruments used in the studies reported above almost universally failed to include items testing expeditious reading (skimming, search reading or scanning) then their claims to have demonstrated that reading is a unitary ability would seem to be questionable. If one does not take the time and trouble to operationalise these strategies carefully in tests, then one should not be surprised that careful reading tests are just that – tests of careful reading with a possible division between global and local. Given the stranglehold this view of reading has had on research due to the different agenda of psychologists, it is perhaps not surprising that, with a few exceptions (Pugh, 1978), little attention has been paid to expeditious reading.

Careful reading models have little to tell us about what happens in expeditious reading. We noted in Chapter 2 that Rayner and Pollatsek (1989: 477–8), who provide one of the clearest accounts of the reading process, had to admit that there is little hard information on this. Paris et al. (1991: 633) confirm this:

> Testing is a mainstay of US education, and students endure a wide variety of criterion-referenced and norm-referenced tests every year. But educational tests of reading have not changed to conform with our notion of strategic reading. Instead, they are surprisingly uniform. The common format of most reading tests requires the students to read brief paragraphs and answer multiple-choice questions about them. Although decoding, vocabulary, syntax and other features of language are often tested, comprehension scores are usually derived from reading several short paragraphs. Most of these paragraphs are disembodied prose – they do not have titles, pictures or structures like the selections used in basal readers or text encountered in content areas.

De Leeuw and de Leeuw (1965) were among early proponents of the need (p. 10) 'to use a strategy of reading', i.e. read in different ways, at different speeds for different purposes. They argued the importance of efficient reading involving selectivity and the use of expeditious reading strategies (see also Pugh, 1976, 1978). Expeditious reading involves the conscious use of strategies to sample a text in the most efficient fashion in line with a particular purpose (see Paris et al., 1991, for a theoretical description of strategies as actions selected deliberately to achieve particular goals).

Top-down processing may help to determine the sampling strategy with a reversion to conventional bottom-up processing when closer attention is paid to the selected parts of the text. The process may well differ from that of careful reading in important aspects (Rayner and Pollatsek, 1989: 477–8).

Van Dijk (1977: 79) suggests:

> ...we also have explicit discourse cues to select correct macro structures. Such clues include titles, initial summaries and declaration of content/intention. The reader by convention interprets such properties as approximate indications of the global meaning of the discourse. Additional cues are provided by expressions that indicate the relative importance of certain thematic propositions, expressions such as *The crucial point is ... And then the most important thing happened ...* , etc. They are textual warrants for the plausibility of some hypothesis concerning the macro-structural ... relevance of some proposition.

These clues may assume great importance in skimming, in particular, where we are attempting to establish expeditiously a macrostructure and, to a lesser extent, in search reading where we are seeking the answers to predetermined questions on the macrostructure. They are the means whereby we can 'graze' the text to select parts which are more important for establishing a macrostructure quickly. Careful reading of text will embrace these but at the same time the whole of the microstructure is taken in as macro-rules are applied to get at an underlying macrostructure in the text.

All this is not to deny that different readers would appear to use different strategies/skills to extract the author's message in a text (Alderson, 1990a: 436, 1990b; Storey, 1995; Weir, 1981: 34 and 1983a: 346). There may also be a degree of overlap in some hypothesised components (Weir, 1983a: 346); for example, it is possible that the act of quickly skimming through a passage to get an overall idea of the content will activate various schemata and establish the basis for closer reading by drawing on both the main ideas and important details (see Lee and Musumeci, 1988). Thus the interactive parallel processing Buck (1990) talks about in relation to listening may also make it difficult in reading to establish the completely separate existence of the types of reading A, B and C above. This is particularly the case where questions from different levels are set on the same passage. It may be necessary, therefore, to use different texts to test the separability of each of these skills and strategies. Basing tests on a single passage may have been a confounding variable for much of the earlier research in this area! At the very least, independence of items must be in doubt in a number of the studies reported above. Strict time controls will also need to be imposed on the passages within these separate tests to ensure that each passage that is meant to be read expeditiously is in fact processed in that manner. Conversely, careful reading tests should allow candidates more time than they will need, as in real life such reading is not normally constrained by time conditions.

Testing at the microlinguistic level

Research often 'testifies' to the importance of word recognition. Stanovich (1991: 423) in a recent survey notes that research studies have indicated that 'word recognition is a fundamental component of reading comprehension'.

The ability to perform reading types A–C above is obviously dependent on a certain level of competence in the microlinguistic skills detailed as type D. Alderson (1984: 19) termed this 'the threshold level' (see also Carrell, 1991; Coady, 1979; Hudson, 1988; Samuels and Kamil, 1988; Stanovich, 1980 and the discussion in Section 2.2).

It does seem improbable that students would be able to work out the main ideas of a text without some baseline competence in the microlinguistic skills, without understanding some of the relations within at least some sentences of that text (Alderson and Urquhart, 1984; Alderson and Lukmani, 1989; Carrell, 1991; Clarke, 1980/1988; Devine et al., 1987; Eskey, 1988; Grabe, 1991: 391; Stanovich, 1980; Storey, 1995; Weir et al., 1990). However, the degree to which the reader needs these lower order abilities is not yet clear and may prove difficult to quantify (Weir et al., 1990: 508). An interactive or interactive-compensatory view of reading (Rumelhart, 1977; Stanovich, 1980) would seem to imply that readers can make differential use of a range of components which we might loosely label 'specifically language related' and 'reason related' (Grabe, 1991; Williams and Moran, 1989).

The simple answer is that we cannot clearly state what the value of the contribution of skills and strategies at the local level is. In those countries such as China where the aim is to encourage learning to bring students up to and beyond this threshold level, there is naturally some concern that solid foundations in lexical/ syntactic knowledge need to be laid. If it is in the test, it will happen. If it is not a recognisable component of the new Advanced English Reading Test (AERT), then it might not.

Given the evidence against both fully unitary views of reading ability on the one hand, and multidivisible views on the other, it is important for those concerned with language test development to reflect critically on the ramifications of operationalising either in reading tests.

Dangerous implications of a unitary view

There is a disturbing corollary of the fully unitary argument that deserves serious attention from all involved in developing language tests. If there are no discernible components in reading – i.e. if it is unidimensional – it should not really matter how we test it, or what operations we try to assess. The inability to provide consistent or conclusive empirical evidence (either quantitative or qualitative) for the separability of components might well encourage us to utilise test formats with a specifically linguistic focus (D-type operations in Table 3.1 above). These are often relatively easy to construct, administer and mark, frequently have respectable psychometric properties and reliability estimates (usually high internal consistency estimates), and frequently correlate fairly highly with more global tests of reading comprehension.

Given that the current consensus on the nature of reading includes microlinguistic elements as important components within reading (Grabe, 1991; Williams and Moran, 1989), and given the evidence for a unitary view of reading (Lunzer et al., 1979; Rosenshine, 1980; Rost, 1993), it is perhaps not surprising that many current reading tests have in fact ventured down this microlinguistic road (quite often for reasons of practical expediency rather than from a principled view of unidimensionality). In the British Council/UCLES ELTS test, one-third of the items in some of the reading modules appeared to be testing at the microlinguistic level, and in the G1 General Reading Comprehension Module, Criper and Davies (1988: 89–97) indicated that over 50 per cent of the items focused on such lower order elements. The more recent IELTS test has a number of items at this level (see Weir,

1990); so do the TEEP test (see Weir, 1990), TOEFL, and many other tests of international standing and good repute. It is thus fairly urgent that the status of such lower order elements in the measurement of reading ability be investigated.

There are serious question marks against the value of testing directly the specifically linguistic D-type operations listed in Table 3.1 above. The evidence from the literature and our own initial investigations throw some doubt on the value of including any items which focus on specific linguistic elements (e.g. individual words or cohesive devices) in tests which purport to make direct statements about a candidate's reading ability. Tests focusing on level D microlinguistic elements may well correlate quite highly with tests that attempt to tap into global facets of that ability, but they do appear to load on a different factor from general reading comprehension in many studies. It is, in our opinion, unarguable that level D elements contribute to level A and C activities, but on their own they may not constitute an adequate predictor of that ability.

The limited data reported below are intended to raise awareness of the possible danger that some candidates might be disadvantaged by the inclusion of such discrete linguistic items in tests of reading comprehension (level D operations in Table 3.1 above) where the purpose is to indicate whether a candidate has understood the main ideas and important detail provided by the writer, i.e. the reader has understood the text (A and C reading types in Table 3.1). Further data sets are also cited which cast doubt on the use of specifically linguistic test items and the formats with which these are commonly associated to test reading ability. We are aware that our argument smacks of the assertive at present and that further data will need to be generated to prove or falsify our fears. It is a purpose of this chapter to generate interest in this issue so that a concerted body of empirical research might throw further light on it.

Dangerous implications of a multidivisibility view

The dangers of a unitary view of reading have been outlined above, in the light of evidence concerning the status of items testing at the specifically linguistic level. Equally serious problems may arise in accepting unthinkingly a multidivisibility view. This 'scattergun' approach to the testing of components in reading, as referred to above in connection with the original TEEP test (Weir, 1983a, 1991) likewise needs to come under close scrutiny. In the past, broadly sampling components across the four types (A–D) seemed a sensible course of action for assessing reading comprehension. By attempting to sample across the range of hypothesised 'skills and strategies', the intention was to take an adequate sample of a construct that could be labelled reading (Weir, 1983a, 1990).

·*The University of Reading data*

Doubts now arise concerning the relative contribution of the various components to measure the construct of reading, at least in terms of the relationship between type D and types A and C. In the placement assessment (broadly styled on the TEEP approach described above) administered to students recently entering the presessional EAP courses at Reading University in July and August (candidates arriving range from roughly around band 5 on the IELTS scale to band 6.5), it was noted that there were a number of students who might be able to cope quite well with reading passages and questions at the global level, but that this was not matched by their performance on test items focusing on more microlinguistic items: cohesion markers, lexis and structural elements. Regardless of the item-type and regardless of their score on the microlinguistic items, students scored overwhelmingly in the top 50 per cent of the available score range on global items; scores on microlinguistic items, on the other hand, were more evenly distributed on either side of the 50 per cent line, with a slight tendency to fall below rather than above the line. This situation initially gave pause for thought as to how to allocate such students to classes.

However, of far greater concern were the implications of using specifically linguistic test items later on in the programme for assessing proficiency in reading prior to entrance into the university proper. Here there was a serious dilemma in interpreting test results. Doubts arose about the wisdom of using tests or items which appeared to focus on microlinguistic elements. To be more precise, there was major concern about the fairness of such tests for the subset of students who did 'well' on the global comprehension items in our reading tests (at the moment for descriptive purposes arbitrarily defined as more than half the items right) but did not do so well on the microlinguistic items (less than half the items right). Such a situation may occur for a variety of reasons, e.g. successful application of background knowledge to the text under review and/or transfer of higher level processing and strategies from the L1 which compensate for deficiencies in lower level linguistic abilities (Coady, 1979; Goodman et al., 1979; Hudson, 1988). This group of candidates must in any case have passed a threshold level of language proficiency necessary for this transfer to take place in order for global questions to be correctly answered (Alderson, 1984; Clarke, 1980/1988; Cziko, 1980; Devine, 1987, 1988).

The low loading of vocabulary on a general reading comprehension first factor in some of the analyses reported earlier in this chapter is consistent with these findings, in that such results may reflect that candidates can comprehend the overall ideas in a passage irrespective of specific linguistic shortcomings. If we try to relate this to the research on the organisation of prose and its effect on memory (see Section 2.2 above), the work of Meyer (1975: 165, 167) shows that:

> the height of information in the content structure influences its recall . . . ideas located high in the content structure are better remembered than ideas low in the structure.

She posits that this may be because central ideas high in the content structure subsume ideas located low in the structure; ideas in high structural positions are more retrievable from memory or readers most likely select ideas high in the content structure to process for long-term storage rather than low level ideas. This may help to explain why we have found that, in many cases in our tests, global comprehension of a text is superior to local comprehension.

The evidence will need to be supplemented by further, more detailed studies. What an adequate performance on the two item types is will need to be more precisely operationally defined. Simply taking a 50 per cent cut-off point on each test, while useful for descriptive purposes at the early stage of our inquiry, is rather crude. Furthermore, it is possible that a group of candidates might perform worse on microlinguistic items as a normal feature of score distribution. Moreover, it needs to be investigated whether the same candidates are similarly distributed over a number of measures of each of the bi-divisible elements identified. Recent data (Khalifa, 1997) suggests this to be the case.

There is also a possibility that the data we present may have been unduly influenced by the formats employed; some candidates may have reacted adversely to the gap-filling format used to assess microlinguistic knowledge. However, synthesis of information available from the variety of sources reported below would seem to suggest that format effect would be unlikely to account for our results. Evidence from short-answer and multiple-choice formats indicates that the items in reading comprehension tests which focus on microlinguistic elements such as lexis or cohesion do not necessarily contribute to the overall measurement of reading in ways similar to items which test more global comprehension, in that they can be shown to correlate more highly with their own subtest or with other microlinguistic elements in a test battery (such as separate subtests of vocabulary and structure).

Data from ESP Centre, Alexandria, Egypt

Similar differential performance is emerging in data from a battery of EAP tests under development by the Testing and Evaluation Unit at the ESP Centre in Alexandria, Egypt. These are short-answer question tests designed to test, separately, reading comprehension types A, B, C and D in Table 3.1 above. Point biserial correlations show that items in section 1 of the battery testing at levels A and C correlate more with their own subtest than they do with level D (the microlinguistic items), and vice versa. Similarly, there is a small subset of students who, while coping well with A and C operations, experience more difficulty with the specifically microlinguistic items. So here again there is the same phenomenon of differential performance on global as against specifically microlinguistic items. It should be noted that, in the Alexandrian case, the reading test format differed from that used in the Reading study.

Data from College English Test (CET), China

Evidence of differential performance appears in further test contexts. Items which focus on cohesion or working out the meaning of words in context appear to be out of place in a recent version of a reading component of the College English Test (CET) used to test over 1.8 million undergraduates across China. Such items, according to item/part correlational data (Pearson Product Moment), would appear to relate more closely to a later section in the test which focuses on vocabulary and structure than they do to the section designed to test reading comprehension. The format used in this test is multiple-choice, so the phenomenon would appear to repeat itself here in a third format. This is further evidence that the results obtained on the microlinguistic as against global focus are probably not the effect of item type.

Data from the Advanced English Reading Test (AERT), China

A new dedicated reading test designed for undergraduates at Chinese universities is also producing data which suggest that all 15 items in the part of the test focusing on careful global comprehension load on a different factor than do all the 15 items in the part testing careful local comprehension at the word level (see Chapter 5, Table 5.2). Additionally items in the skimming and search reading part testing expeditious global comprehension tend to load on a different factor than those items testing slower, careful reading. In fact, varimax rotation of the data generated by the second pilot on 1100 candidates suggests a four-factor structure in line with the four-part division outlined in Section 3.1 above.

Data from Alderson and Lukmani

Alderson and Lukmani (1989: 269) found that:

> ... what seems to be happening is that weaker students overall do somewhat better on higher order questions than lower order questions ... perhaps lower order questions measure language ability whereas higher order questions might be said to measure something like cognitive skills, logic, reasoning ability and so on ... it might perhaps be possible to get a better estimate of a student's reading abilities ... from higher order questions rather than from lower order questions ... one should not perhaps believe that students with lower language levels are incapable of answering higher order questions. In other words, one should not be inferring from poor performance on lower order questions an inability to perform well on higher order questions.

In proficiency tests, the issue of validity is crucial, given the use to which the results of such tests are normally put. If items with a specific linguistic focus are used in the measurement of reading ability, and if the results are then used in taking decisions on entrance to further study or to the professions, unfairness might result. Tests including such items might discriminate against the linguistically disadvantaged but otherwise competent reader. Those students who can understand almost all of the main ideas and important information in a passage – i.e. those who can clearly establish the macrostructure, but are unsure about the meaning of particular lexical items or cohesion devices, such test items selected for inclusion perhaps subjectively or idiosyncratically – may not pass through the entrance gate which the test embodies. To this extent the idea of reading comprehension as either purely unitary or multidivisible would appear to be dangerous.

The only sensible solution until research reveals a clearer picture of this issue is to profile abilities in each of the areas of our framework. In this way both strengths and deficiencies might be revealed rather than being hidden behind a potentially misleading single score or grade. Different candidates will exhibit different strengths and weaknesses, so, in the interests of fairness alone, different sections of the test should be weighted equally. Profiling of ability in the four levels of our taxonomy of tasks will remove the need for weighting. The users of the profile are in the best position to determine how performance at the different levels is relevant to their needs.

As well as clearly establishing the operations we wish our test tasks to involve, there are a number of additional considerations relating to test task development. We turn next to the issue of the conditions under which the operations discussed above might need to be performed.

3.3   TEXT-BASED FACTORS

There has often been a tendency to focus on the reader rather than the text in reading research. With advances in text linguistics over the last twenty years, text should have an equal status in test development with reader, task and output.

Text type

Unfortunately, as we noted in Chapter 2, many text analysis procedures are so detailed and produce so much data that they can be of little value to testers in making decisions on whether or not to select a text for a test. Deciding what are appropriate text types for the test population is a crucial step in test development. This decision is currently best informed by needs analysis of the students' target situations and by careful examination of the texts (and tasks) used in other tests and teaching materials aimed at the particular test population. (See Section 5.3 on page 274 for exemplification from the development of the Advanced English Reading Test (AERT) project in China.)

There has been a consensus for a number of years that texts used both for teaching and testing should be 'authentic', though this requirement has become more a matter of common sense than, as originally, of almost missionary dogma. There has, however, been a suggestion that in dealing with heterogeneous test populations fully genuine texts are not essential. This is a view supported by the work of Lewkowicz (1997) which indicates that texts might only need to resemble those that the candidates will process in the future in terms of salient 'authentic features'. She argues that full authenticity of text may not be necessary, attainable or desirable. However, until such findings are substantiated by stronger evidence than her initial pilot studies, we would be best served by selecting texts which exhibit as many salient features of target situation texts for the population as is possible.

Obviously the skills and strategies it is wished to test will also influence selection: problem/solution, causative or comparison texts from journals or textbooks may well lend themselves better to testing reading carefully for main idea(s) comprehension than more descriptive texts with lots of detailed information. Though, as Carrell (1984: 464) points out, this might be unfair to certain native language groups such as Arabs for whom it is a preferred rhetorical pattern and more facilitative of recall than other patterns. In careful reading the texts may not necessarily have clear main ideas for selection and main ideas might have to be constructed through propositional inferencing, whereas in skimming and search reading they should be explicit.

Where candidates are expected to skim or search read lengthier texts, these would ideally have a clear overt structure and be clearly sequenced with a clear line of argument running through them. A journal article or chapter from a textbook with clear sections and headings, and where paragraphs contain topic sentences in initial position which signal the information to be presented, may prove suitable for testing these expeditious reading strategies. Problem and solution, causative and comparison texts may have the clearest, tightly organised structures (Carrell, 1984; Meyer and Freedle, 1984; Meyer, 1975). One might also look for texts which are overtly organised into sections. Texts without a clear structure may well be authentic but they do not lend themselves easily to use in testing expeditious reading, just as in real life they are difficult to follow quickly, to summarise or to make notes on. A collection of description texts (Carrell, 1984; Meyer and Freedle, 1984) may be the best vehicle for testing scanning for specific detail.

We realise that the guidelines we have presented are, at best, rather skeletal. Lewkowicz (1997) points out that a key area for future research is in determining the text types that allow the best testing of the various skills and strategies. Kobayashi (1995) has in fact made a good start in this area. She found (pp. 266–7) that:

> there seems to be a close relationship between text type and question type. For example, tightly organised texts tended to produce more questions on main ideas than less organised texts. At least, it seemed easier to generate a variety of questions when texts were highly organised. If texts were loosely organised, on the other hand, questions tended to focus on details or literal understanding.

At lower levels, texts employed in tests are often artificially constructed or simplified because of the restrictions imposed by the structures and lexis available to the students. This may seriously constrain the range of strategies and skills that can be tested and it may be that expeditious strategies are simply not testable at this level because of length constraints.

In Section 4.3 we return to the issue of text selection for teaching purposes and a number of criteria for selecting text are explored in detail.

Propositional content

In most test populations we are dealing with a heterogeneous body of people in terms of their interests, backgrounds and occupational, academic or professional situations. Thus we need to select texts which are within the experience of the whole test population. They should be at an appropriate level in terms of propositional content and candidates should be similar to the audience originally addressed by the writer. Weir (1993) emphasises that the relationship between the writer of the text and the reader – e.g. expert : layperson – needs to be considered at the selection stage. A text written for a different audience than the candidates may not be appropriate.

Topic familiarity

Topic familiarity is increasingly seen as one of the criterial determinants of performance in reading tests (Khalifa, 1997; Aulls, 1986: 124–5). This obviously overlaps with the nature of the existing schemata candidates possess (see Section 2.2 for a full discussion of this). Weir (1990, 1993) points out that the topic should be selected from a suitable genre, at an appropriate level of specificity, and should not be culturally biased or favour any section of the test population. The issue of what is a generally accessible text remains with us. In those situations where we are writing tests for heterogeneous groups of students, we are by necessity forced to select texts with a wider appeal than is the case when we have a more homogeneous group. Clapham (1996a/b) suggests that in her research it is only with more specific texts that background knowledge has a significant effect on text comprehension. We might also need to consider the effect of interestingness. The work of Spilich et al. (1979) suggests that this is an important influence on the interaction between readers and text.

The content of a text should be sufficiently familiar to candidates so that candidates of a requisite level of ability have sufficient existing schemata to enable them to deploy appropriate skills and strategies to understand the text.

Royer and Cunningham (1978) suggest that texts selected should be within the knowledge base of the candidates; they introduce the concept of 'tailoring' texts for specific audiences. Such matching may not be available in tests with large heterogeneous populations and a cruder more general strategy may be unavoidable.

As part of the *a priori* validation process the familiarity of the text can be established through survey and we would want to avoid texts at the extremes of a familiarity continuum (Khalifa, 1997). In general, a text should not be so unfamiliar that it cannot be mapped onto a reader's existing schemata. Conversely, the content should not be so familiar that any question set can be answered without recourse to the text itself (Roller, 1990). This should be checked rigorously, whichever of the formats for testing reading are employed. A key pretesting check is to determine if any of the questions are answerable without recourse to the text, and any such questions should be removed. The reader is referred to the discussion of schemata in Section 2.2.

Texts currently employed in testing reading tend to be genuine and undoctored and, as far as possible, are selected with appropriacy for the target situation needs of the test takers in mind (West, 1991). However, it is not always easy to determine which texts are most appropriate for which test takers; a postgraduate in business studies may well have come from a science or engineering academic background; an undergraduate may be studying a variety of subjects. The practicalities of constructing multiple forms for an EAP proficiency test for different subject areas are intimidating, and though there is some evidence that performance is enhanced by background knowledge in the content area of a reading comprehension passage (Alderson and Urquhart, 1985) the evidence is not conclusive (see Clapham, 1994; Ja'far, 1992; Koh, 1985). However, it does appear that the more specific a text the more important the contribution of background knowledge to comprehension (Clapham, 1994: 281–2), the less specific a text the more important the contribution of language proficiency. This would encourage us to select texts with a preponderance of semi-technical as against technical vocabulary. The development of computer programs for concordancing of texts is already in use in the People's Republic of China for checking this facet of texts in test design.

As far as a canonical culture is concerned, students sitting an EAP test, for example, should not, if possible, be faced with texts which are too far outside their academic culture. If the texts are selected well, testees should be inside what Swales (1990) has termed the 'discourse community'. There remains the problem of the extent to which the test developers also belong to the appropriate community.

If general texts are to be selected in Academic Purpose tests, it appears that the non-science texts may be the most suitable as, although non-science students seem to be adversely affected by science texts in tests, the reverse does not appear to be the case. Most science students appear not to be adversely affected by non-science texts in tests as they are familiar with these areas in their own reading (Clapham, 1994: 277).

Grabe (1991) found that a major implication of research in this area is that students need to activate prior knowledge of a topic before they begin to read. If this is absent then they should be given 'at least minimal background knowledge from which to interpret the text'. It is interesting to note that, in our survey of teaching tasks used in coursebooks, prediction was seen as a useful pre-reading strategy. In contrast, in the analysis of testing tasks we carried out, a pre-reading activity was seldom built in.

Vocabulary

Researchers have attempted to differentiate three levels of vocabulary : common core, subtechnical and technical (Inman, 1978; King, 1989). In tests for heterogeneous populations care should be taken to avoid technical terms (Robinson, 1991: 28). For higher level students in particular, we need to examine whether the lexical range is appropriate in terms of common core, technical and subtechnical vocabulary. In EAP tests, where the focus is on lexis, there is a preference for testing subtechnical words which Cowan (1974: 391) defines as: 'Context independent words which occur with high frequency across disciplines' (see also Yang, 1986: King, 1989). Marton (1976: 92) sees subtechnical words as academic vocabulary, 'the words have in common a focus on research, analysis and evaluation – those activities which characterise academic work'. In general, this seems sensible advice but it is not always easy to determine the level of a word unequivocally and reliably.

Channel

Particularly in science texts, diagrams are extensively used to convey information (Ferguson, 1977; Shepherd, 1978). The presence of diagrams affects the way text is written and processed (Hegarty et al., 1991; Koran and Koran, 1980). Test developers need to decide on the nature and amount of non-verbal information that is desirable, e.g. graphs, charts, diagrams, etc.[5]

Size

Johnston (1984: 151) notes that currently texts used in reading comprehension tests tend to be many and brief. The length of text(s) that candidates are exposed to will influence the strategies and skills that the candidate may be asked to deploy. If texts are too short it may not be possible to test expeditious reading strategies (search reading, skimming and scanning), only careful reading.

Difficulty

Here the concern is with establishing the difficulty of the text/ tasks students are expected to handle. The difficulty of the text will be largely determined by its linguistic, organisational, propositional and discoursal attributes (see above) and is obviously relative to individual variation across a number of parameters (e.g. background knowledge, purpose(s) for reading, etc.).

The literature abounds with warnings against reliance on readability formulas for estimating text difficulty (Weaver and Kintsch, 1991). But as these authors note, and accepting the complexity of the conditions noted above, a simple formulaic approach which takes account of these other conditions is not available and is not likely to be. Miller and Kintsch (1980: 348) present some directions in which we need to go:

> ... the best index of readability is a measure that takes both factors into account, that is, reading time per unit recalled ... the readability of a text is determined by the ways that certain text properties – primarily the arrangement of the propositions in the text base, but also word frequency and sentence length – interact with the reader's processing strategies and resources.

but even this analysis did not take account of inferencing ability or macroprocessing.

The amount of work in conducting such analyses is usually beyond the time and resources available in most teaching/testing situations. At best we need to be aware of these factors and a panel of experts familiar with the use of texts for the specified context are the most likely to be able to make sensible judgements about the inclusion or non-inclusion of texts for testing purposes.

The levels of text that candidates will have to process in the target situation are perhaps still the best guide to the types of text that might be included. *A priori* needs analyses may help here. This should be supported by other validation procedures such as eliciting reactions from future candidates, people preparing candidates and future end users of test results to establish, among other things, appropriate levels of difficulty of texts. Farr et al.'s suggestions (1986) for collecting data on functional literacies is in line with this.

Appendix 1 also contains a summary checklist of the conditions appropriate to the assessment of reading ability that a test writer might want to take into consideration. The list is not exhaustive (see Bachman, 1990, for additional categories) and conversely not all the components will necessarily be relevant in all situations.

It is only when decisions have been taken in relation to selection of texts and tasks for a test that the issue of format can be settled. In the next section we briefly review the use of a number of reading test formats from a historical perspective, consider a number of important facets in test design and then examine in detail the advantages and disadvantages of the most commonly employed formats used for testing reading comprehension.

3.4 TEST FORMATS

Origins

Pugh (1978) suggests that silent reading replaced a long tradition of reading aloud only in the nineteenth century, possibly as the conditions affecting reading rooms in libraries supplanted those of the medieval monastery. However, a more probable explanation is that the growth of literacy in that century reduced the numbers of those needing to listen to texts read aloud. Venezky (1984: 21) dates a change in instructional emphasis from oral to silent reading in the USA at around the end of the first decade of the twentieth century as a result of an increased emphasis on meaning in reading instruction accompanying a social need for literacy, matched by an increased availability of cheap paper and high-volume printing techniques. The chief complaints against oral reading being (a) it did not deal with understanding and (b) it was not the most important kind of reading (Johnston 1984: 152).

Venezky (1984: 3) details how Romanes reported the first study of reading comprehension in 1884 (ibid.: 13) in which rapid readers recalled the most. However, he notes that in the seventy-five years which followed, 'the investigation of cognition in reading comprehension was never pursued as systematically as word recognition was . . . the present day importance given to comprehension in reading research is a phenomenon of the last two or three decades'. Historically, then, the focus has been essentially on vocabulary rather than comprehension in general in both the teaching and testing of reading (op. cit.: 14).

Venezky (1984: 16) describes the work of Thorndike (1917) on comprehension processes based on data gathered in field testing a reading comprehension test. He also provides fascinating details of the use of reading tests in school surveys (evaluations) in the USA in 1915–16 (p. 18), the use of survey data to improve teaching methodology (Neal and Foster, 1926) and a model for planned instructional improvement and its evaluation in Chicago schools. Venezky traces the development of standardised reading tests to the early part of this century and details how they became 'an indispensable component of the schooling ritual, a position they still hold today' (p. 19).

However, Johnston (1984: 149 et seq.) sounds a more cautionary note in pointing out that support for testing reading came largely from administrators because of its accountability and gatekeeping function, and met considerable opposition from teachers. Thus from the beginning of this century the standardised, group silent reading product-oriented model for testing was institutionalised. An individualised, descriptive process-oriented model has not emerged (ibid.: 168 et seq.) and a concern for summative as against formative assessment has maintained its dominance (see Calfee and Hiebert, 1991: 291–301, for the argument for more teacher internal assessment to provide the data which will guide instructional decisions).

It should be noted that such summative tests tend to be unidimensional as reliability is a major criterion for inclusion (Calfee and Hiebert, 1991: 286) and the final versions of tests are very consistent internally and, consequently, provide little information about student strengths and weaknesses. Expeditious reading subtests seem to have lower internal consistency figures associated with them, whereas items focusing on the microlinguistic have much higher. One might speculate that this may in part explain why attempts to develop models for expeditious reading, or to include such reading types in research, tests or teaching, has suffered relative to a traditional focus on careful reading, particularly at the local level. Pugh (1978: 20) notes that from about 1910 there was an increased interest in comprehension exercises on texts requiring close careful reading. He contrasts this with an American interest in the speed of silent reading, which is noticeable by its absence in the British literature in the first half of this century. Slow silent reading features in many of the second language tests produced in the earlier part of the twentieth century (Spolsky, 1995: 41; Venezky, 1984: 13), although from a current perspective it is easy to be dismissive about these early efforts (West, 1991). Generally they did not select texts with the target situation of candidates in mind – although in 1934 James Conant is quoted by Spolsky (1995) as arguing for testing reading knowledge in the candidate's own field. Nor did they meet the demand for 'authenticity' in text and task selection; they do not appear to have been based on any theoretical view of underlying reading process; test items do not appear to have been designed in any principled fashion; and no need was felt to demonstrate their statistical properties, such as their reliability.

Farr et al. (1986: 62) note:

> ... the passage was seen simply as a stretch of prose providing language for comprehension ... the concept that readers read in different ways according to their purpose and the type of text was as yet unrecognised.

Spolsky (1995) describes how such traditional descriptive-humanitarian tests, usually short-answer questions (SAQ) or translation, were largely supplanted by rational-empiricist objective measures, most commonly multiple-choice questions (MCQ), on the basis of the superior reliability and psychometric qualities of the latter. Tests produced within this new 'modern' paradigm did little to embrace the criterion of validity, however.

We would now seem to be entering a 'post-modern age' as concern mounts that, though objective reading tests may be reliable, they may not be delivering valid information on the abilities we seek to measure. We describe below how the wheel now appears to have turned full circle. We appear to be moving from the 'rationalist-empiricist' measurement era (Spolsky, 1995: 1) which attempted to make the testing of reading more objective and more reliable through the use of multiple-choice questions (MCQ) and cloze procedure (Weir, 1990). The short-answer (SAQ) format employed in the first reading tests is now regaining currency as it attempts to rectify its earlier deficiencies using techniques such as mindmapping (Sarig, 1989) and introspection (Faerch and Kasper,

1987; Storey, 1995) to establish what is to be tested and to ensure that what is being tested is what was intended. Statistical validation through internal consistency estimates, correlational data and factor analysis has also proved useful in the validation of such tests. The humanistic-descriptive approach they embody, with its concern for what we are measuring, is now supported and enhanced by an additional concern for the accuracy and replicability of measurement (see Spolsky, 1995: 5 and Section 5.3 below).

In the TESOL field much of the discussion about the testing of reading until the early 1980s focused on how we were going to test it. The concern was largely with the formats we might employ to do so and with the reliability of the measurement involved. The format employed as the vehicle for assessing reading ability will certainly constrain the operations and performance conditions we attempt to include. We examine below some of the principal vehicles for testing various types of reading in the latter half of this century.

In the current consensus it is felt that a valid direct reading test should reflect as closely as possible the interaction that takes place between a reader and a text in the equivalent real-life reading activity, where background knowledge, formal knowledge, and various types of language knowledge may all interact with information in the text to contribute to text comprehension in line with the intended purpose(s) and type of reading.

Developers of reading tests need to make sure they do not artificially constrain the processing options available to the test taker either through inappropriate performance conditions arising from texts employed in tests (e.g. topic, text length, discoursal structure, etc., discussed in Section 3.3 above) or through restrictive, insufficient or ill-conceived sampling of the operations (the activities/reading types discussed in Section 3.2 above) the reader is asked to perform on the text(s) selected (Weir, 1993). Lastly, when all of these are sorted, only then can we decide which test formats are most consonant with our specification. For this reason we have left discussion of test facets and formats until last.

Some important facets of reading test design

Speed

The literature abounds with investigations of the question of reading speed (Fry, 1963; Taylor, 1965; Carver, 1985; Haynes and Carr,

1990). Most make suggestions that good readers read at about 300–350 words per minute but there is wide variation in these studies down to 140 and up to 800 (see also Nuttall, 1996: 56). However, these estimates are really meaningless without consideration of the purpose for reading and other considerations such as text difficulty, etc.

If too much time is given, candidates may simply read a passage slowly and carefully, and questions designed to test ability to process text expeditiously to elicit specified information may no longer activate such operations. Establishing time available for reading for various purposes is difficult to establish and is best done by empirical trialling on an appropriate test population with clearly established criteria for successful completion of tasks.

Time control

If the test does not control how much time students spend on certain items/sections this may change the operations that are needed to answer them. Too much time spent on a search reading question may change it into one that only requires a slow careful reading. A similar problem might arise in careful reading tests where too much time on earlier items means that subsequent questions which demand careful scrutiny have to be answered more hurriedly, and a candidate is forced into constructing invalid test-taking strategies to come up with an answer in the restricted time left.

Careful thought needs to be given to grouping questions into sections (and most probably using different texts for different skills and strategies); empirically determining time necessary to deploy the required skills/strategies; and carefully structuring the test through rubrics and invigilation so that timings are adhered to. If more than one passage is used within a section, then time controls need to be applied here as well or there is a tendency to spend more time on the earlier passage especially in expeditious reading. Thus earlier passages might become tests of careful reading and only the final passage is processed quickly in the absence of strict time controls.

User friendliness

How much help is given? A number of factors need to be taken into account, such as the clarity of the rubrics and whether the rubrics are in the First Language (L1) or the Target Language (TL). Shohamy (1984) goes further and suggests that questions set in L1 are easier than in TL and the latter may not give as accurate a measure of comprehension. In monolingual contexts it seems logical that candidates might be permitted to write their answers in their mother tongue as well as having the rubrics and questions in L1. Lee (1986) suggests that recall of a text was significantly better when done in L1 rather than TL.

Format familiarity

Weir (1993) advises that every attempt should be made to ensure that candidates are familiar with the task type and other environment features before sitting a test. Sample tests or examples in test manuals should be available for national examinations, and in the school context similar formats should have been practised in class beforehand. Where such help is not available in the pre-test situation, thought might be given to providing examples at the start of the test paper if item types are not familiar to candidates. Anderson and Armbruster (1984: 659) gave support to this when they argued that 'performance on the criterion task is a function of knowledge of the task'.

Issues in question design

Fillmore and Kay (1983) provide a useful set of guidelines for setting questions (see also Weir, 1993):

- Questions should not contain harder vocabulary than the text.
- Questions should have only one unequivocal answer.
- If the candidate understands the text they should be able to answer the question.
- Rejection of alternatives on grammatical grounds should not be allowed.
- Skills not related to reading, e.g. mathematics, should not be tested.
- Incidental insignificant information should not be tested.
- Questions that require stylistic or other ambiguous judgements should be avoided.

Further consideration might also be given to the following questions:

- How are the questions to be ordered?
- Does the ordering help bring the process of taking the test closer to the way readers would normally process that particular text, or at least satisfy a critical audience that it promotes one reasonable way of doing so?
- Should skimming and search reading questions occur first and be separated from those questions requiring closer reading of the text?

It would seem to be consistent with the literature on processing that candidates may find it helpful to gain an overview of the passage first. Bransford et al. (1984) showed how performance is affected by activation of background knowledge. Graves and Cook (1980) and Graves et al. (1983) found that previewing text helped increase comprehension of explicit and implicit information. Paris et al. (1991) provide further evidence of empirical support in their review of the literature on strategies.

Some writers on the teaching of reading, such as Nuttall (1996) and Grellet (1981: 6), advocate that activities which lead to an overall global view of the text should precede more local detailed understanding. This would suggest that the first activity in tests might be a skimming task that helps them develop a macrostructure for the passage. In teaching materials a prediction activity normally precedes the reading exercises but it is rarely present in test tasks.

In test tasks students should be advised in advance of the purpose of the item(s). This should contribute to the authenticity of the test task by helping students to adopt appropriate strategies/ skills in task completion. It is important that students should see the questions to which they are to find answers before they actually read the text (skimming may be an exception to this as the search for overall meaning is not usually predetermined in any way and the elaboration of a question would affect this). In this way they will be able to approach the text in the desired manner. Therefore, if the questions only demand specific pieces of information, the answers can be sought by quickly scanning the text for these specifics rather than reading it through very carefully line by line.

We need to consider whether to set questions testing different skills and strategies on the same passage. It may be beneficial to separate those items focusing on expeditious reading from those catering for more intensive reading ability by employing different texts for each. Within the expeditious reading section we might also wish to separate skimming (Pugh, 1978: 54) for the discourse topic, search reading for main ideas (see Pugh, 1978: 53; Guthrie and Mosenthal, 1987) and scanning for specific information (Pugh, 1978: 53; Rosenshine, 1980).

The order of questions should be the order in which information occurs in the text for all test items with the possible exception of scanning (Hughes, 1989: 130). This is consistent with work on text processing (Kintsch and van Dijk, 1978; Just and Carpenter, 1980, 1987) which indicates that readers construct referential representation of a text incrementally. The sequential ordering of questions (for search and careful reading) will help candidates mirror this cumulative process.

Recent methods for testing reading ability

It is necessary to be sure that the methods used do not unduly constrain the range of skills and strategies we might want to test. It is likely that different test formats will permit the measurement of different aspects of reading ability (Reder and Anderson, 1980; Kintsch and Yarborough, 1982; Kobayashi, 1995). The limitations in the cloze procedure and multiple-choice questions (MCQ) need to be examined in this light.

Formats should not in themselves adversely affect performance – e.g. do multiple-choice tests test reading and/or the ability to do multiple-choice tests? The measurement of the reading trait should not be contaminated by the method employed.

Another form of muddied measurement might occur if language abilities additional to those of reading *per se* are involved. If short-answer questions are used, to what extent is the ability to write part of the measurement?

Formats should be familiar to the candidates and, if they are not, a practice test should be given to familiarise them. If it is an achievement test, it should reflect the types of text and associated activities that have been practised in class. If it is a proficiency test it should mirror future activities and text types.

The main proviso for testing within a communicative framework is that the test tasks should, as far as possible, reflect realistic discourse processing and cover the range of contributory skills and strategies, purposes for reading, that have been identified as appropriate for the target population.

Selective deletion gap filling

Gap filling is indirect in that it seems to measure only a limited part of our construct of reading proficiency, namely microlinguistic contributory skills (see Table 3.1 above) and normally would not seem to provide any evidence on a candidate's ability to extract information expeditiously by search reading or skimming a text or to read it carefully to understand its main ideas (reading types A and C in Table 3.1 above). To the extent that it does not match the range of operations and the conditions under which reading tasks might normally be performed by the intended target group, then the task is indirect. Weir (1993) points out that the more indirect the tasks, the more difficult it is to generalise from scores on this test to statements about students' reading ability for particular purposes under specified conditions. How much would the student have to score to be deemed to have met the pass grade in reading and be deemed a competent reader?

Weir (1993) suggests that it is probable that this technique largely restricts one to sampling a much more limited range of enabling skills and strategies (i.e. a limited set of those abilities which collectively represent the overall ability of reading) than do short-answer questions on a text. Whereas short-answer questions allow the sampling of a range of reading skills or strategies, gap filling is much more restrictive where only single words are deleted.

He notes that there is even some difference of opinion on what is being tested where only single lexical items are deleted. Is it testing the ability to recognise which form of the word is required and/or lexical knowledge? On its own it is an insufficient indicator of a candidate's reading ability. If the purpose of a test is to sample the range of enabling skills and expeditious strategies, then an additional format to gap filling is essential.

The format is not likely to have a positive washback effect on learning as it is not in itself a direct measure of the reading construct, and it is difficult to see how performing this test or practising for it relates to a normal reading process or provides information that has a broad diagnostic potential. Tests of this type may be more happily described as tests of general proficiency rather than tests of reading and, as such, may have a role to play in placement testing where an accurate description of ability is less important than quickly putting students into roughly similar levels of 'general ability'.

However, if the focus of attention in the reading class is at the microlinguistic level, selective deletion enables the test constructor to determine where deletions are to be made and to focus on those items which have been selected *a priori* as being important to a particular target audience. For example, in EAP contexts computerised concordancing of a wide range of academic texts can identify common and frequent academic semi-technical lexis that occurs in these types of text.

Cloze

Weir (1990, 1993) describes how the term 'cloze' was first popularised by Taylor (1953) who took it from the gestalt concept of 'closure', which refers to the tendency of individuals to complete a pattern once they have grasped its overall significance (Alderson, 1978). Johnston (1984: 151) details how it had its earlier roots in the completion task used by Ebbinghaus in 1897 in his efforts to find a measure of mental fatigue, for which it proved unsatisfactory though its value as a measure of intellectual ability was noted.

In cloze the reader comprehends the mutilated sentence as a whole and completes the pattern. Words are deleted from a text after allowing a few sentences of introduction. The deletion rate is mechanically set, usually between every 5th and 11th word. Candidates have to fill each gap by supplying the word they think has been deleted.

Alderson (1978: 39) described how

> The general consensus of studies into and with cloze procedure for the last twenty years has been that it is a reliable and valid measure of readability and reading comprehension, for native speakers of English . . . As a measure of the comprehension of text, cloze has been shown to correlate well with other types of test on the same text and also with standardised tests of reading comprehension.

Cloze tests are easy to construct and easily scored if the exact word-scoring procedure is adopted. With a 5th-word deletion rate a large number of items can be set on a relatively short text and these can exhibit a high degree of internal consistency, in terms of Kuder–Richardson coefficients. This consistency may vary considerably, dependent on the text selected, the starting point for deletions and the deletion rate employed (Alderson, 1978).

Some doubts have been expressed, especially concerning its validity as a device for testing global comprehension of a text. One of its main flaws is that it seems to produce more successful tests of syntax and lexis at sentence level, comprehension of the immediate local environment, than of reading comprehension in general or of inferential or deductive abilities (Alderson, 1978; Chihara et al., 1977; Kintsch and Yarborough, 1982; Kobayashi, 1995; Markham, 1985). Alderson (1978: 99) found that

> . . . cloze is essentially sentence bound . . . Clearly the fact that cloze procedure deletes words rather than phrases or clauses must limit its ability to test comprehension of more than the immediate environment, since individual words do not usually carry textual cohesion and discourse coherence (with the obvious exception of cohesive devices like anaphora, lexical repetition and logical connectors).

The process underlying successful completion appears to be largely bottom-up with an emphasis on careful passive decoding at the word or immediate constituent level. The focus appears to be on local comprehension at the microlinguistic level rather than global comprehension of ideas encoded by the writer across the text as a whole. Bernhardt (1991b: 198) comments:

> . . . it focuses a reader's attention on individual words to the detriment of a global understanding of the text . . . It clearly has little if anything to do with a reader's understanding of a piece of connected discourse.

In reading for academic study purposes it is difficult to see how it can test the ability to read through a text expeditiously or carefully to extract main ideas and important detail. Cloze appears to have little to do with a reader's understanding of a piece of connected discourse (Markham, 1985), measures information only within clause boundaries (Kamil et al., 1986; Shanahan et al., 1982) and focuses attention on individual words to the detriment of global understanding of a text. That such decoding is seen as the hallmark of a poor reader (automaticity; rapid context free word and phrase recognition being the hallmark of the fluent reader according to Carrell et al., 1988: 94–5 and Stanovich, 1981: 262) may lead us to question its place in either teaching or testing.

Bernhardt (1991b: 197) argues that as far as the construct validity of cloze as a test of reading is concerned, 'cloze testing is profoundly inadequate'.

Multiple-choice questions

In reaction to the earlier 'pre-scientific' SAQ tests, an interest developed in using the more objective MCQ format which still appears in major international second language tests, e.g. TOEFL and UCLES examinations, to this day.

Weir (1993) details how multiple-choice tests exhibit almost complete marker reliability as well as being rapid and often more cost effective to mark than other forms of written test. The marking process is totally objective because the marker is not permitted to exercise judgement when marking the candidate's answer; agreement has already been reached as to the correct answer for each item. The format allows scripts to be machine marked in large-scale examinations, as in China, where over 2 million take the College English Test (CET). Selecting and setting items are, however, subjective processes (Meyer, 1985) and the decision about which is the correct answer can be a matter of subjective judgement on the part of the item writer or moderating committee.

However, even for experienced examiners it is extremely difficult and time consuming to develop a sufficient number of decent items on a passage. Items need to be validated through trialling before we can be confident of their statistical properties, e.g. facility and discrimination. The development of items for the CET in China go through a number of rigorous trialling phases, and even so it takes the national moderating committee ten days to finalise the papers each year. Given how difficult it is to write such items, there must be a serious question mark against teachers using this format to test reading for practical reasons alone.

In more open-ended formats for testing reading comprehension, e.g. short-answer questions, the candidate has to deploy the skill of writing. The extent to which this affects accurate measurement of the trait being assessed has not been established. Multiple-choice tests avoid this particular difficulty.

With the growth of interest in overall text comprehension as against decoding in the 1970s, an interest in top-down processing as against bottom-up decoding, testers also became more aware of assessing comprehension of text at the global level. A comparison of the ELBA test with the ELTS test makes this distinction clear. It is, however, extremely time consuming and demanding to get the requisite number of satisfactory items for a passage, especially for testing strategies such as skimming in the MCQ format. A particular problem appears to lie in devising suitable distracters for items testing the more extensive receptive strategies. West (1991: 63) comments:

> ... while multiple-choice reading items are well able to test isolated details or 'fragmentary' comprehension, they are not very suitable for more global tests of reading. By 'global' reading is meant some broader response to the text – either comprehension across the text as a whole (or at least a considerable portion of it) or an understanding of the text as a text: an appreciation of the characteristics of the text type, the intended audience, the writer's intention, the overall message, or the structure of the text.

Although MCQ items could (albeit with some difficulty) be written in these areas, such items would seem to inhibit the use of top-down strategies (skimming, predicting), not least because it is likely to encourage test takers to try to match the stem and options with words in the text. Heaton (1988) had noted earlier that, for global comprehension activities, it is more helpful to set simple open-ended questions rather than multiple-choice items; otherwise students will find it necessary to keep in mind four or five options for each item while they are trying to process the text.

There must be some doubt about the validity of MCQ tests as measures of reading ability. Answering multiple-choice items is an unreal task, as in real life one is rarely presented with four alternatives from which to make a choice to signal understanding. In a multiple-choice test the distracters present choices that otherwise might not have been thought of. In MCQ tests we do not know whether a candidate's failure is due to lack of comprehension of the text or lack of comprehension of the question. A candidate might get an item right by eliminating wrong answers, a different skill from being able to choose the right answer in the first place. Nevo (1989) details how test-taking strategies can lead to right answers for some candidates and reading strategies to incorrect ones on an MCQ test.

Bernhardt (1991b: 198) raises the issue of passage independence in such tests and cites evidence of candidates being able to determine answers without recourse to the passage (see also Pyrczak, 1975; Jarvis and Jensen, 1982; Barnett, 1986). Evidence of this being a problem is also presented in Katz et al. (1990) .

There is also some concern that students' scores on multiple-choice tests can be improved by training in test-taking techniques and that such improvement reflects an enhanced ability to do multiple-choice tests rather than any increase in language ability. This is a matter which is in need of serious investigation.

Carrell et al. (1989) found that the effectiveness of training in reading strategies varied according to the test format employed. Metacognitive training led to improvement in the sample whose ability was measured by open-ended questions but not for those on MCQ tests.

Weir (1993) draws attention to the danger of the format having an undue effect on measurement of the trait. There is some evidence that multiple-choice format is particularly problematic in this respect. This has been evidenced by low correlations both with alternative reading measures and with other concurrent external validity data on candidates' reading abilities (see Weir 1983a). The scores obtained by candidates might have been affected by the method used. This is not a problem with direct measures of language ability.

Reading tests in this approach were more concerned with the psychometric properties of the test than with the nature of the construct being measured. Thus, in earlier versions of the TOEFL reading test one could find a section of decontextualised vocabulary items being used as indicators of reading ability; this is very much a bottom-up approach to reading and a very limited part of it at that. As Spolsky (1995: 4) points out: 'what can be measured reliably is not necessarily the same as the ability one is interested in'.

A more recent variant of this technique termed 'multiple matching' (where the answers to all questions plus a number of distracters are all provided in the same list for the candidate to select from) appears in a number of recent ELT exams produced by UCLES. Its advantages are enumerated by West (1991). However, its proponents still do not explain how the underlying processes that help select the right answer from the many available equates with normal processing for the reader. It is nevertheless an improvement on traditional MCQ and in those situations where tests need to be machine scored because of huge populations its potential should be investigated.

Information transfer tasks

Direct language tests which aim to measure ability to perform authentic tasks (e.g. extracting main ideas quickly) under real-life performance conditions (e.g. reading undoctored texts from the real world) provide the tester with information which can more effectively be translated into statements concerning the candidate's ability to cope with reading in the target language situation.

All of the conditions identified in Appendix 1 can be taken account of in this format and in contrast to the indirect formats discussed above, the normal purposes for which people read can be more easily accommodated.

In testing reading comprehension there is a potential problem of the measurement being 'muddied' by having to employ writing to record answers. Weir (1993) provides examples of how, in an attempt to avoid this contamination of scores, several examination boards in Britain have included tasks that require information from written texts to be translated into a non-verbal form, e.g. by labelling a diagram, completing a chart or numbering a sequence of events.

However, a good deal of care needs to be taken that the non-verbal task the students have to complete does not itself complicate the process or detract from the authenticity of the experience. In some of the more sophisticated tasks using this format, there is sometimes a danger that students may be able to understand the text but not be totally clear what is expected of them in the transfer phase. There is also a danger that in order to fit more neatly into such formats, texts are sometimes expressly written for this purpose.

Weir (1993) details how the questions set in this format can cover the important information in a text (overall gist, main ideas and important details) and understanding of structures and lexis that convey this. The nature of the format and the limitations imposed by capacity at lower levels of ability will constrain the types of things students might be expected to read for in the early stages of language learning. In the first year of learning a language, reading will normally be limited to comparison and contrast of the personal features of individuals and extracting specific information from short non-personal texts. At higher levels more complex texts will be used and most of the skills and strategies in Table 3.1 above – involving search reading and reading carefully to understand the main ideas and important detail – can be assessed.

Weir (1993) describes information transfer tasks as a useful variant of short-answer questions which require candidates to write down answers in spaces provided on the question paper. These answers are normally limited in length either by using short lines to indicate the number of words, restricting the space made available to candidates through boxes, or by controlling the amount that can be written by deleting words in an answer that is provided for the candidate. All of these techniques help keep the answers brief and reduce writing to a minimum in an effort to avoid possible contamination from students having to write answers out in full.

Short-answer questions

This was one of the earliest forms of testing and predates MCQ and Cloze. In its earlier incarnation it suffered from the fact that the texts were often short and in many cases artificially constructed (see West, 1991). Texts now tend to be genuine and undoctored (see Weir, 1990, for examples) and as far as possible are selected with appropriacy for the target situation needs of the test takers in mind.

Developments in test validation techniques have also contributed to making better use of the SAQ format. Through meaning consensus techniques (Sarig, 1989) a more principled basis for arriving at test items is now available. If the focus for such questions is determined in a principled fashion, for example, by textmapping to form a consensus framework of the main ideas and important details a reader might be expected to extract from a text (Sarig, 1989), idiosyncrasy in content selection can largely be avoided (see Section 5.3 for details of this procedure). The immediate recall protocols advocated by Bernhardt (1991b: 200–10) for testing individuals might alternatively be used for helping to decide what a candidate should be able to take away from a text.

Expert judgement and introspection (Storey, 1995) by appropriate readers enhance the probability that the required operations are being tested, and introspection in particular can illuminate the extent to which the behaviour that test items produce equates with the behaviour identified in the theory-based model as being representative of the real reading which occurs outside the test itself (see Section 5.3 for details of how these procedures were used in the development of a recent EAP reading test). Storey (1995) shows how introspective validation can help identify the proportions of construct-relevant and construct-irrelevant variance generated by test items.

Dubin et al. (1986: 163) point out:

> . . . interactive models (of the reading process) suggest a need to test skills at many levels, since all these skills are assumed to play a

significant role in the reading process. They include everything from rapid identification of vocabulary and syntactic structures, to the interpretation of larger discourse patterns, the making of inferences, etc. In addition, since interactive models are defined by the interaction of various skills and strategies, ideal assessment strategies would involve combining skills.

Weir (1993) describes how, with careful formulation of the questions, a candidate's response can be brief and thus a large number of questions may be set in this format, enabling a wide coverage. The SAQ format lends itself to testing all the types of reading identified earlier in Chapter 2 and discussed above in Section 3.2 (search reading, skimming for gist, scanning for specific information and reading carefully to extract the main ideas and important details from a text). Activities such as understanding implicitly stated ideas, recognition of a sequence, comparison and establishing the main idea of a text, often require sentences in a text to be related with other elements which may be some distance away in the text. This can be done effectively through short-answer questions where the answer has to be sought rather than being one of those provided as in multiple-choice. Consequently, correct answers are more likely to result from comprehension of the text rather than from test-taking strategies such as guessing, matching, etc.

The main disadvantage to this technique is that it involves the candidate in writing, and where candidates are required to use their own words rather than language supplied in the text, there is some concern that a significant amount of difficulty may be added (Pollitt and Hutchinson, 1986; Bensoussan and Kreindler, 1990: 59), and there is accordingly interference with the measurement of the intended construct. Care is also needed in the setting of items to limit the range of possible acceptable responses.

Weir (1993) claims that if the number of acceptable answers to a question is limited, it is possible to give fairly precise instructions in the mark scheme as to the range of semantically acceptable answers. In those cases where there is more debate over the acceptability of an answer, in questions requiring inferencing for example, there is a possibility that the variability of answers might lead to marker unreliability. However, careful moderation and standardisation of examiners should help to reduce this. Mechanical accuracy criteria (grammar, spelling, punctuation) should never feature in the scoring system as this affects the accuracy of the measurement of the reading construct.

The attraction of SAQ over all other formats is that texts can be selected to match performance conditions appropriate to any level of student, and the format allows the testing of all the operations that might be required in a test of reading.

Recall measures

The measures we have discussed so far for assessing comprehension have been the choice of educators: write questions about information in a passage and then evaluate readers' responses to them. Meyer and Rice (1984: 320) describe how psychologists have tended to get readers to write down all they can remember from texts. They point to difficulties in marking such protocols, not least the difficulties of establishing marking frames, especially where inferences are made.

Kobayashi (1995: 111), in reviewing recall protocols, comments:

> Recall protocols can be classified as either oral or written in terms of the language mode, or either immediate or delayed in terms of time of recall, or either free or probed, i.e. with or without cues for recalls. First a text is analysed in terms of idea units (or propositions) and this analysis becomes a template for scoring recalls. The number of propositions recalled after listening or reading will be counted as scores.

She notes that the method has not yet gained much ground in testing but is increasingly common in second language research studies (see also Lee, 1986, and Lund, 1991). She points to the difficulty in establishing propositions and a hierarchy of relative importance within these. The difference between reproduction and comprehension is also noted. More mature readers who integrate ideas and synthesise may be penalised because their protocols lack details and they may have used their own words.

Bernhardt (1991b: 200–10) proposes immediate recall as an alternative to traditional testing measures, drawing on her experience in cognitive psychology and L1 reading research. However, at present the analysis of protocols necessary to determine an estimate of performance would take far too long for this technique to be feasible for either classroom or large-scale testing, particularly if the recall protocols are to be written in the native language of each author.

Developing a marking scheme even on a relatively small passage can take up to 50 hours (Bernhardt 1991b: 202) and marking individual protocols, an hour for relatively short passages. She does, however, suggest a revised and more efficient scheme, based on breaking the propositions into pausal units, which is quicker but there must still be some concern that scoring is based on very small units of information and often single lexical items; this raises again the central issue of construct validity.

As well as problems in efficiency there is a serious question mark against the validity of this procedure for testing reading comprehension. Kobayashi (1995: 113) draws attention to the fact that readers may not be able to remember all they have understood. Comprehension is not necessarily equatable with remembering.

3.5 CONCLUSIONS

In Chapter 2 we looked at the theory relating to componential and process models of reading. We noted that a comprehensive model of the processing involved in different types of reading is not yet available and that, for the present, L2 researchers, teachers and testers might be better served by focusing on the components of reading ability. In Section 2.2 an *a priori* case was made for there being more than one component in reading and a preference was stated for a three, as against a two, component model. In Section 2.3 we translated these components into terms of skills and strategies which are more familiar to testers and teachers.

In Chapter 3 we have examined test-driven research for empirical evidence relating to the componentiality issue in terms of what strategies and skills can and **should** be assessed. The data emerging from such studies offer some tentative but encouraging support for the theoretical view of the components favoured in Chapter 2.

The rigorous requirements of validation in language testing have necessitated a closer examination of the parameters of texts than in Chapter 2, Section 2.2. The need for explicit specification in testing means that we also have to establish any performance conditions that may affect the product of reading comprehension and perhaps even processing itself. We believe that these text-based facets must form part of any definition of reading objectives or any definition of reading proficiency. All skills and strategies are performed under certain performance conditions and not in the vacuum or text neutral position purely theoretical work sometimes assumes. We do not just read expeditiously but rather we skim/search read/scan a certain type of text, of a certain length, of a certain degree of familiarity, under certain time constraints, etc. (see Section 3.3 above). Altering the conditions will alter performance in comprehending a text and possibly the way we process the given text.

In terms of the test data presented in this chapter, the argument as to whether reading is multidivisible, consisting of a number of components which can be identified clearly, or whether it is an indivisible, unitary process, is still not fully resolved. The ubiquitous call for further research is necessary. If a unitary view is to be convincingly rejected, future research will need to demonstrate the consistent presence of at least a second component in repeated analyses across a range of samples of ESOL candidates. Secondly, future research will need to investigate whether such components are identifiable. Finally, it will have to establish the extent to which each component has a meaningful effect on the measurement of reading comprehension. How much of the overall variance does each component explain in a reading test? It will be important to use more exigent statistical techniques to test whether the presence of each component is statistically significant.

There is cause for immediate concern that wholesale adherence to either the unitary or the multidivisible view in language testing may be problematic. As a matter of urgency we need to develop tests which are **maximally valid** tests of the skill components at levels A, B, C and D in Table 3.1. If, in constructing tests of expeditious and careful reading strategies, test constructors faithfully mirror these in the mapping of texts for testing purposes, then we might be able to make a stronger case for suggesting that we are actually testing these skills or strategies. Student introspection at the piloting stage might lend further credence to our efforts. Statistical analysis of data from a normally distributed test population, in particular principal components analysis, might add further weight to the success of operationalising the constructs. A full account of a systematic and principled methodology for researching the construct of reading through language test data is presented in Section 5.3.

Such research may not, of course, run as smoothly as we would like. It may prove impossible to operationalise the posited four types of reading separately in a test. It may be that reading is such a massively parallel interactive process that we will not be able to distinguish clearly between such components. It may be that, at certain levels of ability – for example, weak and strong readers – reading is indeed unitary; divisibility may be a function of the level of student being tested. For readers linguistically proficient in the target language and already competent readers in their L1, reading in the target language may well be uni-componential, whereas this may not be the case where either of these conditions is not met (see Downing and Leong, 1982).

However, Johnston (1984) rightly emphasises the need to view validity as the interpretation to be made from test results rather than residing in the test itself. We must not lose sight of the emerging evidence that there is doubt about the status of items that focus on specifically linguistic operations at level D as part of the assessment of a candidate's general reading ability. As a matter of urgency, it is necessary to investigate whether testing D-type reading does in fact give us sufficient information about a candidate's ability to handle global comprehension tasks A and activities C. We must address the implications of evidence that there may be groups of candidates who are capable of type A and C reading but who are severely challenged by type D test items. There must be serious concern that test items which focus on the specifically linguistic/individual word level may not be good predictors of general reading ability, i.e. they do not give us an accurate picture of the reading ability of all the individuals who sit a test.

We believe that utilisation-focused tests of reading need to be based on a clear specification of the target situation needs of candidates and an attempt will have to be made to identify the skills/strategies which are needed to carry out their future activities. A representative sample of those reading types should be incorporated into the test in a number of different sections with their own specific configurations of performance conditions. Kintsch and Yarborough (1982: 834) argue in a similar vein:

> It is clearly false to assume that comprehension is an ability that can be measured once and for all, if only we had the right test. Instead, 'comprehension' is a common sense term for a whole bundle of psychological processes, each of which must be evaluated separately. Only a collection of different tests, each tuned to some specific aspect of the total process, will provide adequate results.

Crucially, a profile of appropriate abilities would indicate whether or not the candidate is likely to be able to function effectively in the target language situation in respect of each of the identified skills/strategies. Everything we have said in our earlier review of models in Chapter 2 and in the empirical review of test-based research in Chapter 3 supports the case for profiling. Spolsky (1994) succinctly adumbrates the complex and multidimensional nature of comprehension and stresses the need for full description in reporting results as against a single grade or score. He argues (1994: 151):

> ... we will need to design and use a variety of reading assessment procedures (not only tests) to allow us to report on a variety of aspects of the student's ability to understand, and to establish some systematic way of reporting the results on all of them. The differences the student shows across this range of results will inform us at least as much as will the result of adding them together. However good our tests are, a single score will always mislead.

Given the distinct possibility that different skills and strategies can be taught and tested, and an acceptance that it is worth while investigating these, then some form of profiling of these abilities is essential rather than collapsing scores into a single score or grade for reporting purposes.

Lastly, we have argued that, as well as carefully considering operations and the conditions under which they are performed, the test developer must pay due attention to selecting appropriate formats for assessing performance. Kobayashi (1995) has clearly demonstrated that the formats used for testing reading comprehension may well influence performance. Such method effect should be limited, as far as possible, by the inclusion of a range of task types which replicate real-life performance (Johnston, 1983) and which have been shown to be suitable instruments (valid, reliable and utilisation focused) for measuring posited reading skills and strategies.

Notes

1. We must be careful not to fall into the trap of thinking that these two types of variation are separable. Clearly the dimensions intersect: readers' careful reading may be expected to produce a different product from their expeditious reading, but their careful reading may also produce different interpretations from other readers' careful reading.
2. It will be recalled that Hoover and Tunmer adopt this course when describing the components of reading *ability*.

3. Testers' assumptions can so easily be thwarted. One of the authors once set a JMB test apparently requiring a detailed background knowledge of horse-shoes to a group of British adults. One student performed brilliantly, only to confess that in his youth he had passed a lot of time in a farrier's workshop.

4. As pointed out in Chapter 2, Kintsch and van Dijk's description is best suited to careful reading.

5. The provision of such a categorisation should not be taken as pre-empting the question as to whether multicomponent categorisations are valid.

4

The teaching of reading

4.1 TEACHING AND TESTING

A few years ago it was a commonplace to assert that a great deal of testing reading went on but little teaching. With a lot of justification, it was held that a typical reading lesson consisted of the teacher, with little or no prior discussion or any other kind of preparation, presenting the students with a text, which the students then read. After this stage, the teacher asked questions and the students answered. Feedback was limited to the students being told that their answers were right or wrong. Variations existed: the teacher might read the text aloud, while the students followed it on the page; or the students might be asked to read it aloud. The teacher might use a textbook which contained the questions, and sometimes the answers.

If such a depiction of the typical reading lesson is valid, and it is our experience that not only was it virtually ubiquitous some years ago but it is still prevalent in many parts of the world, then the accusation that reading was tested but not taught is justified. The sequence of activities described above amounts to an informal assessment of students' reading performance, i.e. a test. Teaching would involve, among other aspects, more structured feedback as to why responses were acceptable or not, some instruction in how to arrive at the desired response, in addition to more global instruction in how to set about the task, alternative strategies which might prove helpful, etc.

In the past few years, a great deal of work has been done on these and other aspects of teaching, as opposed to testing of reading. This work will be reviewed below. Before we proceed to it, however, we shall look more closely at similarities and differences between testing and teaching.

Similarities

Both testing and teaching involve students being given a written text or texts, and being required to read it. Usually, they are also expected to respond overtly to some task requirement (though in classroom 'silent reading', this requirement may be dropped). Apart from such an obvious overlap, the following similarities can be discerned.

We noted in Chapter 3 that a feature of the British approach to communicative testing is that the tasks and the conditions under which they are performed should approximate to real life performance as closely as possible (McNamara, 1996; Weir, 1993). We feel that the same should apply to the teaching of reading, at least as far as comprehension activities are concerned.

Consideration of the types of task discussed for testing reading in Chapter 3 and the performance conditions under which they are performed, such as

- purpose
- nature of the texts
- length of text
- rhetorical structure
- topic area
- background knowledge
- writer/reader relationship
- speed of processing
- range of vocabulary
- grammatical complexity

are of equal relevance in the reading classroom in determining activities and selecting texts.

For example, as far as purpose and texts are concerned, reading genuine texts for authentic purposes is held to be crucial in motivating learners to read (Nuttall, 1996). In both teaching and testing, coping with genuine text is likely to be an important objective at a certain stage for many learners. A key objective for both the materials writer and the test developer should be to give the students a realistic purpose for every reading activity (see Moran and Williams, 1993: 68). Personal interest may be difficult to cater for in a course book or a test, but instrumental purposes are relatively easy to simulate in information-giving texts (see Paran, 1991 and 1993, for examples of this). Such purposes enable the activity to move beyond the ubiquitous post-text comprehension question(s) demanding a ritual show of understanding (ibid.).

A feature of modern textbooks on reading is to try to provide a clear purpose for reading a text and Paran (1993) provides some nice examples of how this might be set up through pre-reading activities such as: an initial questionnaire followed by reading to compare findings; a quiz and a reading to check how much you know; prediction of content from title, words, illustrations, etc., and checking text to see how right you are; discussing own opinions and comparing with opinions in the text.

The question of text length is another aspect shared by testing and teaching. It is clear that people learn to read by reading not just by doing exercises. Learners must therefore read enough in a programme for it to make a difference (see Mahon, 1986). So just as longer texts are necessary in tests where the interest is in expeditious reading, so too in learning to read. The tendency to employ short texts in tests and course books meant to cover the range of reading skills and strategies is questionable (for example, note the limited length of texts in McGovern et al., 1994). Obviously, in a teaching situation the length of texts that it may be possible to use is far greater, especially if out-of-class work can be given. At this point differences between teachers and testing begin to emerge.

Activities and performance conditions discussed in Chapter 3 are criterial for both teaching and testing; it is in the use made of the data generated by the reader interacting with these that differences emerge.

Differences

It is universally accepted that, in testing, reliability of measurement is of crucial importance. Any factor that reduces reliability must be isolated and, if possible, eliminated or at least minimised. In the teaching situation, however, reliability of measurement is far less important. This is the major difference between testing and teaching, from which all the other differences, set out below, derive.

Interpretations

We have argued that traditional testing aimed at forming a reliable estimate of an individual reader's performance. In order to achieve this, a consensus as to what constituted an agreed standard performance in a particular context had to be agreed in advance by the testers. Alternatives to this standard had to be eliminated. In other words, the test had to be constructed in such a way that for each task there was a right answer. Scenarios, even if reflecting situations in the real world, where either there was no agreed right answer (as in reading for enjoyment) or where different answers were arguably equally valid, had to be avoided.

In Chapter 2 we discussed different styles of reading and contrasted the submissive versus the dominant reader. We argued in Chapter 3 that in testing there was little room for dominant reading or challenging the texts as this would certainly defeat any attempts to assess such activities reliably. In addition, no account could be taken of the way in which the response offered had been arrived at. In other words, testing at present is concerned with product, and not process. Teaching, on the other hand, since reliability of measurement is not as important, can take differing products, interpretations, into account. Also, since it must be concerned with how one goes about solving a reading task, it is also permitted to encompass process.

Thus, reader-specific responses to text are possible and to be encouraged in the teaching situation, whereas for reasons of test reliability they were excluded from consideration in testing (see Section 3.1). In learning to read, activation of relevant schemata is seen as a key part of the reading process. Pragmatic inferencing (Chikalanga, 1992) is also viewed as an important aspect of the reading classroom, particularly at more advanced levels (see Section 4.2 below for a discussion of this type of reading, and Nuttall (1996: 121 and 167) for discussion of classroom procedures and exemplification). Inferencing may indeed promote effective learning (Pearson and Fielding, 1991).

Training

Recent textbooks (Paran, 1991, 1993) build in cognitive and metacognitive training as a central part of each unit. Their exercises go beyond mere answering of comprehension questions and attempt to teach strategies for coping with texts at the pre-reading, while-reading and post-reading stages. Sometimes learning is paid lip service in testing tasks, but this is not common. It is this developmental rather than accountability function which distinguishes summative testing from teaching.

Formative testing in the classroom is different, however, in that the purpose, the use to which the results are put, should be diagnostic. Teaching cannot proceed without reliable information on what students can or cannot do. Formative testing has a crucial role in providing such data for developmental purposes and, as such, the distinction between teaching and testing tasks is blurred in such formative use of tests.

Tasks

We have already said that testing is fundamentally concerned with tasks. The testees must perform overtly, in response to a task set, and their performance is assessed. Tasks, of course, occur in the teaching classroom too, but there are differences. While there are numerous definitions of tasks in teaching (Nunan, 1989, 1993; Candlin and Murphy, 1987; Crookes and Gass, 1993a and b; Skehan, 1996; Skehan and Foster, 1995) we are happy to take Williams and Burden's (1997: 167) simple description as our working definition for teaching purposes:

> *Basically, a task is anything that learners are given to do (or choose to do) in the language classroom to further the process of language learning.*

We would want to extend tasks to include such activities outside the classroom and limit it for our purposes to reading, e.g. reading a book at home for pleasure. We would also see formative test tasks as falling under this umbrella. We also accept that Nunan's elements of a task – input data, activities, goals, role of learners and role of teachers – are all important and all interact with each other (Nunan, 1993). Consideration of one will necessarily involve some consideration of the others. For ease of description the role of the learner and goals are considered in Section 4.2; input data, i.e. texts and activities, are discussed in Section 4.3; and we examine the role of the teacher in Section 4.4.

Staging tasks

Unlike the test, in the reading classroom tasks may well be broken down, staged or scaffolded to help the less able reader. The teacher provides help to enable students to complete tasks they would not be able to do on their own. In contrast to the driving test itself, in learning to drive one would not expect to do everything in a single lesson, at least not in the early stages. So too with reading; at some stage it might be necessary to focus on certain strategies or skills, or analysis of sentence functions or text structures (see Nuttall, 1996: 100–24).

Microskills

There may well be a necessity to bring some students up to a threshold level of linguistic ability whereby they are enabled to establish, expeditiously or carefully, the macrostructure of a text. Activities promoting global comprehension may not be sufficient for this. Learning the important skills of word recognition and decoding may involve less direct, less global activities. Whereas in testing we have suggested that successful expeditious and careful reading for global comprehension must indicate a minimally adequate knowledge of lexis and structure, and thus make testing at the word level unnecessary except for diagnostic/placement purposes, the teaching situation is different. We may have to provide the opportunities to practise activities promoting word recognition and decoding skills in reading classes although, as such, they may never appear in proficiency or achievement tests of comprehension.

Co-operation

We noted above that in summative testing the teacher and fellow students are removed from the interaction, and the help that can be provided by both in learning to read is not available to the student. The interest in the test situation is in what the student is capable of comprehending unaided. In testing, some students might be expected to fail; whereas in teaching, the agenda is to try to ensure that nobody does.

In the test situation the reader is isolated from contaminating sources, such as help from other students or from the teacher, in an attempt to measure his or her ability in a construct unmuddied by other influences. In the reading classroom pedagogical input exists in terms of instruction and mediation that is absent from the test context: i.e. advice on strategies and skills, practice in their use and discussion of their value. The aim here is to bring about understanding rather than just measuring it in a statistically reliable fashion.

The agenda of the classroom is more formative, co-operative and developmental. Thus the methodology, the activity of the reading classroom, can be wider and richer. The tasks available for learning to read are more diverse and may involve working with others, students or teachers, in both pairs and groups. The learners are not being asked to demonstrate how well they can use strategies or skills but rather to develop and improve their use of these. The tasks employed may be similar in the reading lesson to those of the test but differ in the way they are used.

In the classroom, comprehension questions set on texts are often done in groups which promotes effective discussion concerning how the answer was arrived together with feedback for individuals in a non-summative manner. By verbalising about their own reading they come to understand better the processes involved. Nuttall extols the value of buzz groups (1996: 201): small groups work on the task for a short period, and report back in plenary followed by whole group discussion.

Conclusion

While there are a number of similarities between teaching and testing there are also marked differences which necessitate considering teaching separately.

Background issues in the teaching of reading

Bernhardt (1991a: 173), in a broad survey of L2 reading research, argues that

> Research has not yet firmly established how to teach comprehension (or for that matter whether it is teachable). Neither has research provided substantial insights into the process of second language learning.

Research into L2 reading is certainly a relatively new field. As we saw in Chapter 2, most of the serial models of reading were developed for L1 learners by psychologists. In L2 it has mainly been applied linguists who have been responsible for research, and this is clear from their focus on componential models with a direct link to pedagogy, as against serial models which are more concerned with internal workings of the brain.

Given the limitations of our understanding in this field we concentrate below on reading activities and accompanying cognitive behaviour which research has indicated as leading to measured improvement in comprehension. Obviously any activity in the right hands in the right circumstance may result in better performance. However, we are interested in consistency of empirical evidence and we have used Barr et al. (1991) and Bernhardt (1991a) to guide our selection, as their reviews of reading research in L1 and L2 provide a wide empirical and theoretical base for selecting teaching/learning activities for the reading classroom.

The comparative lack of research in L2 reading has encouraged us to draw on research in L1 settings where this seems appropriate. In addition, we have had to rely on examining methods and classroom textbooks to inform us about what goes on in the L2/EFL classroom in the comparative absence of observational studies of L2 reading training (see Siedow et al., 1985).

To teach or not

A car sticker in Britain carries the message: '*If you can read this, thank a teacher.*' The implication is clear: if you are not taught to read, you will not learn. It is, however, perfectly likely that some L1 children, at least, learn to read with little or no formal teaching, and it is certainly the case that L2 readers learn to read the second language without formal instruction. Whether explicit instruction is any more effective than simply encouraging students to read and form their own rules remains unproven. We would, however, agree with Pearson and Fielding (1991), in their excellent review of comprehension instruction in L1, that the danger of the non-interventionist approach is that the good readers get better and the poor do not. The gap widens.

In some classes students will not lack ability in the skills and strategies discussed below, and until problems become evident in these areas they may well be avoided. The time to practise these skills and strategies is in response to needs or lacks that become evident.

What is also clear is that comprehension teaching effectiveness may differ from context to context and there are no generic classrooms (Bernhardt 1991a: 173); those of young bilinguals will be very different from adult second language readers preparing for postgraduate study in an overseas context. Because of the great diversity of reading contexts we shall not be providing multiple examples of reading activities and texts; there are stimulating collections of these already available to which we would direct the reader (Grellet, 1981; Nuttall, 1996; Wallace, 1988; Williams, 1984) and a plethora of reading textbooks aimed at specific audiences. We will instead focus on the evidence from principled reading research and instruction to formulate generic suggestions for teaching. We will attempt below to determine what research indicates as being the most productive activities across diverse situations. The discussion below is therefore for the most part in terms of principles rather than commentary on specific examples of classroom tasks. Reference will, however, be made to sources the reader can consult for practical exemplification.

4.2 FOCUS ON METACOGNITIVE STRATEGIES

As we noted above, one of the major differences between teaching and testing is the presence in the former of teacher input in the form of training, in which strategy training has become of increasing importance in recent years (see discussion in Sections 2.3, 2.4 and 3.2 on strategies and skills). Cohen (1998) provides a comprehensive and clear account of strategies for using and learning a second language. A useful distinction can be made between cognitive and metacognitive strategies.

Cognitive strategies are the more familiar mental processes that enable us to read, ranging from working out the meaning of words in context through to skimming a whole text quickly to extract the gist. Metacognitive strategies are more concerned with thinking about the reading experience itself and are seen to involve

> . . . learners stepping outside their learning, as it were, and looking at it from outside. Such strategies include an awareness of what one is doing and the strategies one is employing, as well as knowledge about the actual process of learning. They also include an ability to manage and regulate consciously the use of appropriate learning strategies for different situations. They involve an awareness of one's own mental processes and an ability to reflect on how one learns, in other words, knowing about one's knowing.
>
> (Williams and Burden, 1997: 148)

Cohen (1998: 7) describes metacognitive strategies as dealing with:

> pre-assessment and pre-planning, on-line planning and evaluation, and post-evaluation of language learning activities and of language use events. Such strategies allow learners to control their own cognition by coordinating the planning, organizing, and evaluating of the learning process. There is a rather extensive literature demonstrating that the higher proficiency students are more likely to use metacognitive strategies than the lower-proficiency ones and to use them more effectively as well.

He details distinctions that may be made between general approaches and specific techniques or actions. He suggests (1998: 10):

> A solution to the problem would be to refer to all of these simply as strategies, while still acknowledging that there is a continuum from the broadest categories to the most specific or low level.

He also acknowledges that the distinction between metacognitive and cognitive strategies may not always be clear cut and there may on occasion be some overlap (op. cit.: 12) and both may be legitimate interpretations of some actions.

Williams and Burden (1997: 155–6) draw attention to the importance of knowledge of tasks (see also Cohen, 1998: 14):

> Knowledge about task refers to an awareness of the purpose and demands of the task, as well as an ability to assess the information provided, and to select what is relevant from what is irrelevant. Knowledge of strategy involves an understanding of what strategies should be used for different types of task.

They also detail (1997: 145–6, 156) a number of preplanning and planning-in-action metacognitive strategies drawing on the work of Nisbet and Shucksmith (1991) and Wenden (1987b), namely:

- determining objectives
- selecting methods
- predicting difficulties
- asking questions
- planning
- monitoring
- checking
- revising plans
- evaluating outcomes.

Cohen (1998: 14) outlines the areas of metacognitive strategy use in a similar fashion:

(1) *a goal setting component* where the respondents identify the tasks and what they are going to do;
(2) an *assessment component,* whereby the speakers (listeners, readers or writers) determine what is needed, what one has to work with, and how well one has done; and
(3) *a planning component,* whereby the respondents decide how to use their knowledge of the topic and their language knowledge.

From their perspective of education as a life-long process, Williams and Burden see one of the main aims of the educator as being to help students cope with self-directed, autonomous learning. Teaching students to read effectively unaided would seem to be potentially a powerful contribution to this, if not the single most important. If we can help students to read carefully and expeditiously on their own for their own purposes, then this would be success indeed.

There is evidence to support such metacognitive training. Alvermann and Moore (1991) cite research studies which demonstrate the value of learning strategies initiated and directed by students. They detail how, through metacognitive training and self-questioning, students can be taught to monitor comprehension (see also Carrell et al., 1989; Cohen, 1998; Williams and Burden, 1997: 144–66). Oxford and Crookall (1989) report on a number of studies where the experimental group received training in metacognitive strategies and subsequently outperformed a control group who did not.

As far as strategy training is concerned, Williams and Burden (1997: 156–66) offer sound advice on how best to go about it (see also Cohen, 1998: ch. 4). They present (pp. 158–9) a strategic teaching model developed by Jones et al. (1987), which has the following guidelines:

- Assess strategy use (through think aloud, interview, questionnaire).
- Explain strategy by naming or telling how to use it, step by step.
- Model strategy by demonstration or verbalisation of own thought processes while doing it.
- Scaffold instruction by providing support while students practise; adjusting support to suit students' needs; phasing out support to encourage autonomous strategy use.

- Develop motivation by providing successful experiences; relating strategy use to improved performance.

Williams and Burden (1997: 162) suggest that most of the procedures for strategy training they surveyed:

> generally involve a sequence of first helping students identify or become aware of strategies they are already using, then presenting and explaining a new strategy, with a rationale for using it. At this stage the teacher might model the strategy. This is followed by practising it, at first with substantial support or 'scaffolding' but gradually reducing this to encourage autonomous use. Finally, students are helped to evaluate their success.

This would seem appropriate also for training in the cognitive strategies such as skimming, search reading and scanning, discussed in Section 4.3 below.

Cohen (1998: ch. 4) offers a comprehensive discussion of the various forms that strategy training can take, and the reader is referred to this for a full discussion of this area. He also provides an informed consideration of extending the role that teachers can play. In this he develops a view of a role for teachers as learner trainers as well as language instructors (p. 97):

> One potentially beneficial shift in teacher roles is from that of being exclusively the manager, controller, and instructor to that of being a *change agent* – a facilitator of learning, whose role is to help their students to become more independent, more responsible for their own learning. In this role, the teachers become partners in the learning process.

The teacher's role is seen as one of gradual withdrawal with the objective that, by the end of the course, the student should be able to apply the strategies independently. The difficulty seems to be deciding when to start turning over more responsibility to the students, for example, by reducing coaching or scaffolding. Palincsar and Brown (1984) describe a technique, called reciprocal teaching, which they used with retarded readers where initially the teacher does a lot of the work although still in a co-operative format and gradually learners assume more responsibility as they improve until they are able, finally, to work independently.

As yet there is little evidence on the long-term effects of strategy training or transferability to novel contexts. However, there is some support for their immediate impact on reading performance (see Cohen 1998: 483 et seq. and ch. 5). Different readers will have different perceptions of their usefulness and part of the training would be enabling learners to explore this relevance to them. As Williams and Burden (1997: 164) point out:

> they will employ particular strategies if they have a sense of ownership or choice in the strategies used, they are clear why they are using them, and they want to complete a task to achieve a goal that they have identified as worthwhile.

Cohen (1998: 12) rightly warns that:

> . . . the effectiveness of a strategy may depend largely on the characteristics of a given learner, the given language structure(s), the given context, or the interaction of these,

and suggests that a strategy may work in one particular case but not necessarily in all cases. He also indicates that strategies may need to be related to learning styles and other personality related variables (op. cit.: 15–16).

Some potentially useful metacognitive strategies

Having briefly surveyed the nature of metacognitive strategies and how, in general, to present them in training we would now like to examine in closer detail a number of such strategies that appear to be of some value. We adopt the now conventional distinction between *pre-reading* (planning) strategies, *while-reading* (monitoring) strategies and *post-reading* (evaluation) strategies.

Pearson and Fielding (1991: 836–9), on the basis of a wide survey of the L1 reading research literature, identify two generic *while-reading* strategies and practices to support students to engage independently and actively with text. These are **self-questioning** and **self-monitoring**.

We would like to add two *pre-reading* strategies: namely **previewing** and **prediction** which relate to Pearson and Fielding's generative learning. Generative learning describes how comprehension occurs when learners build relationships between parts of the text and between the text and their background knowledge: associations improve comprehension. The two pre-reading strategies discussed below can help activate schemata prior to the reading process and can contribute to this process. We also look at **post-reading** activities which involve evaluation of the text, relating it to one's own experiences or context.

Pre-reading activities

Previewing

Previewing can be used to make a decision whether to read a book, an article or a text. Where appropriate to text type it might involve:

- thinking about the title
- checking the edition and date of publication
- reading the table of contents quickly
- reading appendices quickly
- reading indices quickly
- reading the abstract carefully
- reading the preface, the foreword and the blurb carefully.

Hamp-Lyons (1984: 305) adds that previewing helps students recognise the difficulty level of a text and comparative difficulty with other texts in the same field, helps them judge the relevance/irrelevance of a text for a particular topic, and helps them decide which book from a set of possibilities would be more appropriate to read for a specific purpose. Its value for teaching is the amount of time it might save if it prevents prolonged reading of something of no value (see Nuttall, 1996: 45–8).

It is of particular use in deciding whether textbooks or parts of a textbook are of value, though browsing through a novel at the airport bookshop before deciding to purchase is another manifestation. The reason that it seldom features in tests is on the grounds of efficiency and reliability. It is difficult in the exam situation to provide the same textbook(s) for large numbers of candidates. Additionally, the number of items that can be usefully written are often limited with implications for test reliability. Similarly, how would one evaluate *x*'s decision to purchase a particular book?

However, in the classroom context, previewing may be very useful, particularly for English for Academic Purposes Students. Previewing has obvious links with expeditious reading strategies, particularly skimming for gist, discussed in Section 4.3 on cognitive strategies.

For exemplification of previewing, see Grellet (1981: 58–61), Hamp-Lyons (1984) and Trzeciak and Mackay (1994: 5–10).

Prediction

After taking the decision to read a text, this strategy is used to anticipate the content of a text; to make hypotheses about the macropropositions it might contain. It is a form of psychological sensitising, thinking about the subject and asking oneself related questions.

In theoretical terms it accords with the hypothesis advanced earlier in Section 3.3 that establishing a macrostructure for a text is an aid to more detailed comprehension. One might also hypothesise that the activation of relevant schemata should facilitate the reader's interaction with a text (see Section 2.2). Finally, this activity has the potential to clarify for the reader what the purposes for reading the particular text might be.

It is often a case of supplying or activating appropriate background knowledge, and this might best be done through pre-reading activities: lectures, discussion, debate, real-life experiences, text previewing or introduction of vocabulary. It makes use of top-down processing to activate different kinds of schemata in common with many pre-reading activities.

Haines (1988) uses surveys and questionnaires to encourage discussion and activate and build up background knowledge pre-reading, and Paran (1993) uses surveys to similar effect. Tomlinson and Ellis (1988) offer a range of pre-reading activities aimed at activating formal knowledge of text.

Williams and Moran (1993: 66) suggest:

> Perhaps the most effective of these activities are those which elicit factual information or a personal response and ask the students to pool such information in pair or group work. Preferably, this is followed by a task which relates the discussion to the first reading of the passage.

In comparing teaching and testing tasks currently in use it is noticeable that, whereas prediction activities are now a common feature in textbooks on the teaching of reading, they seldom feature in tests. Part of the reason for this is presumably that such data do not lend themselves easily to assessment. The open-ended and idiosyncratic nature of such prediction, based as it is on already existing constructs, is obvious.

Williams (1984: 36–51) provides useful advice and examples of pre-reading activities that can be employed in the language classroom. Swaffar (1981) and Carrell and Eisterhold (1988) describe key word and key concept pre-reading activities. See also Glendinning and Holmström (1992: 20–4), Langer (1981) and McGovern et al. (1994: 11–12) for further exemplification.

While-reading strategies

Self-questioning

This is identified by research as a characteristic of good reading when it promotes cognitive processes such as inferencing, monitoring understanding and attending to structure. Alvermann and Moore (1991: 961) detail how 'generally, instruction in self questioning improves student processing of text' and note that 'poorer readers tend to benefit most from such training. Scaffolding of instruction leading to gradual control appears to be beneficial.' Nuttall (1996: 37) describes this activity as interrogating texts; text talk. For students unfamiliar with this activity the teacher interrogating the text aloud can provide a valuable example, particularly where the focus is put on important problematic aspects of a text.

Organised methods involving self-questioning have been in use for some time (see Nuttall, 1996: 129; and Richards, 1989 for details of SQ3R). Palincsar and Brown (1984) focused on teaching summarising, questioning, clarifying and predicting skills, arguing that these activities, if engaged in while reading, enhanced comprehension, and, at the same time, gave the student the opportunity to monitor whether comprehension was succeeding.

Self-monitoring

Monitoring one's own comprehension – checking that comprehension is taking place and adopting repair strategies when it isn't – is seen as a hallmark of skilled reading. It is important that students are aware of how various strategies will help them. Self-verbalisation was also seen as important (Pearson and Fielding, 1991: 838).

The connection with schema theory is clear: by asking themselves whether they understand, learners are asking whether it fits in with what they know already. Thus they learn how to understand what they read in the process of learning how to monitor their comprehension (Pearson and Fielding, 1991: 847).

Alvermann and Moore (1991: 962 et seq.) sound a note of caution in that many of these studies were achieved under experimental rather than field conditions with consequent threats to their ecological validity: they were decontextualised; an experimenter rather than the normal classroom teacher introduced the intervention; texts were specially prepared and were often shorter than normally met texts; and students were often not prepared in the use of the strategy before the intervention. They argue (p. 974) that we need to develop a research methodology which would actively involve teachers and carefully document baseline data of the situation preceding the decision to implement an innovation and also collect data to monitor its effect.

Post-reading strategies

Evaluation and personal response

Questions of evaluation and personal response are also seen by teachers and course book writers as a valuable post-reading activity, relating the text to the outside world (Nuttall, 1996: 167, 188–9). The work may be done either orally or in writing, though Nuttall (p. 167) favours the former because of the importance of discussion and exchange of views. Research suggests that in learning to make the text their own the readers will better comprehend it. Readers can be encouraged to relate content to their existing schemata and to evaluate it in the light of their own knowledge and experiences. This promotes greater interaction with text and may lead to more successful reading encounters. Orlek (1996) provides a thorough and stimulating case for teaching readers to challenge text rather than submissively trying to recreate the author's intended message.

Training in metacognitive strategies is a relatively new departure in L2 teaching of reading but it seems to have potential cash-in value for enhancing the reading of particular texts and, more importantly, carrying over to future reading experiences. Cohen (1998: ch. 4) provides a detailed and useful review of strategy training, focusing primarily on strategies-based instruction aimed at increasing learners' awareness of the benefits that such strategies might have for them. More familiar to teachers is training in cognitive strategies and skills and most of the textbooks we surveyed attempt to cover a range of these with varying degrees of success.

4.3   FOCUS ON COGNITIVE STRATEGIES AND SKILLS

Introduction: purpose determines choice

An awareness of top-down (reader-driven) and bottom-up (text-driven) processing strategies can benefit teachers. It should help them to incorporate classroom activities which encourage L2 readers to use appropriate combinations of such strategies in reading for different purposes (Carrell, 1988; Richards, 1989). Information on effective and ineffective reading strategies can help inform and improve students' reading efficiency. For example, we will argue below that some of the time devoted in class to working out the meaning of words in context might be better spent on activities promoting automaticity. An excessive focus on the former might actually impede developing fluency!

Over-reliance on either top-down or bottom-up processing to the neglect of the other may hamper readers; efficient and effective second language reading requires both top-down and bottom-up strategies in different combinations for different purposes (Carrell, 1988: 240–1; Rumelhart, 1977, 1980). For example, it would be mistaken only to rely on word by word bottom up processing in a skimming exercise designed to extract quickly the gist from a text. However, some careful processing of textual clues to overall meaning might be necessary once these are located through more expeditious strategies.

Cognitive strategies may range from macro activities, such as skimming a text quickly for gist, down to micro activities, such as working out the meaning of a word in context through cognates, translation, etc. (see Jimenez et al., 1996 and Hosenfeld, 1984). As we saw in Section 2.3, strategies have the following characteristics:

- they are essentially problem solving on whatever level, macro or micro
- they are goal oriented

- they are purposeful
- they involve efficiency and selection
- in the case of expeditious strategies, they also involve speed
- they are consciously adopted (in contrast to subconscious use of skills)
- they are, by implication, directly teachable.

Williams and Moran (1993) point to an increasing eclecticism in the strategies in the course books they surveyed. A similar picture emerges in the more recent textbooks we surveyed. This has not always been the case. Following the introduction of top-down approaches there has been a tendency to overlook the crucial importance of word recognition and decoding in the early stages of learning to read and in training those not brought up on the Roman script (see Paran, 1996).

Williams and Moran (1993: 67), in their review of reading course books, argue:

> It would in most second language teaching situations clearly be misguided for teaching to focus exclusively on top down processes. As Eskey (1988: 98) puts it, 'If we can no longer afford to teach reading as a kind of linguistic analysis, we also cannot afford to teach it as a kind of cued speculation.'

Individual tasks at the local level

Word recognition: a neglected area

Bernhardt (1991a: 174) points out that an assumption is often made in L2/EFL classrooms that students can already read and that

> ... reading is just a slower form of first language reading, reading instruction per se really does not exist.

One of the problems, especially in the L2 teaching of reading, is that we are accustomed to teaching students who will already have learned to read in their L1. As a consequence, the skill of word recognition may not receive as much attention as has global comprehension of text for example. This may mean that second language reading students who do not share a common orthographic script may be placed at a disadvantage (see p. 54). The additional processing time they require for word recognition may have a knock-on effect in other areas of the reading process.

Additionally we tend to have little experience of emergent literacy, early reading and writing development (Sulzby and Teale, 1991) as many of our students in the UK tend to be adults rather than very young children and an assumption is made either that they will have gone through this stage, or that acceptance procedures of overseas students on courses preclude such recognition problems. Williams and Moran, in their review of course books, call for more research into initial reading in a foreign language and refer to Wallace (1988) as one of the few serious pieces of work in this area.

Juel (1991: 759) argues that we know little about the transition from emergent to beginning L1 reading largely due to a focus on 'higher order' reading processes by the research community arising in the USA from a concern over the poor performances of older students on national assessments of higher order reading skills. She details how they already felt they were doing an adequate job teaching lower order decoding skills. She then queries how good a start children in the USA are actually given with the dire consequences this may have for later development as the L1 research evidence mounts that there is a strong link between early progress in reading and later reading ability and comprehension. She also notes that most of the models we have are for the skilled reader and little attention has been paid to developing a comprehensive model of the reading acquisition process.

Automaticity

We pointed out in Chapter 2 that a strong criticism of so-called top-down models was that they attributed too much importance to hypothesising, or guessing, whether of lexical items or larger units. Stanovich (1980) points to the implausibility of hypothesis testing being of much value to the skilled reader as it take so much less time to recognise a word than to go through a complex guessing game. In one of the most important contributions by cognitive psychologists to reading research (and potentially the teaching of reading) in recent years, it was repeatedly found that good readers used context much less often than poor readers when recognising printed words. In fact they appear to be able to recognise words without any conscious thought, i.e. at the automatic level.

Juel (1991: 771) cites important evidence that early attainment of decoding skill/word recognition is a very accurate predictor of later reading comprehension in L1 children. Those who do poorly in the first year of learning to read are unlikely to improve their position as compared to those who do well. Poor decoding skill may delimit what the child can read and the differences are further compounded by out of school experiences.

Automaticity in L2

The increased importance attributed to automatic word recognition in L1 reading has been extended, though with less empirical support, to the L2 reading area. Previously in L2, a great deal of faith had been placed on decoding by means of context. Haynes (1984), however, points out that we need to get the level of automaticised vocabulary up rather than focusing on decoding in context. Haynes points out (48):

> Rapid precise recognition of letters and words, that is, bottom up, more input constrained processing, must be mastered before fluent reading can take place.

She cites evidence from L1 studies that fluent reading is achieved by increasing one's bottom-up processing of print and decreasing semantic and syntactic guesswork, though this is not as yet proven for L2. She questions the emphasis given in textbooks to guessing the meaning of unknown words from surrounding context as the main approach to learning vocabulary. Context often proved inadequate to support accurate inferencing and encouraging the guessing from context strategy might well lead to frustration in these cases.

There is some negative evidence for this position in the L2 area. Bensoussan and Laufer (1984) found no evidence that better readers are able to use context more effectively for lexical guessing than less proficient students. More crucially, they argue that in many cases only a minority of word meanings can be recovered from the context. Working out the meaning of words in context is only a part of the vocabulary skills needed for fluent reading and it appears that it may actually interfere if a student over-relies on this strategy.

Beck (1981) argues that 'basic recognition exercises to improve speed and accuracy of perception may constitute an important component of an effective second language reading programme'.

If, as appears likely, automatic word recognition is more important to fluent processing of text than context clues, the large-scale
development of recognition vocabulary may be crucial to reading
development (van Dijk and Kintsch, 1983; Perfetti, 1985). Poor
readers have simply not acquired automatic decoding skills. Poor
readers spend too much processing time thinking about words
and relating them to the surrounding context, rather than automatically recognising them.

Bernhardt (1991a: 235–6) argues that the ultimate goal is automaticity. Good L1 readers process language in the form of written
text without thinking consciously about it, and good L2 readers
must also learn to do so. It is only this kind of automatic processing which allows the good reader to think instead about the larger
meaning of the discourse – on the one hand, to recover, the
message that the author intended to convey and, on the other, to
relate that new information to what the reader knows and feels
about the subject, and to his or her reasons for reading about it.
In short, it is only this kind of local processing that allows for
global meaning with true comprehension.

L2 reading speed

Bernhardt (1991a: 234) argues that a major bottom-up skill is
reading as fast in that language as their knowledge of it will allow,
in relation to their reading purposes. Where appropriate we need
to dedicate some time for rapid identification of lexical and grammatical form. Juel (1991: 771) quotes Chall (1979): '. . . (learners)
have to know enough about the print in order to leave the print.'

It is noted in the literature that L2 readers often read texts
more slowly than L1 readers. One of the most striking differences
between L1 and L2 readers of English texts is their speed. Haynes
(1984: 50) and others have identified the root of the problem as
the length of the fixation slowing down the reading rather than
number of fixations or regressions. Haynes (1984: 50) notes:

> There is no clear experimental evidence explaining these longer
> visual fixation times, but a strong possibility involves the time re-
> quired for lexical access, that is the time it takes for a reader to
> match the printed word to a word meaning in memory.

It seems likely that it takes longer to access lexical meanings,
remember what a word means, in L2 than it does in L1. L2 readers

of English do not have large well-practised vocabularies and years of experience of recognising words in print. Hence, it takes them longer to decide whether a word is known or unknown and, in the latter case, whether to skip it or not.

Developing automaticity in L2 reading

Although the importance of automaticity in decoding is gaining general recognition, there is less agreement on how to achieve the goal in L2 reading. Haynes (1984: 59) argues that:

> The importance of word unit processing needs to be recognised in ESL teaching. First, precision of encoding spelling and pronunciation can be increased through oral and written practice of important vocabulary from reading.

Haynes also advocates dictionary work as a method of separating words which look familiar. The aim is to help the student distinguish new words efficiently in lexical memory. Nuttall (1996: 62) is less sanguine about the use of dictionaries and warns that it can slow down reading considerably and reduce effectiveness in reading. Occasional rather than constant use is advocated. She also cautions that all of this does not mean that guessing from context is not essential but should be seen as one of a number of bottom-up as well as top-down strategies that can help the student to reach a meaning.

Juel (1991: 783) points out that automaticity in most skills comes from overlearning:

> repeated practice frees up one's attention so that it does have to be focused on the mechanics involved in the specific activity . . .

though she does admit that we do not know exactly what it is about word recognition that becomes automatic, i.e. is it recognition of common sound spelling patterns, recognition of high frequency words, etc?

Paran (1996), in a recent article, makes a strong case for developing exercises to help EFL students recognise vocabulary more automatically. He puts the case for a greater focus on bottom-up processing (p. 25): 'good readers do not rely on hypothesis formation and prediction as much as is commonly thought. Visual input and bottom up processing during reading are of great importance.' He argues that the top-down approach (Goodman, 1967:

75, 78) has permeated ELT reading materials and teacher training despite the advent of more comprehensive interactive models and cites Grellet (1981), Nuttall (1982) as important books illustrating this bias. While accepting the value of interactive compensatory approaches which allow learners to compensate for lack of developed automaticised skills, Paran feels we need to go further. Though providing context or activating background knowledge is important to compensate for poor automaticity, readers need to be weaned off this support and be trained to do without it.

Paran (1996: 29) claims:

> . . . one of the goals of L2 reading instruction is to make readers less reliant on top down processing and help them progress towards greater reliance on bottom up strategies as they become more proficient.

Guessing may well take place on a global level, but Paran argues that this is not an appropriate strategy for word or phrase recognition; the lower levels of processing (p. 30). Top-down approaches would seem to be more suited to expeditious reading such as skimming or search reading where the focus is on the macrostructure of the text. We note along with Paran the absence of such activities from most course books on the teaching of reading.

Paran also points out the limited variety in the exercise types for automaticity; basically matching identical words in lists and suggests that they might not go down well at advanced level. Bloor (1985: 345) sees little use for it beyond an elementary level. However, if we relate it to the activity of scanning discussed later under expeditious reading, it may well be that practising this strategy has important spin offs for automaticity and widens the base of exercise types that concerns Paran and Bloor. Scanning is an activity suitable for advanced readers as well as elementary!

It may also be the case that one major value of extensive reading (see p. 215 below) lies in its value for developing automaticity of word recognition. Familiarisation with a large number of words through extensive practice is likely to free up processing time.

For further exemplification the reader is advised to look at Mahon (1986) and Nuttall (1996: 54–61) for useful suggestions concerning building L2 reading rates and de Leeuw and de Leeuw (1990) for L1. For further discussion on automaticity in L2 reading teaching, see Nuttall (1996: 45–61), Dubin et al. (1986) and Silberstein (1994).

Vocabulary acquisition

As we have discussed so far, automaticity has largely been concerned with decoding. The L1 readers, given that they are reading appropriate material, can be assumed to have lexical entries previously established for the items encountered. In other words, they 'know' the words; they just have to make automatic recognition of the orthographic rendering of these words. This is particularly the case with adult or near adult readers. This situation cannot, of course, be assumed in the case of L2 learners. Here the readers may well frequently face items which they not only have difficulty decoding, but with which they are simply unfamiliar; the item may not yet have a place in their lexicon. Thus, except in fairly unusual cases where the L2 readers are very fluent in the spoken language before they are introduced to the written form, L2 readers have to acquire vocabulary items before they can begin to make recognition of these items automatic.

How best to acquire a large stock of vocabulary is a problem. It has often been argued that vocabulary is best acquired through reading. Thus Nuttall (1996: 62) claims: 'An extensive reading programme is the single most effective way of improving vocabulary.' However, according to Nation (1997), extensive reading is unlikely to lead to large increases in our vocabulary knowledge unless we read a very large amount so that new words are repeated sufficiently in context for us to learn them (apparently 12 times is the recommended dose, based on Saragi et al., 1978). Thus extensive reading may not be the panacea for vocabulary acquisition that it is often thought to be. For acquiring vocabulary we may have to rely also on instruction in intensive mode.

Many teachers see one of their key roles in the reading classroom as expanding vocabulary knowledge and developing learners' ability to continue to increase their vocabulary. It is generally accepted (see Nuttall, 1996: 63) that a vocabulary of 5000 words is needed to start independent reading, although the empirical evidence for this is slight (see Laufer, 1989). If this figure were accurate it would seem to be beyond many of the students we teach and we would need to be extremely careful in selecting texts for the majority of our students (i.e. ensuring the lexical load is below their level) and/or focus on language work for a longer period with those only possessing a restricted vocabulary of, say, less than 2000 words.

The desire to expand student vocabulary is supported by the L1 literature on the effects of vocabulary knowledge on comprehension. Correlations between knowledge of word meanings and ability to comprehend passages containing these words are high and well established in L1 reading studies (Anderson and Freebody, 1981) and in the L2 literature (Laufer, 1989). Such correlational evidence, of course, fails to establish knowledge of word meanings as a cause of comprehension but suggests that the two are distributed in a similar manner in the population. Stahl and Fairbanks (1986) provide a meta-analysis of studies concerned with effects of vocabulary instruction on comprehension and on learning of word meanings.

Clarke (1979, 1980/1988) and Cziko (1978) hypothesise that competence in the second language (grammar and vocabulary) may place a ceiling on second language reading ability. Implications are that 'good reader' top-down reading skills may be parasitic on language to a larger degree than in first language reading. However, Hudson (1982: ch. 2) has found that schema production, top-down processing, is very much implicated in the so-called short circuit of second language reading, and that schemata can override language proficiency as a factor in comprehension. This would accord with data we put forward from language testing studies in Chapter 3.

Beck and McKeown (1991) argue that before we can talk of the value of instruction we need to have a clear idea of what it means to know a word and how we are to measure vocabulary size and development. Like many before them, they suggest that knowledge of a word is not an absolute but rather a continuum from not knowing to 'rich decontextualised knowledge of a word's meaning, its relationship to other words, and its extension to metaphorical uses' (p. 792). The distinction between receptive and productive vocabulary has a long history. We need to recognise that there is a difference between becoming aware of a new word and learning it. Obviously size of vocabulary is determined by how a word is defined; what knowing it means and what corpus (and sample from that corpus) of words are used to test it (p. 793). Despite these problems it is clear that high-ability students have much larger vocabularies than lower ability students.

Much of the research on vocabulary knowledge is based on multiple-choice question tests; however, this format obviously suffers from the drawbacks listed in Chapter 3 and raises a question mark about much of the research. In particular, such tests do not distinguish between words that are known well and those which are only vaguely familiar, etc.

We need to develop measures/tasks which reflect the point along the continuum of word knowledge at which we wish to elicit data and determine the measures to be introduced optimally at each point. Do we want to test minimal degree of familiarity or discrimination among related concepts or completeness of word understanding as in accurate definition? It also seems likely, according to Beck and McKeown (1991: 808), that the effect of vocabulary instruction on comprehension may well be qualitative rather than quantitative. Studies focusing on qualitative understanding may well demonstrate clearer effects than the latter.

A case for direct instruction

Direct instruction cannot account for all the vocabulary acquired by learners and so it is often argued that learning vocabulary from context in written text is likely to promote vocabulary learning. We expressed some reservations concerning this in the previous section. The research evidence on the value of attempting to teach the ability to use context is mixed (Beck and McKeown, 1991: 802–3) but the ubiquitous finding is that 'learning word meanings from context does not seem to occur with particular ease'.

Finding ways to encourage learners inside and outside the classroom to extend their reading is another contender, although as we pointed out above (Nation, 1997) this may not be the panacea for vocabulary deprivation it was once thought. Getting students to read more is not likely to be a problem with the skilled reader as nothing succeeds like success. The problem lies in encouraging less able students to do so, and in recognising that wider reading may simply not be enough for them to get their vocabulary knowledge up to a critical mass. For these students direct instruction may be necessary.

This may involve classroom activities where word meaning information is intentionally given to students either through definition from recourse to a dictionary (Nuttall, 1996: 62–3) or explanation in context. More recently, the key word method, semantic mapping and semantic feature analysis have appeared in the literature (Beck and McKeown, 1991: 804). Again research has not indicated a best method across studies. Part of the problem lies in the way methods are labelled but there is also some degree of overlap which may interfere with experimental enquiry. However, what is clear is that instruction does have an effect (Beck and McKeown, 1991: 805) on word learning and 'there is advantage from methods that use a variety of techniques . . . there is advantage from repeated exposures to the words to be learned'.

There is little indication that vocabulary instruction leads to increased comprehension, i.e. little evidence of a causal link, despite strong reported correlations between the two. Beck and McKeown (p. 806) argue that this may be because the semantic processes in reading comprehension required fluency of access to word meaning and richness of semantic network connections, in addition to accuracy of word meaning knowledge.

To have an effect, research indicates that successful instruction 'provided more than one or two exposures to each word, presented both definitional and contextual information, and engaged students in deeper processing' (ibid.: 806). Semantic features analysis and semantic mapping involve active processing by getting students to examine the relationship between words. Both involve active processing, e.g. comparing and combining with known information to establish meaning. They go beyond simply entering new information in memory as per use of a dictionary.

Rudzka-Ostyn (1986) introduces students to a range of techniques, including semantic fields, componential and collocational analysis, and semantic relationships such as synonymy. Similarly, Beck and McKeown (1991) advocate the use of semantic feature grids to discuss the relationships between items. For a discussion of semantic-based vocabulary teaching methods see also Pearson and Johnson (1978).

Such direct instruction cannot obviously teach all words. A strategy which focused on high-frequency words in a mature vocabulary which also have a high utility across discipline areas, e.g. semi-technical vocabulary, might prove to be the most effective and efficient strategy.

Nuttall (1996: 64 et seq.) offers useful advice on how to get students to ignore unknown words and provides a series of practical techniques for helping in this, e.g. understanding gapped texts: shows students they can get the gist of a text without understanding every word. Nuttall also provides a number of valuable activities for developing word attack skills for dealing with words which are important for comprehension (pp. 69–77):

- looking for structural clues
- grammatical function: its place in the sentence
- morphology: its internal structure
- inferencing its meaning from context
- using a dictionary for unknown key words not accessible by other means.

Paran (1991, 1993) offers a wide variety of exercises for helping learners to understand strategies they might use for acquiring the meanings of words, for example:

- relating a new word to a known word
- contrasting a word with another word in the sentence
- understanding the sentence as a whole
- employing knowledge of the world
- relating a word to a word in L1.

It is noticeable that top-down techniques are being used here on occasion.

As in all exercises we must be aware that we can never be sure that, on the basis of meeting a word once, we know what it means. Bright (1965) stresses to students the multiple meanings of common words: 'The way a word fits into the language and life of the people who use it is not a simple thing. Hardly any words except technical ones have one simple meaning.' Like many others, he recommends extensive reading as a method, not of acquiring new words, but of broadening one's knowledge of the multiple meanings of already known items. While seemingly sensible advice, there is little empirical support for this in the literature, as is the case for the other techniques mentioned here.

The place of vocabulary teaching in the reading lesson

Reading classes should principally be for reading and not language work. We recognise there is a paradox that enhanced vocabulary will aid reading, so where should it occur? A conventional solution is offered by Paran in his Burlington Proficiency Series books. He saves the first reading of text for comprehension activities. Towards the end of a reading unit, after the second reading, he considers it legitimate to focus on linguistic features such as lexis or cohesion as well as further away activities such as appreciation or evaluation.

For further reading on vocabulary in EFL the reader is referred to Carter and McCarthy (1988), McCarthy (1990) and Nation (1990, 1997).

Grammatical skills

Surprisingly in the vast literature on reading there is relatively little on the relationship between grammatical knowledge and reading ability and we will make some suggestions in the next section on research as to how this might be rectified (see Section 5.2, p. 255). Understanding syntax can help the L2 readers to comprehend text more readily. Increasing syntactic knowledge may help them to deal with more complex sentences and increasing their automaticity in recognising syntactic structures should free up processing time.

Nuttall (1996: 78–99) argues the case for paying close attention to language, particularly syntax and cohesion in order to interpret difficult text. She sets this in a wider context of trying first with top-down strategies to establish meaning and, if this does not prove sufficient, suggests resorting to the additional information such as examining the syntax and matching this with top-down insights to consider differing interpretations. Its problem-solving nature might make this a candidate for the term *strategy* rather than *skill*.

Nuttall suggests a number of fairly complex exercises designed to help students to

- remove optional elements from sentences systematically until only the core remains and the bare structure of a sentence is clear;
- paraphrase optional elements of complex sentences one by one, and fit them into the whole structure to make sense of them.

Cohesion

Chapman (1979a) found a relation between reading ability and ability to complete anaphoric relations in a cloze test and concluded that mastery of such textual features is a central factor in fluent reading and reading comprehension. Weir (1983a) found that gap-filling tests including items on cohesion, discourse markers and structure correlated well with general reading comprehension tests. Mackay et al. (1979) and Cowan (1976) have argued that recognition of conjunctions and other intersentential linguistic devices is crucial to the information-gathering skills of second language readers.

Williams (1984) discusses the importance of recognising cohesive ties and has suggested teaching materials for this. Nuttall (1982/1996: 86–98) provides a number of useful exercises for recognising and interpreting cohesive devices and discourse markers.

For exemplification of grammatical work, see Morrow (1980: 63–4), Nuttall (1996: 79–86), Silberstein (1994: 63–6) and Sim and Laufer-Dvorkin (1982: 59–61). For work on cohesion, see Williams (1983).

Work on the place of microlinguistic elements, in particular the role of grammar, has an important role, which has tended to be neglected in the recent past. In class, we must of course distinguish between vocabulary and grammar work, which is aimed at improving reading, and the use of texts to teach vocabulary and grammar. Both are important aspects of teaching an L2, but we have to concentrate on the first. What we turn to now – the recognition of main ideas and important information in a text through either careful or expeditious reading strategies – is more exclusively a part of reading activities in the classroom.

Individual tasks at the global level

Comprehension instruction: the process of reading text carefully

In Chapter 3 we considered how we might test some aspects of reading a text carefully. In testing we felt constrained to limit ourselves to careful reading for explicitly stated main ideas and to propositional inferencing. We felt that pragmatic inferencing was beyond the remit of the tester as it goes beyond text-based comprehension. However, a strong case can be made for the value of the latter in the classroom.

We briefly expand on our earlier descriptions of these three aspects of careful reading below as they are all criterial for developing reading ability in the classroom. We describe them in accordance with a taxonomy developed in the reading research group of the TEU at CALS Reading University. Practice in these activities should form the backbone of any careful reading programme and should be particularly effective when supplemented by activities for activating background knowledge and summarisation skills discussed in the following section. We then focus on text selection and a number of activities which we see as important for promoting attention to comprehension instruction in the reading classroom.

Reading carefully for explicitly stated main ideas

Careful and thorough reading of text for explicitly stated main ideas and important information is an important purpose for reading. We often need to decode the whole of a text to understand it or to establish its macrostructure. In this mode the reader has to read a text at a careful rate from beginning to end in a linear and sequential fashion with regressions as necessary. This will mainly be a bottom-up sequential process with some limited top-down processing, and might involve:

- separating explicitly stated main ideas from supporting detail by recognising topic sentences or by recognising lexical indicators of importance
- generating a representation of the text as a whole
- understanding the development of an argument and/or logical organisation.

Further exemplification is provided in Glendinning and Holmström (1992: 52–3), Grellet (1981) and Nuttall (1996: ch. 9).

Reading carefully for implicitly stated main ideas

In some texts the ideas may not be explicitly stated and students can be alerted to the nature of propositional inferences. These are made when the reader uses explicit statements in the text to form an inference without recourse to knowledge from outside the text (Chikalanga, 1990). This might involve making

- propositional informational inferences which are either referential, typically answering questions beginning with what and which, or spatiotemporal, typically answering questions beginning with where and when;
- propositional explanatory inferences which are concerned with motivation, cause, consequence and enablement and will often answer questions beginning with why and how.

All the information required to make such propositional inferences is recoverable from the text. Readers' activities might include

- discovering writer's intention
- understanding writer's attitude to the topic
- identifying the addressee
- distinguishing fact from fiction.

For exemplification see Ellis and Tomlinson (1988: 71–2, 86–8), Glendinning and Holmström (1992: 54–6), Grellet (1981: 98, 239–44) and Paran (1991: 3–4, 44).

Inferring pragmatic meaning related to a text

Pragmatic inferencing takes place when readers rely mainly on their own schemata and/or opinions to interpret a text (Chikalanga, 1992). This might involve making

- pragmatic informational inferences which are either referential, typically answering questions beginning with what and which, or spatiotemporal, typically answering questions beginning with where and when;
- pragmatic explanatory inferences which are concerned with motivation, cause, consequence and enablement and will often answer questions beginning with why and how;
- pragmatic evaluative inferences where the reader makes an evaluation on the basis of the content of a text
  - applying the main idea(s) in the text into other contexts
  - evaluating a point of view
  - expressing own opinion on the subject.

With reference to their own background knowledge and experience, the readers would try to interpret, respond to, evaluate and possibly apply the writer's message(s) contained in the text.

A recent story had the headline 'Who baas wins'. It was a story of how sheep had crossed a cattle grid (a device for preventing animals from crossing, consisting of horizontal metal bars with gaps between) by one of the flock lying across it and the rest walking over it to greener pastures. The title would be unintelligible to anyone who did not know the motto of the Special Armed Services (SAS) 'who dares wins'.

For further exemplification see Glendinning and Holmström (1992: 25–7), Grellet (1981: 28–9, 34–8, 41–2, 45–6, 245–9) and McGovern et al. (1994: 12–13).

Promoting careful reading skills in the ESOL classroom

First, we need to avoid specially written texts constructed to illustrate specific language points. The reading text is frequently seen as the conduit for lexical and syntactic learning rather than the source of new content information for the student.

Text selection

Williams (1984: 15) discusses the shortcomings of the types of text used solely for learning language and sees, as its key failing:

> There is little attention to reading as a skill in its own right that might need to be developed in different ways for different purposes.

He concludes (p. 125):

> ... although it is very tempting to use written text as a basis for the learning and teaching of language, an approach that goes no further not only neglects reading as a skill but also neglects the ultimate purpose of learning a language which must surely be to use that language. Being able to read skilfully and flexibly is an important use of language.

Nuttall (1996: 30) argues in a similar vein for focusing on using texts to convey meaning rather than as a convenient vehicle for conveying language:

> partly because this is often neglected in the language classroom, partly because treating texts as if they meant something is more effective in motivating students and promoting learning.

She offers a number of criteria for text selection including:

- suitability of content: it is essential that text should interest the reader;
- exploitability: facilitation of learning. How well can it help develop reading ability; this is not a language lesson or a content lesson but rather 'how language is used in conveying content for a purpose' (p. 172).

Appropriate texts, for example in terms of:

- intended audience
- intended purpose
- source
- length
- lexical range
- rhetorical structure
- topic familiarity
- relationship to background knowledge
- channel of presentation

should be chosen to enable students to practise careful reading. The same selection criteria apply to the other strategies and skills we discuss below. It seems that careful reading can accommodate implicit text structure and ideas, whereas expeditious reading is more dependent on explicitness in text structure or ideas. This is what Hamp-Lyons (1984) called a 'text strategic approach'. The focus here is on exploiting generalisable features of text 'in order to help learners develop skills for approaching any text'.

This is an area in critical need of attention by reading teachers. What are the salient features of text selection which will facilitate selecting texts to best practise appropriate activities? What is a principled set of procedures to determine whether texts appropriate in terms of the above conditions actually allow the practising of intended activities, purposes for reading. An attempt to draw up a specification for text selection for an advanced reading test in China is presented in Appendix 1. The same categories of description are applicable to text selection for teaching purposes. In addition, in Section 5.3 a text-mapping procedure is described which offers a systematic method for the development of tasks once a text appropriate for the intended purposes of reading has been identified.

It is also important that students are exposed to the range of materials they might later have to cope with for either informational or entertainment purposes. For example, it is no use basing EAP reading materials solely on texts taken from newspapers, though obviously the introduction of target texts will only occur when it is appropriate to do so both in terms of background knowledge and linguistic readiness. Hamp-Lyons (1984: 308) cautions:

... our readings in schema theory ... convinced us of the need to choose texts which the students would be easily able to integrate with their own prior experience and knowledge of the world.

Authenticity was also discussed in Chapter 3 with regard to testing. Nuttall (1996: 177) argues:

> To pursue the crucial text attack skill we need texts which exhibit the characteristics of true discourse: having something to say, being coherent and clearly organised. Composed (i.e. specially written) or simplified texts do not always have these qualities.

This is not to say that texts may not be modified with due caution (see Lewkowicz, 1996). For example, difficult words can be substituted or complex syntax unravelled. Williams and Moran (1993: 66) note that the claims for authenticity are not taken as literally as they once were and simplified or specially written texts have a place in the reading course books they reviewed. Lewkowicz (1997) makes the point that as long as salient performance conditions, e.g. appropriate rhetorical structure, are present full authenticity may not be essential in the texts employed for teaching or testing specified skills and strategies.

Williams (1984: 18–19) makes a number of points about the linguistic difficulty of the text selected:

> ... it should not contain a large amount of language that is too difficult for most of the class ... if too difficult, then either the pace of the lesson will be slow, and boredom will set in, or the pace will be too fast, and the learner will not understand enough, and frustration will result.

Nuttall (1996: 174–6) deals with this under the heading of readability (see also discussion of text difficulty in Section 3.3). She sees it as a combination of structural and lexical difficulty though recognising the influence of conceptual difficulty and interest. Texts selected should take the level of the students in terms of vocabulary and structure into account. In multi-level classes, self-access work at different levels may be an essential supplement if the provision of differentiated reading materials is not available for regular classroom instruction (p. 174).

Nuttall (1996: 36) talks of the 'next step' level, i.e. one step further than where the student currently is, but no more, as the target for pushing them on. The teacher provides 'scaffolding' to help them take this extra step. Nuttall describes this as never doing anything for them that they can do themselves with a little support. This is discussed by Williams and Burden (1997: 65–6) as the zone of proximal development from the field of educational psychology:

> ... it suggests that the teacher should set tasks that are at a level just beyond that at which the learners are currently capable of functioning, and teach principles that will enable them to make the next step unassisted. Bruner and others have used the term 'laddering' to refer to this process.

Williams (1984: 34) also advocates using a range of materials, selecting texts 'that deal with the same topic or theme, since this will result in consolidation and extension of language and language use in a way that is comprehensible to the general learner'.

Vygotsky (1962: 78) is one of the earliest writers to deal with mediation in the sense of using tools to achieve goals, and his work previews much of the current discussion in this area.

If learners can choose their own texts, this is likely to be highly motivating; but in those cases where textbooks are prescribed, this may not be possible, and how the teacher uses texts becomes crucial. Walker (1987) offers a proforma set of activities for students who bring their own texts to the classroom so that even though the instruction is individualised in terms of text the activities being practised are common.

In addition to work focusing on the careful reading activities detailed at the start of this section, there are a number of other interventions which should help to ground these skills properly.

Interventions designed to build or activate background knowledge

The role of background knowledge in reading was discussed in Section 2.2 and its relationship to testing was considered in Sections 3.1 and 3.3. Whereas in testing we argued for trying to minimise its influence, the reverse might be said to be true in teaching. In the section on metacognitive strategies above we considered ways in which the students might consider the relationship between their existing state of knowledge and information to be found in a text at the pre-reading, while-reading and post-reading stages. Here we look more closely at how understanding the structure of a text can aid main ideas comprehension in careful reading mode.

We focus on two activities in the classroom, *understanding text organisation* and *writing summaries of main ideas*, which appear to be particularly beneficial for successful careful reading.

Text organisation

Students with varied profiles appear to benefit when teachers help them activate or build formal knowledge of text structure: structural relations between main ideas in a text. Pearson and Fielding (1991) provide examples of story structure and expository text structure instruction. They describe ways of activating knowledge of the structure of the text itself, e.g. of a story grammar. This might involve consideration of its abstract hierarchical structure: setting, problem, goal, action, outcome; and giving practice in identifying category relevant information.

Comprehension, particularly inferential comprehension, is also helped when connections are made between readers' background knowledge and experience and the content of the text under review (Pearson and Fielding, 1991: 847). This may happen prior to reading. Invoking knowledge structures aids comprehension. Making predictions before reading and confirming them during reading, and asking inference questions during and after reading, improves comprehension – particularly inferential comprehension (ibid.).

As well as formal knowledge of text structure, knowledge about specific topics and themes related to a story is important. The role of pre-reading discussions to generate expectations in this respect has been shown to be effective (Pearson and Fielding, 1991: 822). Other methods include using writing to anticipate story information and developing a short list of key words, and such a cognitive engagement has been found to help poor readers (p. 823).

Longer texts, or a number of texts on the same theme, are seen by Williams and Moran (1993) as another way in which authors have tried to build up background knowledge in a certain area (see Haines, 1987, and Tomlinson and Ellis, 1988, for examples of these).

Additionally, inferential questions and prediction questions – a focus on important ideas (central events in a story), on constructing an interpretation and on summary – are seen by these reviewers as useful techniques for improving the understanding of a story.

As far as expository text structure is concerned, it has been suggested that visual summary is a useful tool. What was said earlier in Sections 2.2 and 3.3 about the organisational structure of a text is relevant here. The importance of summary (see below), schematic representation of a text, and rating the importance of ideas related to the text to comprehension, learning and remembering, are noted by Pearson and Fielding (1991: 827) as they promote attention to text structure. The effectiveness of teaching students to use text structure to identify main ideas is confirmed by Alvermann and Moore (1991: 960), though they point out that students' familiarity with the topic appears to mediate instructional effectiveness.

It is clear that readers who are knowledgeable about, and who can follow the author's text structure, recall more of a text than those who lack these attributes (Pearson and Fielding, 1991: 827) and they note that more good readers than poor follow the writer's structure in recall of texts. Hierarchical summaries using discourse clues and visual representations (networking, flowcharting, conceptual frames) are also seen as useful in helping recall text information better and improving comprehension, particularly for lower ability students who need more help in developing strategies. Nuttall (1996: ch. 12) offers a variety of information transfer task examples that might be used in the reading class. Also the section on information transfer in Section 3.4 on testing offers advice on the use of this task type.

Pearson and Fielding (1991: 832) conclude:

> It appears that any sort of systematic attention to clues that reveal how authors attempt to relate ideas to one another or any sort of systematic attempt to impose structure upon a text, especially in some sort of visual representation of the relationships among key ideas, facilitates comprehension as well as both short term and long term memory for the text.

It appears that while most strategies are of value across the ability range:

> ... the more able readers benefit the most ... (but) regardless of ability level, the teaching strategies have their greatest effect when students are actively involved in manipulating conceptual relationships and integrating new information with old knowledge.
>
> (Alvermann and Moore, 1991: 960)

Nuttall (1996: 100–24) provides useful advice and sound practical exemplification of a range of text attack skills: recognising functional value of sentences; recognising text organisation; recognising presuppositions underlying a text; recognising implications; and making inferences. A particularly interesting example is where students are given parts of a chapter or of a text and they have to put the parts in the right order. This is best done in groups. It involves an integration of many of the skills and strategies discussed in this chapter.

Creating text diagrams to illustrate the way ideas and information are presented in a text is probably best done by the students working in groups with classroom discussion later. Not all texts lend themselves to this technique, so input texts need to be chosen carefully. The section on mindmapping in Section 5.3 offers some insights into how students might go about this process and learn something more about skills and strategies at the same time. Nuttall notes of text diagrams that

> Their great advantage which outweighs the disadvantages . . . is that they demand close study of the way the text is put together and promote text focused discussion. They are useful either to display common patterns of paragraph organisation or to elucidate the structure of complex text.   (p. 109)

Useful discussion of networking can be found in Danserau et al. (1979); flowcharting in Geva (1980, 1983) and for work on top level rhetorical structures see Meyer (1975) and Bartlett (1978), who show how, through diagram, ideas and their relationships are represented within the text. Williams (1984) provides a useful basic survey of text structure and some ways of introducing it to students.

Careful reading into writing: a product from the reading process

Summarisation is perhaps the verbal equivalent of the visual diagrammatic representation of text structure discussed in the previous section, which could easily be subsumed under the broad umbrella of summary. In contrast to earlier work on summarisation, where research results were confounded by the use of low-level multiple-choice items as criterion scores, Pearson and Fielding cite positive support for summarising including improved comprehension on the texts involved, increased recall and even improvement on standardised reading test scores by students involved in this activity (1991: 833). There is also evidence that summarisation training transfers to new texts. They argue for its value as a broad-based comprehension training strategy.

> Students understand and remember ideas better when they have to transform those ideas from one form to another. Apparently it is in this transformation process that author's ideas become reader's ideas, rendering them more memorable. (p. 847)

In Chapter 3 we discussed the aim in testing of measuring reading unmuddied by the contaminating influence of other variables, e.g. writing. Measurement considerations such as this do not loom as large in the teaching situation. A good case can be made for the fruitful interaction between reading and writing in the language classroom, both activities being seen as potentially complementary to each other. Zamel (1992) argues that reading and writing instruction benefit each other in an integrated approach and argues for 'writing one's way into reading'. Silberstein (1994: 70–1) argues that by integrating instruction students come to understand the way in which both readers and writers compose text. Smith (1988: 277) comments that 'writing is one way of promoting engagement with a text which leads to better comprehension'.

The student has to establish the main ideas in a text, extract them and reduce to note form and then rewrite the notes in a coherent manner in their own words. Brown and Day (1983) identified a number of rules for summarising which match the rules of Kintsch and van Dijk for establishing macropropositions (see Chapter 2, p. 80):

- delete trivial information
- delete redundant information
- provide a superordinate term for members of a category
- find and use any main ideas you can
- create your own main ideas when missing from the text.

Pearson and Fielding (1991: 834–5) report that such training enhanced summarisation and increased scores on reading tests when compared with control groups. Exemplification of summary tasks can be found in Grellet (1981: 233–6), Paran (1991: 5, 27, 41) and Trzeciak and Mackay (1994: 26–8, 33–55).

We expressed concern about what actually happened as regards reading in the L2 classroom at the start of this section. The evidence suggests that little attention is devoted even to teaching the skills and strategies necessary for successful careful reading for global comprehension of text. The situation may be even worse as regards expeditious reading strategies. Leaving aside the prevalence of short texts in most course books, less attention is devoted to these strategies in comparison with careful reading.

Teaching expeditious reading skills

We noted in Section 2.4 and Chapter 3 that, in contrast to intensive careful reading, expeditious reading activities such as skimming, search reading and scanning were often overlooked in the past, certainly by testers, researchers and reading model builders. Nuttall (1996: 39) makes a similar point in relation to teaching materials:

> Moreover, longer texts are liable to get forgotten in the classroom, since it is easier to handle short texts which can be studied in a lesson or two. But the whole is not just the sum of its parts, and there are reading strategies which can only be trained by practice on longer texts. Scanning and skimming, the use of a contents list, an index and similar apparatus are obvious ones. More complex and arguably more important are the ability to discern relationships between the various parts of a longer text, the contribution made by each to the plot or the argument, the accumulating evidence of a writer's point of view, and so on.

and devotes an entire chapter to efficient reading in the 1996 revised edition of her book on the teaching of reading skills. Williams and Moran (1993) make a similar point in relation to the length of reading texts in course books.

Hamp-Lyons (1984: 305) notes the paucity of materials available in teaching at the macro-level in English for academic purposes reading. Needs analyses have made it clear (see Weir, 1983a) that one of the biggest problems for overseas students studying in a second language context is the sheer volume of reading that is required (see also Hamp-Lyons, 1984; Robb and Susser, 1989). Thus, as well as needing to read texts carefully to understand all in the text, they also have to read expeditiously to extract main ideas quickly or to establish whether it is relevant to their purposes (see Sections 2.4 and 3.2 for earlier discussion of these expeditious strategies, and also Nuttall, 1996: 39, 44).

Previewing and predicting were dealt with earlier in this part of the book in the section on generic metacognitive activities and practices. We addressed the expeditious strategies of skimming, scanning and search reading in Chapter 3 and the tasks used to test these are equally suitable as teaching tasks though, in the latter case, they may be mediated by teacher or students co-operating on them and their results put to a different use.

These strategies were introduced in Chapter 2 and the reader is asked to forgive a limited amount of repetition necessary to contextualise the taxonomy under development in the TEU at CALS Reading University (see Appendix 1). In this section we will expand our definitions of these strategies by exploring the purposes for which they might be employed and the actual operationalisations that might be focused on in classroom activities. These are the key areas that future research will need to focus on as such mediation by the teacher may help students to read more efficiently.

Skimming

This involves processing a text selectively to get the main idea(s) and the discourse topic as efficiently as possible, which might involve both expeditious and careful reading and both bottom-up and top-down processing. The focus may be global or local and the rate of reading is likely to be rapid, but with some care. The text is processed quickly to locate important information which then may be read more carefully. Purposes for using this strategy might include:

- to establish a general sense of the text
- to quickly establish a macropropositional structure as an outline summary
- to decide the relevance of texts to established needs.

Where appropriate to text type it might involve one or more of the following operationalisations:

- identifying the source
- reading titles and subtitles
- reading the abstract carefully
- reading the introductory and concluding paragraphs carefully
- reading the first and last sentence of each paragraph carefully

- identifying discourse markers
- noting repeated key content words
- identifying markers of importance
- skipping clusters of detail
- glancing at any non-verbal information.

Readers would be taught to be flexible as not all strategies would work with all texts. Also, some attention might usefully be paid to metacognitive strategies discussed above such as prediction and monitoring; the former to facilitate the use of existing knowledge, the latter to help separate less important detail from main ideas. Practical exemplification can be found in Grellet (1981: 71, 73–5, 81–2), Paran (1991: 79–81) and van Dijk (1977: 79).

Search reading

This differs from skimming in that the purpose is to locate information on predetermined topic(s), for example, in selective reading for writing purposes. It is often an essential strategy for completing written assignments.

The process, like skimming, is rapid and selective and is likely to involve careful reading once the relevant information has been located. Like skimming, bottom-up and top-down processing are therefore involved. Unlike skimming, sequencing is not always observed in the processing of the text although it is likely to be more linear than scanning. The periods of closer attention to the text tend to be more frequent and longer than in scanning. It normally goes well beyond the mere matching of words to be found in scanning activities, and might include the following operationalisations where appropriate:

- keeping alert for words in the same or related semantic field (unlike scanning, the precise form of these words is not certain)
- using formal knowledge of text structure for locating information
- using titles and subtitles
- reading abstracts where appropriate
- glancing at words and phrases.

Examples of search reading activities can be found in Ellis and Tomlinson (1988: 86–7), McGovern et al. (1994: 12), Morrow (1980: 15, 17, 37, 39) and Paran (1991: 55).

Scanning

This involves looking quickly through a text to locate a specific symbol or group of symbols, e.g. a particular word, phrase, name, figure or date. The focus here is on local comprehension and most of the text will be ignored. The rate of reading is rapid and sequencing is not usually observed. It is surface level rather than deep processing of text and is mainly reader-driven processing. There is a rapid inspection of text with occasional closer inspection. Pugh (1978: 53) describes it as:

> finding a match between what is sought and what is given in a text, very little information processed for long term retention or even for immediate understanding.

The operationalisations involved might include looking for/ matching

- specific words/phrase
- figures/percentages
- dates of particular events
- specific items in an index/directory.

The Crescent Series, designed for use in the school systems in the Middle East, offers a useful general procedure for scanning (O'Neill et al., 1996; Teacher's Book 8, xxii). For further exemplification of scanning, see Grellet (1981: 83), Morrow (1980: 18) and Nuttall (1996: 49–51). Nuttall (pp. 51–3) also provides some interesting ideas and examples on how graphic conventions – print size and style, layout, spacing, indentation – help the reader navigate a text and sometimes can signal, e.g. through different type faces, how the text is structured.

Extensive reading

The distinction we have been drawing between careful and expeditious reading can easily be confused with another, earlier, distinction between *intensive* and *extensive* reading. While there is undoubtedly an overlap, there are significant differences between the two dichotomies. The careful/expeditious distinction, taken together with the distinction between *local* and *global*, results in a number of different reading styles, or strategies, which can be employed either alone or, more often, in conjunction to accomplish a range of reading tasks. While expeditious reading is likely to be directed at lengthy texts, there is no reason why careful reading must be restricted to short texts. In fact, there are cogent reasons in academic contexts as to why it should not be.

The intensive/extensive distinction, on the other hand, is largely a pedagogical construct. Bright and McGregor (1970), for example, see them as being distinguished in terms of the number of questions the teacher decides to ask about a text:

> For the sake of convenience we shall discuss and exemplify extensive and intensive reading as though they were opposites. This will, however, be misleading unless we think of them as lying at opposite ends of a scale determined by question density. The point on the scale at which we decide to work will depend on:
>
> (i)   how much there is in the passage waiting to be discovered. Not all passages are worth meticulous attention.
> (ii)   how much time is available. By no means all the passages worth serious attention can be tackled.
> (iii) how much the class is capable of seeing and how well they respond.
> (iv)   how much is essential to a minimum worth-while response.
> (v)   how hot the afternoon is – and so on.
>
> (Bright and McGregor, 1970: 65)

Bright and McGregor (p. 80) remark that

> . . . it is not whole lessons but parts of lessons that may properly be so divided. In the middle of a chapter, we may stop to dwell on one word. This is intensive study.

However, our experience in a wide range of countries suggests that the distinction has become fossilised, with *intensive reading* being confined to the classroom, where it involves the teacher asking a large number of questions about a short text, while *extensive reading* refers to either 'silent reading' in the classroom, or reading done unsupervised in the library or at home, the aim being pleasure or practice, or both.

Hafiz and Tudor (1989: 1–2) see the goal of this type of extensive reading as 'to "flood" learners with large quantities of L2 input with few or possibly no specific tasks to perform on this material'.

Nuttall (1996: 127) describes it as 'the private world of reading for our own interest' and offers some valuable suggestions for organising such activities. She argues that reading extensively is the easiest and most effective way to improve reading and it is easier to teach in a climate where people enjoy the activity as well as value it for pragmatic reasons.

Davis (1995: 329) defines an extensive reading programme (ERP) as:

> ... a supplementary class library scheme, attached to an English course, in which pupils are given the time, encouragement, and materials to read pleasurably, at their own level, as many books as they can, without the pressures of testing or marks. Thus, pupils are only competing against themselves, and it is up to the teacher to provide the motivation and monitoring to ensure that the maximum number of books is being read in the time available.

Williams (1984: 10) sees extensive reading as the 'relatively rapid reading of long texts' (see Hedge, 1985) and emphasises that it should normally be at the level of the student's reading or below it. This contrasts with careful intensive reading where the aim is often to stretch the student slightly.

Bamford (1984: 218) claims that 'for all but advanced learners, the best way to promote extensive reading is by graded readers'.

Graded readers

In terms of contributions to the teaching of reading in this century, Howatt (1984: 245) singles out the work of West in Bengal in the 1920s who argued against the prevailing orthodoxy for the greater surrender value of basic literacy as against training in spoken language. West developed a system of readers using the principles of lexical selection and lexical distribution, the latter giving the reader more practice material between the introduction of new words – a distinct problem with earlier primers which introduced too many new words too quickly.

Hill and Reid-Thomas (1988a: 44) describe a graded reader as follows:

> A graded reader may be either a simplified version of an original work or a 'simple original', i.e. an original work written in simple English. In either case it is written to a grading scheme which may be set out in terms of vocabulary, sentence structure, and, in some cases, content.

Nuttall makes the distinction between needing to read, which can be instigated in the classroom, and wanting to read (1996:

130), which is a greater incentive to more people. She provides helpful advice on how to promote this, including choosing appropriate suitable books at the right level, short, appealing, varied and easy; on how to organise a library (pp. 133–41); on how to organise an extensive reading programme (pp. 141–4) by creating interest, developing incentives to read; and devising appropriate monitoring and assessment procedures.

Survey reviews by the Edinburgh Project on Extensive Reading (EPER) staff in *ELT Journal* (Hill, 1992, Hill and Reid Thomas, 1988a, 1988b, 1989, 1993) give advice on graded readers in terms of levels, readability level, appearance, text subject matter, aids to reading, recommended reader age, and a quality rating on a scale of 1 to 5 (an interest rating in the 1988 reviews). Hill and Reid-Thomas (1989) note a trend to shorter books and advise publishers that these books may be too short and possess insufficient meat to be used as class readers. They make a plea for some longer readers (more than 72 pages at the upper level and more than 40 at the lower).

Davis (1995: 331–5) provides some useful advice for development of extensive reading programmes:

- the watchwords are quantity and variety, rather than quality
- books should be attractive and relevant to students' lives
- books should be more than sufficient in number
- books should be graded and colour coded by reading level but students should be encouraged to move between levels
- try to make ERP school policy
- try to get it built into the timetable
- try to get financial support at least for a book box
- integrate with library studies where appropriate, for example, through parallel grading of fiction books in the library
- develop a simple system for using the books
- develop a quick and painless system for monitoring the use of the books.

Very similar advice can be found in Bright and McGregor (1970).

The class reader: sustained silent reading

A similar but slightly different form of extensive reading is the silent sustained reading which may take place in class with a class set of books. Nuttall (1996: 145–8) describes how to select class readers and outlines a number of useful activities that can be done in class and outside class. What is clear is that it is fine if the students enjoy such extensive reading; however, if they do not enjoy a particular story, drop it immediately. Davis (1995) suggests that the class reader may be seen by administrators as a cheaper alternative to ERPs and one easier to handle in the classroom.

The teacher's role

Williams (1984: 19) points out that extensive reading in class is important in giving learners uninterrupted quality time to read and reflect and, just as important, it gives teachers time/breathing space to reflect on their teaching. He comments: 'Teachers should not feel that they are neglecting their job if they are not constantly explaining something or organising classroom activities.'

Does extensive reading work?

In common with the rest of this chapter, we are concerned that any advice we give should where possible be supported by evidence of positive impact. Surprisingly little negative comment appears in the literature concerning extensive reading. On the downside are:

- the cost of extended reading programmes
- the amount of time setting them up and running them efficiently
- the fact that curriculum time is required for private reading.

Nuttall (1982: 62) asserts that

> an extensive reading programme . . . is the single most effective way of improving vocabulary and reading skills in general. You can organise a programme of vocabulary building, but greatly increasing the amount of material they read is the best way of all.

She repeats the same in the 1996 revised edition of her book but limits the effect to improving vocabulary in the revised edition.

Rodrigo (1995) argues that there is some evidence for enhanced progress in reading comprehension and vocabulary development as a result of extended reading courses (see also Day et al., 1991, and Pitts et al., 1989). This is a view supported by Krashen (1993) for whom the dominant mode of language learning is acquisition. Hafiz and Tudor (1989: 5) argue that comprehensible input in large quantities in a tension-free environment satisfies a key condition for acquisition to take place. Extensive reading programmes can provide large amounts of reading in L2 for personal interest reading. They quote the claim by Krashen and Terrell (1983) that comprehensible input gained in reading may contribute to a general language competence that underlies both spoken and written performance.

In Rodrigo's study students were encouraged to read as much as they could that was comprehensible during a semester, with a chance to choose what interested them and focus on meaning rather than linguistic form. Certain readings were done in class, often in the library, and others were personal readings. As well as the experimental reading course there was a discussion group where readings were discussed and presented orally. The control group focused on grammar and vocabulary. The reading material was divided into three levels:

- Graded books: 'edited, simplified and/or abridged so that they can be used at certain levels . . . excellent for competence and confidence building' (Rodrigo, 1995: 6).
- Light reading or easy ungraded native reading: 'unabridged not classical literature or technical'.
- Literature or information texts: 'more complex unabridged reading material, such as literature, adult books, bibliography, history and technical and informational books' for those who had succeeded at the stage of light reading.

Rodrigo (1995) compared the two groups using performance on a vocabulary recognition test and the experimental group did outperform the control, but the results were not significant, probably because of low sample size. Qualitative feedback from the students clearly indicated that they had enjoyed the extensive reading course.

Robb and Susser (1989) report on the value of extensive reading as against a skills focus in experimental work they conducted in Japan. Elley and Mangubhai (1983) offer evidence of the impact on reading of an ERP used in Fijian primary schools. They showed that subjects receiving extensive reading improved meaningfully in reading and word recognition at the end of the first year of the study. Hafiz and Tudor (1989) report how an extensive reading programme using graded readers in a control group experimental design resulted in a statistically significant improvement in the experimental (the extensive) group, especially in terms of their writing skills. The improvements in reading scores, though significant, were small.

Hamp-Lyons (1985) offers some evidence that students taught by a text-strategic approach evidenced higher gains in a pre-test/post-test design than students who followed a traditional approach. Nation (1997) cites empirical evidence to show that there are many benefits for extensive reading 'in quality of language use, language knowledge and general academic success'.

The value of extensive reading receives some support in the literature (Davis, 1995; Elley, 1991; Hamp-Lyons, 1985; Krashen, 1993; Nation, 1997; Robb and Susser, 1989; Tudor and Hafiz, 1989). However much more research needs to be done to provide a firm empirical base to convince a wider audience of its value. Lunzer et al.'s massive L1 study (1979) quoted in Nuttall (1996) showed that in British classrooms right across the curriculum little sustained reading occurred and it accounted for less than 15 per cent of class time. It involved more writing than reading work. Nuttall (p. 128) suggests that the situation had not improved by 1989 according to inspectorate reports. Williams and Moran (1993) comment:

> . . . the rather curious situation has arisen, whereby, despite universal acceptance of the view that one becomes a good reader through reading, reading lessons where most time is actually spent on reading (as opposed to discussion, answering questions, etc.) are relatively rare.

It is clear that what is important is how much learners read and the degree of enjoyment derived. The challenge is to access students to such literature and provide the means/incentives/opportunities for them to read it and to carry on reading.

So from the research we have a picture of what might be useful in terms of reading strategies. How teachers take this and make use of it in the classroom is the challenge for the next decade. What is clear from the research is that these strategies as yet do not play a large part in the L1 reading classrooms in the USA (Alvermann and Moore, 1991: 974). The picture is brighter, however, in the L2 situation in the UK.

Working together

We have indicated above that an obvious difference between testing and teaching is that the teaching situation allows for co-operation between students, whereas testing virtually never does (not officially, at least). We also referred to a survey of US secondary classrooms by Alvermann and Moore (1991) which found little group work in evidence. By contrast, we next examine some ways in which students have been encouraged to work co-operatively.

Peer interaction

Research supports the view that working together co-operatively benefits all levels of students in mixed ability groups or pairs. It may be used as follow up to teacher-directed activities (Pearson and Fielding, 1991: 839). They comment:

> In general, successful groups work towards group goals while monitoring the success of each individual's learning as a criterion of group success; also associated with positive growth are peer interactions that emphasise offering explanations rather than right answers.

It might, however, be the novelty of working with each other, rather than the activities engendered, that has produced the results.

Nuttall (1996: 161–6) offers advice on how students might be guided during the reading process itself, and while emphasising the value of individuals reading in silence on their own (this is what reading actually is), perhaps in a self-access system, she points to some advantages of working in a group: motivation, individuals participate more actively because it is less threatening than whole class activity and partly because of reciprocity, the recognition that everyone in the group should contribute. It all makes students aware how others read and promotes thoughtful discussion on reading strategies and skills.

What is clear is that motivation has a very strong influence on strategy use. Williams and Burden (1997: 154) argue 'increased motivation and self-esteem lead to more effective use of appropriate strategies and vice versa'. Motivation appears to be enhanced by co-operative learning experiences (Roehler and Duffy, 1991: 867).

Jigsaw reading is a good example of the more innovative developments that have taken place in the EFL classroom (see Grellet,

1981; Geddes and Sturtridge, 1982; and Nuttall, 1996: 209 and 257). The class is split into groups and given only partial information on a topic situation or story. The groups are then reorganised so each member has a different piece of information from which the new group has to reassemble the whole. Unless you have information from all of the texts you cannot understand something important in the story or situation or perform a key task. Williams (1984: 115–11) provides some good examples of this technique and also of what he terms *enquiry strategy*, where the groups decide what information they would like to find out as a pre-reading task.

Grouping students for reading instruction: does it work?

For a long time it has been accepted wisdom to group students on the basis of ability for reading classes. Barr and Dreeben (1991), however, on the basis of some recent L1 studies, cast some doubt on this: according to them, in general the results are 'equivocal and inconsistent' (p. 895). The authors feel that the research in this area has neglected the properties of ability groups, the principles underlying their formation, the nature of instruction received and the connection between grouping and other aspects of the educational enterprise. The consequence has been that studies have produced results which are inconclusive, inconsistent, and not particularly interesting. They argue that we need to focus on how knowledge is imparted through instruction to various populations of students, e.g. what the nature is of tasks and instruction provided to similar and different groups or tracks across schools; how these differences influence attitudes and learning.

Nuttall (1996: 164–5) offers sound practical advice for this activity. She suggests that groups should not be more than five in number; non-participators might be put together; members of the group should face each other; mixing or streaming groups can be varied from activity to activity; the teacher should take a consultant's role and not interfere; tasks must be explicit as only one group can be attended to at a time; tasks should aim to involve all members of the group.

We have now looked at texts, goals, activities, and roles of students in the learning to read process. We finish by considering what should happen in the reading classroom in general and what actually happens.

4.4 WHAT SHOULD HAPPEN IN THE READING CLASSROOM?

What actually happens in the reading class? Alvermann and Moore (1991: 964) detail the more usual L1 classroom practices in American schools as lecture, textbook assignment, and classroom recitation. They found that reading activities tended to occur only in short bursts of about 15 minutes and were connected with other forms of classroom communication: listening, writing and speaking in a supportive role; 'continuous reading is rare' (p. 965). They found that research suggests considerable variation in practice across teachers with regard to activities, textbook use and academic tracks.

In their survey they also discovered the following aspects of the reading classroom. These are for the most part traditional and date back to the turn of the century (p. 969):

- predominance of textbooks
- emphasis on factual textual information
- teachers in control of students' encounters with print; student initiated comments or questions are rare
- very little work in groups
- little planned reading instruction in terms of teaching skills and strategies.

They argue that this approach is maintained for institutional reasons such as maintenance of order, accountability, socialisation (conveying a sanctioned body of knowledge) and resources such as time (to prepare and deliver and own expertise) and materials (pp. 979–82). It is an environment that rewards control. In the end teachers may well teach in the way they have been taught themselves as this is what they know best.

Bernhardt (1991a: 175–6) presents a similar picture for the L2 EFL reading lesson. Here she suggests that texts are often specially written to illustrate use of lexis, structures and syntactic features rather than for teaching comprehension. The shortness of the texts employed restrict the reading styles that can be applied and encourage a focus on lexis and structure. There is usually some pre-teaching of vocabulary and the reading selection is usually assigned for homework with a commitment to answering the comprehension questions set by the author. Follow-up in class often takes the form of oral reading plus answering the questions.

Some additional focus might be given to vocabulary or pronunciation errors. Exercises on grammatical elements of text occur either before or after the reading text is studied and, similarly, encourage a microlinguistic focus.

Bernhardt argues that this picture is based firmly on the textbooks which teach teachers how to teach. She notes how little time or attention is available for teachers on how to teach reading in these methodology books (1991a: 177).

Hamp-Lyons (1984: 307) notes:

> ... the traditional approach to reading comprehension in ESL classrooms, in which students are asked to read short passages very carefully and expected to understand them in minute detail, being tested on this comprehension by questions mainly at the lexical level, reinforces concrete level process strategies ... it also reinforces the tendency to read slowly and discourages the development of sufficient reading speed to synthesise meaning from the passage (Smith 1971) ... ESL readers spend much longer on each fixation than native language readers do.

Robb and Susser (1989) present a similar picture of the situation in Japan, with reading largely taught by the translation procedure so that many are only able to decode at the sentence level and are denied reading books for pleasure.

Pearson and Fielding (1991: 815) note that there are now a plethora of reviews of research about L1 instruction intentionally designed to improve reading comprehension. They point out that much that passes as comprehension instruction is little more than doing tests or answering questions on passages, with little advice on how to perform such tasks, i.e. instruction intentionally designed to improve reading comprehension.

Often it is a case of 'procedural display' – getting the lesson done, rather than substantive engagement in some academic content (Bloom, 1985, quoted in Bernhardt, 1991a: 181). Hoffman (1991: 939–41) details a number of studies which produced similar findings of very little comprehension instruction happening and also an absence of such instructions in manuals and textbooks in use.

Bernhardt (1991b) describes how L2 students learn to 'look literate': putting hands up to answer questions, looking at the book while another reads aloud but (p. 182) 'they did not learn how to use or interpret printed discourse for meaning ... are rarely asked to display nonteacher-mediated understanding . . .'. She quotes Duffy and Anderson (1981):

> . . . the primary concern of teachers is maintaining the flow of ongoing classroom activities rather than thinking about students' instructional needs and adapting lessons accordingly.

Getting through the lesson (Bloom, 1985) and avoiding lesson breakdown often compel teachers to mediate learning through conversational interaction, often supplying the answers themselves. Students who threaten to impede the flow of a lesson, say, by not understanding, are ignored because they slow it down. Thus, Bernhardt notes, it is the learners who have the most difficulties who often receive the least attention. Those who help promote the successful achievement of the teacher-decided activities receive the most reward.

The way forward: some general considerations

Drill and practise were common procedures and they still have a value in the training of automaticised outcomes. This traditional approach of the teacher giving controlled guidance and then students practising the various skills appears to receive support from high student performance on standardised tests in research studies (Roehler and Duffy, 1991: 861). However, L1 research now suggests the value of moving beyond the exercise model with its emphasis on repetition. Roehler and Duffy (1991) point out that cognitive psychology and information processing have demonstrated the importance of organisation, coherence and connectedness in transmission of knowledge. To reach long-term memory, information needs to be transformed 'into meaningful concepts that can be referenced and stored in an organised way' (p. 861).

Secondly has come an understanding of the importance of metacognition; conscious control of cognitive processing with self-regulation and a focus on understanding (p. 862). As a result, drill and practice are no longer seen as adequate and a more co-operative and cognitively based approach is advocated 'where teachers provide information and mediate student mental processing' (p. 863). So, as well as providing information, importance is also now placed on mediating student learning; helping students to learn about learning (see Section 4.2 above).

The value of explicit instruction on how to comprehend has long been recognised, but now it is felt that it is the nature and content of these interactions in the reading classroom that count (Pearson and Fielding, 1991: 841). Pearson and Fielding's review of L1 research suggests that activity and involvement on the part of the students is as important as instruction; shared reciprocity for interactions and negotiation of meaning rather than monologue are to be encouraged (see Bernhardt, 1991a: 181–9). Williams and Burden (1997: ch. 4) advocate a social constructivist approach and see mediation by the teacher as central to the learning process; '(its) influence is both powerful and profound' (p. 84). Their focus is on what teachers can do to help their learners become effective and independent. They see mediation as being concerned with empowering (p. 68):

> . . . with helping learners to acquire the knowledge, skills and strategies they will need in order to progress, to learn more, to tackle problems . . . to meet new and unpredictable demands. It is also concerned with helping learners to become autonomous, to take control of their own learning, with the fundamental aim of enabling them to become independent thinkers and problem-solvers.

Will it work?

Where teachers' messages convey how to construct meaning in reading, a positive effect has been found. Pearson and Fielding (1991: 848) detail how this might involve focus on text structure; encouraging students to connect background knowledge to text ideas to make inferences, predictions, and elaborations; or prompt students to ask their own questions about the text. In their wide review of the research, Pearson and Fielding (1991) found such interventions to be at least moderately successful although transferability was not tested for. Hoffman (1991: 942–3) also provides data which show a positive result on achievement measures for explicit teacher explanation.

The effective teacher will help students develop an awareness of reading strategies necessary for successful encounters with text. Explicit instruction in strategies and skills discussed in Sections 4.2 and 4.3, and in the section on testing, were found by Pearson and Fielding (1991: 849) to be helpful, particularly where the focus is on ensuring that students understand when and why they might be employed (see also Roehler and Duffy, 1991: 867 et seq. and Paris et al., 1991). Cohen (1998: 19) reports:

> The findings of the study would suggest that explicitly describing, discussing and reinforcing strategies in the classroom – and thus raising them to the level of conscious awareness – can have a direct payoff in student outcomes.

Following instruction by questions that help mediate and build up student understanding was also found to be of value by Roehler and Duffy (1991: 872) in their review of the L1 research literature. Nuttall (1996: 181–91) also examines the value of questioning in the classroom and argues that it provides a window into the students' mental processes; especially where answers are wrong, opportunities arise for learning through 'thoughtful searching'. Questions which make the reader work are advocated as these focus attention on difficult elements of the text, especially where follow-up questions get students to reveal how they arrived at their answers. The use of MCQ format may have a place here, especially if the distracters perform this function and useful discussion may result. Any questions which promote discussion have a valuable role to play as they get learners thinking about reading and developing interpretative strategies (see Paran, 1993, for examples of these in teaching materials).

Roehler and Duffy (1991: 864–6) outline the importance of planning by teachers to identify critical features for their students, to simplify the tasks and create effective examples. The selection of tasks students are asked to do will constrain the operations students acquire and how they interpret learning experiences. To motivate students, tasks should encourage students to engage in cognitive activity appropriate for the intended outcome and students should be aware of the purposes behind these activity structures. Teachers should specify clearly how the learning experience is intended to be useful, and the expectancies they have of their students. Hoffman (1991: 923) provides some empirical evidence for the positive effect of the latter on student performance.

Remediation

What happens when they do not learn? Hoffman (1991: 915) refers to a frequently cited frustration for teachers as dealing with and meeting the needs of students experiencing difficulty in the reading classroom. He presents data to suggest that the slow pacing in low ability groups 'does not appear to hold any promise or pay off in terms of successful reading development' (p. 936).

The high incidence of teacher correction often at the point of error in reading aloud in low-ability groups is also seen as debilitating and helps create an even wider gap between high- and low-ability groups (pp. 937–8).

Johnston and Allington (1991: 985–6) feel that the very use of the term 'remediation', with its connotation of sickness of the child, creates an unfortunate role structure for the children tagged in this way. They suggest that we would look at the situation differently if we used the terms 'children with different schedules for reading acquisition' or 'children we have failed to teach'. They question taking students out of mainstream programmes and show how those in many remedial programmes often receive less reading instruction than those in the classes they have been taken from; read less text and spend less time reading any text. In such programmes teachers' expectations of students are lowered with consequent effects on the way teachers interact with the students and the results obtained. Those who get off schedule in remediation hardly ever get back on (p. 998) and it may be the nature of the instruction they receive, e.g. a focus on decoding, rather than meaning which keeps them that way (p. 999).

Johnston and Allington (1991) argue that the only way to deal with it is to eliminate the need for it in the first place and most effectively by early intervention before problems are compounded. Class sizes might be reduced but the solution is likely to lie in higher quality instruction and the creation of non-competitive tasks involving concepts to increase involvement and co-operation – in fact, through many of the co-operative procedures discussed above and below. In this way remediation might become intercession or friendly intervention by consent or invitation (p. 1005).

Nuttall (1996: 144–5) offers some sound advice for those who simply read too slowly in the EFL classroom. She also argues that special attention may be needed and the provision of lots of easy readers is insufficient on its own.

Simply the best? Is there a best way to teach reading?

This is a question that is always asked but which is almost impossible to answer despite a predominant accountability orientation in school evaluation. Hoffman (1991: 917 et seq.) provides an extensive review of the L1 literature, comparing different methods of teaching reading, and no one method of teaching reading showed itself to be superior to others. Perhaps looking for answers to such big questions is always likely to be unrequited. A particular problem with these earlier studies was that they did not collect any process data and so faithfulness of implementation of a particular method was seldom available in the interpretation of product results; for example, no data on actual time spent in reading were available. Hoffman (1991: 921) cites later studies which showed the importance of this independent variable.

Hoffman's impressive survey of effective teaching studies (1991: 921–30) suggested

> ... the important role teachers play in organising and managing the instructional environment in a way that serves to maximise student engagement in academics ... the important role teachers play in presenting academic content in a way that promotes learning.

He also provides a model for effective academic teaching (p. 930).

Useful taxonomies of advice for teaching reading are also provided by Hamp-Lyons (1984: 308), Hoffman (1991: 921–30), Bernhardt (1991a: 186–7) and Nuttall (1996: 32–3). Similar lists are suggested by Grabe (1991), Richards (1989), Williams (1996) and Williams and Burden (1997: 69).

However it is clear from the evaluation literature (Weir and Roberts, 1994) that any attribution of causality will be difficult. It may prove impossible to single out any of the features of mediation or activities listed by these authors and directly trace its impact on reading in the classroom.

Effective schools

Successful reading instruction is more than just an interaction between teacher, students and materials, however. The context in which learning takes place can have an important effect and it is necessary to consider this wider environment for learning as well, even if the teacher can do little about it outside the walls of his or her own classroom.

Hoffman (1991) surveyed research into effective schools, as defined by performance on standardised reading test scores, and identified a number of features that are potential contributors though reservations are expressed about methodology, generalisability and validity. They included:

- clear school mission
- strong curriculum leadership usually from a head
- instructional efficiency: 'utilisation of resources to achieve maximal student outcomes'
- high expectations for students
- good atmosphere; safe, orderly and positive
- commitment to improvement
- individualisation
- careful evaluation of student progress
- reading identified as an important instructional goal
- breadth of material available
- attention to basic skills
- communication of ideas across teachers.

Three steps forward

In the end all of this is an empirical issue, and in the field of L2 reading such data are noticeable by their absence. As we mentioned above, the reflective teacher is constantly alert for what works and what does not in the reading classroom. What we do not have is broad-based evidence of what works and what does not work in the teaching of reading. In L2 reading we have only a handful of studies which have attempted to investigate empirically the effectiveness of teaching various strategies or adopting a particular approach in the classroom.

The situation as regards L2 testing of reading is similar. What is the status of the various strategies and skills we have considered? Can we demonstrate their separate existence in the tests we write? What methods will enable us to do this?

We also need a serial model or a number of models which will provide a clear theoretical base for L2 reading for different purposes, especially one for expeditious reading. What are some ways in which we might investigate this?

In the next chapter we will make some suggestions as to how these areas might be investigated. Chapter 5 is titled 'future research'. We shall not attempt to survey the field in the manner of Bernhardt (1991a) for L2 reading or Barr et al. (1991) for L1 reading, but we have attempted to incorporate their research findings and those of others where available in our overview of theory, testing and teaching of reading in the earlier chapters of this book. The literature on reading is so vast that we are sure to have missed a number of important pieces of research in the welter of references available on L1 and L2 reading in general. We would be glad to be made aware of any omissions.

Our aim in Chapter 5 is to identify some key areas from our review of the field in Chapters 1–4 and suggest how these might be investigated through small-scale research studies to help shed light on areas badly in need of sustained attention.

5

Future research

INTRODUCTION

Throughout this book so far, we have tried to indicate our preference for claims and conclusions based on empirical data, rather than rhetoric and good-hearted sentiment. We finish, therefore, with a chapter devoted to considerations of some future research directions for teaching and testing reading in an L2.

The relationship between research and teaching is complex, and worthy of a study by itself. A single publication by Goodman (1967) had what some consider to be a disproportionate amount of influence on the teaching of reading both in the L1 and L2. It remains to be seen whether the work of Stanovich and others has anything like the same effect. The huge change in L2 from a focus on linguistic structures to emphasis on communicative use was not motivated by empirical data as is normally understood by the term; it seems to have occurred at least in part by an upswelling of dissatisfaction among the teaching community with the previous paradigm.

The characteristics of the participants involved in teaching and testing on the one hand, and research on the other, are again of interest. Both sides have their virtues and vices. Teachers and testers are usually in contact with real learners, and often form hunches regarding these learners based on extended experience, which may well be valid, even if difficult to substantiate. They often lack, however, an explicit theoretical framework against which to relate these hunches, and thus evaluate them and extend them. Researchers, on the other hand, usually operate within a theoretical framework. However, they may not bring experience to bear on this framework. Moreover, they sometimes rely uncritically on not well-substantiated or repeated experimental results. Here we make an attempt to bring the two worlds together, to evaluate teaching and testing methods in the light of theories, and vice versa.

It is sometimes fashionable in teaching circles to sneer at 'theory' (which sometimes seems to extend to everything except methodology). To the extent that some teacher trainers, having escaped from the classroom themselves, have appeared to exclude 'practical' considerations from what they tell students, this reaction is understandable. We, however, do not go very far in our sympathy. Teachers and testers need both a sound grasp of practical matters, and an educated framework on which to base and to evaluate their methods. We firmly believe that without such a framework, the teacher or tester is trapped in a particular set of practices, with no motivated criteria for making alterations. Often they are reduced to evaluating teaching practices in terms of whether the students enjoyed them or not.

Two research communities

Many of the readers for whom this book is intended, as well as the authors themselves, can be said to belong to a professional group termed 'applied linguists'. We shall attempt to define this group and establish some boundaries though we are aware that many might disagree with our efforts. Our definitions, like all others, are partial. The group is rather amorphous: a recent letter from the Secretary-Treasurer of the American Association for Applied Linguistics describes the association's '1200+ members' as working in 'many language-related areas, including language education, second language acquisition and loss, bilingualism, discourse analysis, literacy, rhetoric and stylistics, language for special purposes, psycholinguistics, second and foreign language pedagogy, language assessment, and language policy and planning'.[1] The section of the group with which we are particularly concerned consists of people who are involved in some way with the teaching and testing of an L2. They are quite a large group; Sampson (1997) attributes the rise in importance of linguistics in the 1960s and 1970s to an influx of such people.

While the book is directed towards this group, we have very frequently referred to another academic group concerned with reading – namely, cognitive psychologists. The two groups are indirectly related, both owing their existence, or preoccupations, at least in part to the reaction against Behaviourism in the 1960s (see Gibson and Levin, 1974). They are, however, fairly distinct. Applied linguists, as indicated above, are fairly widely spread, both in terms of professional interests and places of work; cognitive psychologists seem on the whole to operate in psychology departments in universities.

In this section, we shall briefly compare the contribution made by the two groups to research into reading behaviour. The comparison is not, on the whole, flattering to the applied linguistic community, ourselves included. We shall suggest some reasons related to our respective work situations which serve to some extent to excuse this. However, the main reason we have for making the comparison is to suggest ways in which applied linguistic research into reading may improve by study and use of the psychologists.

The first thing to be said about the contribution of the cognitive psychologists is that the database it has to refer to is very large. Rayner and Pollatsek (1989) list around 850 entries in their bibliography, the vast majority taken from their own field. By contrast, surveying the L2 reading literature, Bernhardt (1991a) could find only 121 articles concerned with empirical research into the reading process. But it is not a matter just of number of articles: their research tends to be cumulative, one experiment building on another, proceeding by criticism and extension. For example, early work on word and letter recognition was criticised, the method refined, then the work repeated until the results are able to stand up to critical scrutiny (Rayner and Pollatsek, 1989: 76ff). The general approach seems to be refreshingly empirical, with a strong drive to discover details of what is happening at different points in the reading process. For example, Rayner and Pollatsek (p. 265) comment that 'everyone agrees that real-world knowledge has to actively intervene in reading for comprehension to take place; the question is how'.

In addition, there is considerable emphasis on method. Rayner and Pollatsek frequently introduce a topic by describing the methods used to investigate it, e.g. the methods used to measure the time involved in word recognition (pp. 63ff). The same methods can be used by successive researchers, enabling results to be compared. The range of methods is impressive, and the details are often ingenious (e.g. some of the work on phonological decoding) and even entertaining: 'Crude Jude chews food' rings in the mind (see Section 2.2).

Inevitably, there are aspects of the cognitive psychologists' work about which we have reservations, and which we shall mention here, to show we are not totally overawed. There is, for example, the use in some experiments of so-called 'unpronounceable' words, used to determine, for example, whether a reader is attempting a phonological or direct route in accessing the lexicon. Gibson and Levin (1974), discussing the use of 'unpronounceable' words with young L1 (English) readers, point out that 'unpronounceability' and orthographic 'illegality' are often confused (pp. 201ff). With L2 readers, another factor is likely to emerge, the phonological rules of their L1. For example, Koda (1987) used two sets of pseudo-words, pronounceable and unpronounceable, with Japanese students learning English. Strings like 'mastib' were classed as 'pronounceable', and strings like 'msatbi' as 'unpronounceable'. The dangers seem clear: an initial sequence of [ms] would be perfectly possible and pronounceable for a speaker of Swahili, and many other languages. Consonant sequences which might be unpronounceable for speakers of Japanese might seem normal for, say, a Polish speaker. There is, it seems to us, no such thing as 'unpronounceability'.[2]

Then there is the problem about so-called 'regular' versus 'irregular' words, i.e. words which are spelled 'regularly', e.g. 'doom' [duːm] versus 'blood' [blʌd] (cf. Rayner and Pollatsek, 1989: 87; Suarez and Meara, 1989: 352). The argument is presumably that 'oo' is the regular spelling of the phoneme [uː] in monosyllabic words of the structure CVC. What, however, is the 'regular' pronunciation of the spelling '-ough'? A concordancer check of a 50,000 word text found 19 occurrences of words pronounced [oʊ], (although, though), 10 of words pronounced [ʌf] (rough, tough, enough) and 31 of [uː] (through). It would be hard on this evidence to establish which the 'regular' pronunciation was. In fact, claims as to 'regularity' are fundamentally statistical, based (probably intuitively) on a large number of words from the total English lexicon. But the L2 learner is operating with a much smaller base. What the learner thinks of as 'regular' may be affected by the actual words in his or her lexicon.

A more serious question concerns the 'naturalness' of many of the experiments carried out in psychology laboratories. The laboratory allows careful control of the experiment, and the use of special equipment, for, say, timing responses to the millisecond. It does, however, leave open the possibility that the results are restricted to the laboratory, and cannot be carried over to 'real reading'. The fact that experimental subjects can be shown to vocalise single words flashed on a screen is not, it seems to us, very good evidence that they do the same thing when reading a long text quickly. It is arguable that, in the laboratory situation, vocalisation is the only response subjects have open to them. Rayner and Pollatsek are very aware of this problem; it is why they attach such importance to using eye movements as evidence of reading activity, since they do not disturb normal activity. On the whole, although laboratories are 'unnatural', so too are classrooms and examination halls, and as long as we are aware of the problem, this is something we have to live with.

Finally, it could be argued that the cognitive psychologists haven't got very far. They know a lot about word recognition but not much else. This is very unfair, but there is an element of truth in it. As we noted in the discussion on bottom-up models in Section 2.1, Gough's model, first proposed in 1972, contains a component called 'Merlin', which handles syntax and semantics in a suitably mysterious way. Rayner and Pollatsek (1989: 263) admit that 'our present knowledge of how sentences are read is meager'. However, they are optimistic about future developments, and it has to be said that if cognitive psychologists know very little about how higher level processing occurs, they know more than anyone else.

All in all, from consideration of the contribution to reading research by the cognitive psychologists one gets the impression of a lot of data, obtained by well-established research methodologies, and organised by means of models, which not only make sense of the existing data but point to further areas of research.

The applied linguistics contribution

When we look in turn at the experimental data gathered for L2 reading, usually by researchers who would be classed as applied linguists, the following aspects emerge:

- The database, as Bernhardt (1991a) points out, is small. As an example partly separate from Bernhardt's analysis, *Reading in a Foreign Language* classifies articles into Reading Process, Text Analysis, Course Design, Graded Readers, Materials and Methodology, Lexis, and Testing. Up to Volume 11 (1), there have in all been 91 articles. Suppose we class as experimental data any paper containing a description of a controlled experiment.[3] Of our total of 91 papers, roughly 30 per cent can be classified as experimental, with most of these being found in Reading Process (14/18) and Testing (6/12).

▪ The research is often not cumulative; i.e. as Bernhardt points out, many of the experiments are one-offs. For example, Pegolo (1985) and Dhaif (1990) both published in *Reading in a Foreign Language*. Both papers reported experiments in which reading silently was accompanied by an oral input, in Pegolo's case, prosodic information only, in Dhaif's case, the text read by a teacher. The language of the first experiment was French; of the second, English. The comprehension of the experimental groups improved significantly in both cases. These results are interesting and of apparent pedagogical significance but, at least as far as that publication is concerned, were not repeated. It is interesting that when an experiment is repeated, as in Nesi and Meara's repetition (Nesi and Meara, 1991) of a study done by Bensoussan and Laufer (1984), one of the authors, Meara, has training in psychology. Even when a topic is repeated, as with, say, Background Knowledge, the different methodologies employed by different experimenters, as Bernhardt says, make comparisons difficult.

▪ There is no established body of experimental methods which the applied linguists can fall back on. In addition, the methodology used tends to be uninspiring. We cannot all be Bransford and Johnsons, but there is more to experimental design than matching two groups reading different texts. The methodology used by Meyer (1975) to investigate the effect of rhetorical organisation on recall, is elegant – pairs of texts being produced by embedding the same target paragraph in two different organisational contexts. One has to assume that she, again, has a background in psychology. Many applied linguists, setting out to experiment, obviously believe that when one can handle ANOVA on a PC statistical package, one has completed one's apprenticeship.

▪ There seems to be a tendency for applied linguistic researchers to accept a theoretical construct without further analysis, definition, or even empirical investigation. *Cohesion* and *schemata* come to mind, while we have commented in Section 2.3 on the way in which 'a reading problem or a language problem' was taken up without much discussion or definition of what constituted 'reading skills' or 'language ability'. As far as sustained empirical investigation is concerned, it is striking how Goodman's claim about 'a psycholinguistic guessing game' was accepted by applied linguists, without very much testing of the claim with L2 readers (see, however, Rigg, 1988).

Causes for the differences

When we look for reasons why the applied linguists, including ourselves, do so comparatively poorly, one is tempted to fall back on the excuse that their attention is diffused over a number of loosely related areas. If we revert to our initial description of the work situations of the members, we find a rather wide range of occupations and pre-occupations, from language planning to stylistics to second language acquisition study. It is a very broad area, with a potentially misleading subject name, and a lack of core focus. In addition, many members spend a considerable proportion of their time actually teaching language, or training language teachers. Profit or perish is often a more immediate imperative than publish or perish.

Even when we restrict the focus to reading, the spread of interest for applied linguists can be wide, extending from studies of the effect of different scripts to the effect of dictionary use to the influence of different text types. Reference to the quick count from *Reading in a Foreign Language* above suggests that some of the areas in which applied linguists operate are less oriented towards experiments than others. For example, while *Reading Process* contains 18 papers, of which 14 contain experiments (78 per cent), *Text Analysis* contains none. Research need not be restricted to experiments.

However, we must be wary of any rather self-pitying excuses for ourselves. Cognitive psychologists have interests other than reading. The reasons for the poor database must be found elsewhere.

The principal reason seems to be that while cognitive psychology is an experiment-centred study area, applied linguistics is not. The typical applied linguist will not have come formally into contact with experiments during his or her undergraduate training, and while an applied linguistics course in Britain, at least, may include a small research design component, it is seldom a major part of the course. Hence it tends to be the case that when graduates of such courses design experiments, they lack the grounding the psychologists have had in method, particularly the depth provided by knowledge of conventional types of experiments which have already been used in investigating similar areas.

A secondary reason is that many experiments in applied linguistics have been done, as it were, on the side, so that, for example, a teacher teaching reading may set up a reading experiment. It is not, in other words, a mainline part of the teacher's professional duties.

A concentration on experiments in psychology is accompanied by a major interest in theory and in models of the reading process. Until recently, L2 reading research has, as Bernhardt says, been atheoretical. Applied linguists have paid comparatively little attention to formal models, particularly process models. Bernhardt comments that a disproportionate amount of the references in the applied linguistics area have been to Goodman, at the expense of, say, Gough, or Just and Carpenter, or Kintsch and van Dijk. She has a point, though in defence of the applied linguists, they are often personally involved in teaching reading, or feel a responsibility to the L2 teaching community. Neither Rayner and Pollatsek nor even Just and Carpenter have much immediate relevance for the classroom teacher. Goodman had a major effect partly because it was easy to apply his main precepts.

The value of a model, for researchers, is that it has the ability to gather together previously diverse experiments and can focus attention on different aspects of a problem, and prevents the emergence of a rash of experiments without any organising principle. If we look, for example, at Gough's bottom-up model, we can see how it invites experiments in areas such as feature recognition, phonological processing, and grammar. The fact that the psychologists have made little headway in experiments with grammar does not invalidate this claim.

The way forward

1. We think applied linguists should become more familiar with the cognitive psychology literature.
2. In particular, we should concentrate on experimental methods, and on a wider range of models. To this extent we agree with Bernhardt.

3. With all respect to Ridgway (1996), we do not think it is useful for applied linguists to put forward rival models to account for low-level processes. On the whole we have neither the equipment nor the training.
4. We think we would be justified in proposing new models, if necessary, for higher level operations. We are better versed in the methodological procedures appropriate for such strategy research.
5. We should concentrate on maximising our advantages in the strategies field: access to readers in real learning situations, familiarity, even expertise, in certain areas of use.

This chapter contains three sections. In Section 5.1, we start by suggesting a set of possible criteria for judging models of the reading process from a utilisation-focused perspective, i.e. what value do they have for improving teaching, testing and researching reading? We then look at how one could obtain empirical data concerning the types of reading we have described earlier in the book. We discuss this in terms of the ad hoc model we adopted in Section 2.4, which includes a goalsetter, a monitor, as well as a sentence processor.

In Section 5.2 we suggest research that applied linguists and classroom teachers can conduct on the relationship between reading and grammar. We have criticised applied linguists for not defining their terms with sufficient rigour. In response to this – and also in response to 'grammar' tests which contain material we do not think is appropriate – we devote a considerable amount of time in this section to defining the scope of syntax.

Finally, in Section 5.3 we focus on the use of language testing to investigate the componentiality of reading in a second language. In Section 3.2 above we voiced our concerns about the methodological shortcomings of a lot of previous research in this area. In particular, we were troubled by the narrow careful view of reading most earlier studies were premised on. It is the belief of the authors that testing procedures are a valid and reliable way of improving our understanding of the components of reading in L2 and the relationships between them in terms of both construct overlap and level of ability. The findings of such test-driven research should enhance both the teaching and the formative and summative evaluation of these abilities. A principled set of procedures is offered for such investigation.

5.1 MODELS AND DIFFERENT TYPES
OF READING

We have mentioned in the introduction to this chapter the desirability of operating with models of reading. A very ad hoc model has been referred to in Section 2.4, and use will be made of it in the second part of this section. We begin, however, with a discussion of the criteria for evaluating models, since not all are suitable for research in the areas of teaching and testing. In the second part of the section, we look at possible research aimed at discovering what reading behaviours are available to L2 readers.

Criteria for judging models of the reading process

The criteria we propose here do not constitute an exhaustive list for judging how perfect a model is in describing the complex process of reading, but serve to judge the operationalisability of the models of the reading process for the purpose of improving the teaching and testing of reading.

One of the valuable sources for our discussion of the judgement criteria is from Samuels and Kamil (1988) who raise a number of questions that should be considered in evaluating models of the reading process. Their criteria emphasise the generalisability of the models: 'Because of the interactive nature of the variables in a study, we must attempt to evaluate the different models in terms of their generalisability' (Samuels and Kamil, 1988: 26).

De Beaugrande (1981) also proposed sixteen criteria for model designing. Using these criteria, he characterised ten alternative models of reading or understanding, including Chomsky, the Clarks, Gibson, Kintsch, Meyer, Frederiksen, Schank, Rumelhart, Woods, and the author's model. But he laid emphasis on proposing

> a set of design criteria that can serve to construct comparative profiles of process models for reading research . . . they are useful in promoting functional consensus by allowing diverse domains to be characterised in a common descriptive idiom.
>
> (de Beaugrande, 1981: 263)

We are concerned with the implications of the process models for the practice of teaching and testing. We shall therefore focus on those criteria that help us judge if a particular model can serve the purpose. However, some of the ideas in de Beaugrande's design criteria and in Samuels and Kamil's evaluation criteria are valuable for our discussion and are thus incorporated into the three broad categories of judgement criteria we propose, that is, accessibility, comprehensiveness and falsifiability, which are summarised in the following list, developed with Jin Yan of Shanghai Jiaotong University, PRC.

CRITERIA FOR JUDGING MODELS OF THE READING PROCESS

(A) Criteria of accessibility
The accessibility criteria evaluate the practical value of the reading process model. In the study of teaching and testing of reading, the first and foremost concern is that the model should be accessible to teachers, teaching material developers, syllabus designers, and test developers.

(A1) *Clarity of the process*
Does the model unpack the complex process of reading in terms of the practical concerns of teachers and testers such as language skills, processing strategies and knowledge sources so that it is within the grasp of the majority of teachers and testers?

(A2) *Implications for teaching and testing*
Can the model directly shape the teaching and testing objectives and provide guidance on teaching task design, teaching methodology, test formats, item types and text selection?

(B) Criteria of Comprehensiveness
Comprehensiveness judges the extent that a model can be applied to various targeted processes of reading, that is, different readers in different reading contexts. It addresses the problem unsolved in many models, that is, for different types of readers, for different purposes of reading, and for different types of texts, the processes of reading in terms of strategies and skills may vary.

(B1) *Types of reader*
Does the model adequately describe both fluent readers and beginning readers?

(B2) *Purposes of reading*
Does the model describe reading across a variety of tasks and purposes?

(B3) *Types of text*
Does the model describe the reading process for different types of reading materials?

(B4) *Scale of processing*
Does the model describe the word recognition process as well as higher level comprehension processes?

(B5) *Transferability*
Is the model of the first language reading process generalised enough so that it can be transferred to the second language or foreign language reading process?

(C) Criteria of falsifiability
Falsifiability refers to the degree that a model can be subjected to empirical tests and thus be supported, proved or improved by the evidence.

(C1) *Empirical evidence*
Has the model been substantiated by empirical evidence?

(C2) *Predictability*
How well can the model predict and explain the reading behaviour in psychological experiments?

(C3) *Replicability*
Are the experiments on which the model is based replicable by other researchers?

(C4) *Openness*
Can the model accommodate new insights accrued from empirical studies without requiring a fundamental change of the design?

Investigations of types of reading

Here we research into the different styles of reading available to L2 readers. We use as a reference point the model we proposed in Section 2.4, and the classification of reading styles put forward there. We see this research as taking place largely in the L2 reading classroom; this affects the resources and equipment suggested, since any experimental techniques must be confined to those practical in the normal classroom. The focus, however, is not on teaching methodology, but on the application of a description of different reading styles, our 'model', in an L2 context. In general, we are concerned with such questions as:

- Do the learners have access to all the different styles mentioned in the model?
- If not, do they have access to some, or are they restricted to one style?
- Are some styles more accessible than others?

In addition, in light of what was said in the introduction to this research section, we are concerned with possible methodologies for investigating these questions.

We should reiterate that our model presented in Section 2.4 is not intended to be a 'proper' process model of reading – that is, it is not fundamentally based on empirical findings about the reading process. To some extent, it is in part indirectly based on such findings, since it is derived from Just and Carpenter. The intent of setting it out, however, is primarily to direct attention towards certain aspects of reading behaviour which we consider fundamental for our readers, and to focus attention on possible areas of empirical investigation.

As we mentioned in Section 2.4, we have added to the Just and Carpenter model two additional components, namely a *goalsetter*, and a *monitor*. We have included the goalsetter to emphasise that there are different purposes for reading, and that different purposes are likely to result in different reading behaviours. Many writers agree in principle that readers should be flexible about their reading behaviour. Thus Gibson and Levin (1974: 548) argue that 'flexibility of reading style is of the greatest importance' and Rayner and Pollatsek (1989: 452) say that it is 'generally accepted ... that the ability to be flexible in reading is a characteristic of better, more mature readers'. The decision by the latter writers to concentrate on careful reading was taken largely because that sort of reading is best researched, and also, possibly, because it is the easiest to observe. However, statements such as 'When you read a passage of text, your primary aim is to comprehend the passage' (Rayner and Pollatsek, p. 449) tend to obscure the differences between different reading behaviours, and hence, we think, justify our emphasis.

While agreeing with the view that readers should be flexible, Baker and Brown (1984: 30) suggest that 'there are students who still fail to set their own purposes, reading everything at the same rate'. It is our experience, and that of many L2 teachers, that L2 readers often exhibit this sort of reading deficit. In Section 2.4 we suggested five fairly conventional types of reading – namely, scanning, search reading, skimming, careful reading at a local level, and careful reading at a global level – and the research proposed below is designed to find out how many of these types are available to L2 readers (see also Sections 3.2 and 4.3 for an extended discussion of these).

The goalsetter

The goalsetter represents the readers' purpose. In life outside the classroom and examination hall, readers choose their own purpose in reading. In the examination hall, in particular, however, the readers have little choice but to conform to the wishes of the examiners. Hence we can relate purpose to test task. This near equation of goal and task is of particular importance to us in that we consider the importance of task to have been underrated in aspects of the literature, e.g. in discussion of skills transfer. For us, 'comprehension' can best be described as the successful accomplishment of a particular reading goal or task. If there is no real purpose in reading, then the outcome cannot be measured. In this we agree with Kintsch and van Dijk (1978: 374):

> In many cases, of course, people read loosely structured texts with no clear goals in mind. The outcome of such comprehension processes, as far as the resulting macrostructure is concerned, is indeterminate.

We would add, however, that the text need not be 'loosely structured', and that it is not just the macrostructure which is likely to be indeterminate. As said before, it is for this reason that we eliminated from our list this reading style, which we termed 'browsing'.

The monitor

The notion of cognitive monitoring has been part of the reading construct for more than a decade. Baker and Brown (1984: 22) define it as:

> The ability to use self-regulatory mechanisms to ensure the successful completion of the task, such as checking the outcome of any attempt to solve the problem, planning one's next move, evaluating the effectiveness of any attempted action, testing, and revising one's strategies for learning, and remediating any difficulties encountered by using compensatory strategies.

They add that:

> Since most of the cognitive activities involved in reading have as their goal successful comprehension, a large part of cognitive monitoring in reading is actually comprehension monitoring.

In our model, the monitor is closely connected to the goalsetter. Its principal task is to keep a running check on whether the goal(s) are being achieved. Thus, it is important to realise that the monitor varies in what it considers successful activity, in terms of the task set by the goalsetter. To drop for a moment into a fashionable computer analogy, the monitor may be 'set' at different values.[4] Thus the monitor should demand different standards of behaviour when the reader is, for example, scanning, as compared to when the reader is engaged in careful global reading. If readers do not vary the 'setting' of their monitor, then in many cases their goal will not be achieved.

Modes of measuring

In theory it should be possible to investigate the reading process at all the relevant points along the line. We could, for example, investigate the activity of the goalsetter, of the monitor, the success or failure of the sentence by sentence processing activity, as set out in our model, or the product. In practice, it is likely to be difficult to distinguish the contribution of the different components: the product, for example, may be deficient either because the initial formulation of the task was defective, or because the monitor did not operate efficiently while reading was going on. However, we can suggest general areas of investigation, and be more specific when we discuss particular reading styles.

The *goalsetter* may be investigated by interviewing readers as to how they interpreted the task. Alternatively, the relationship between goalsetter and product may be examined. There is ample evidence in the literature of different tasks resulting in different products (Thomas and Augstein, 1972; Rayner and Pollatsek, 1989: 452–3).

Baker and Brown (1984: 23ff) suggest various ways of investigating the *monitor*, including:

- observation of readers
- analysis of oral reading errors
- assessing certainty concerning responses
- cloze procedure
- text disruption.

We are happier with some of these than with others: oral reading has, in our opinion, to be handled very carefully, if at all, in the

L2 classroom. Nevertheless, it is useful to know that some progress has been made towards an established range of investigatory methods.

Since we are distinguishing between expeditious and careful reading, an obvious area of observation is *speed of reading*. In the absence of any more sophisticated method of assessing reading speed, there are two general ways of going about this in the classroom: either the students read a text and are timed doing it, then reading speed is measured in terms of words read per minute (cf. Fry, 1963), or the students are given a reading task and a fixed time in which to accomplish it. On the whole, in the investigations suggested below, we favour the first method. It brings with it, however, the problem of whether to include some measure of success on a reading task, as well as simply speed of reading. Fry, for example, uses multiple-choice comprehension questions to be answered after reading. Since no reference back to the text is allowed, this introduces a memory factor. It may be best simply to instruct readers to read a text at their 'normal' speed, and time their performance. However it is done, when we go on to compare, say, scanning speed with a more careful reading speed, we need some estimate of 'normal' reading speed to use as a base line.

We now proceed to look at the different reading styles, with a view to making suggestions as to how their existence or non-existence may be investigated among L2 readers. We begin with scanning, which might be considered an extreme case.

Scanning

We have already defined scanning as 'reading selectively, to achieve very specific goals', e.g. finding the number in a directory, finding the capital of Bavaria (in a geography or history book). Nuttall (1982) defines it as:

> glancing rapidly through a text either to search for a specific piece of information (e.g. a name, a date) or to get an initial impression of whether the text is suitable for a given purpose (e.g. whether a book on gardening deals with the cultivation of a particular vegetable).

Consideration of these definitions suggests that scanning is not quite the simple concept that we originally thought. The definition we had originally in mind covered instances like finding a solitary numerically expressed date, or finding the word 'Munich'. Neither of these activities, however, seems very natural. A more natural event, such as being asked 'Find the date of the battle of Waterloo', might involve a search for the collocation of Waterloo and a date, but once the reader had found the general area, it also involves a scan towards the beginning, where such introductory information would be likely to occur. A similar situation would arise if one were given a book on the geography of Germany and asked to find the capital of Bavaria.

It looks as if scanning merges with what we have called 'search reading'. In what follows, however, we will stick to examples of what one might call 'extreme' scanning, i.e. activities similar to those carried out by the computer on the instruction '*Find*'. We might add that such activities are very different from 'normal reading'. Rayner and Pollatsek, discussing 'proof reading', query whether the activity has implications for normal reading. We think that scanning, as defined above, may have such implications in an L2 context – a point we discuss below.

When we consult our model, it might seem that all that is involved in scanning, as defined above, is word recognition; there is no need in the cases above for processing the syntax or semantics of the sentence containing the search item, and no need, apparently, for the reader to bring background knowledge into play. In fact, one might conceivably argue that the reader does not even need to access the lexicon, since it would presumably be possible to 'scan' a text for a nonsense word. Certainly, numbers in telephone directories do not require access to the lexicon. We referred above to the facility most popular word processor programs contain for 'finding' particular words. The computer accomplishes this by a process of running through the text, matching each word it comes across with the search item. There is no need for meaning. We don't know of any research involving readers scanning in a language unknown to them; it seems likely that it would be an exhausting experience.

Our principal research aim in this case is to determine whether our L2 readers can scan as well as read 'normally', in other words whether they have access to more than one strategy. A secondary aim, given that the answer to the first question is 'Yes', is to investigate how they are doing it.

The obvious way to investigate the first question would seem to involve comparison between scanning and, say, normal reading. If one just gave the students a text, and told them 'Find the following words in the text', there is nothing to prevent them from plodding through at normal speed, identifying each target word in the course of normal reading. In fact, if they have only one strategy, then this is what they will do. According to our classification of reading behaviours, scanning belongs to the 'expeditious' group, i.e. it should be carried out at a faster speed than normal reading. Hence one way of establishing whether students can scan is first to find out their normal reading speed (which is best done over a number of trials), then find out whether their scanning speed is faster. There are several elementary precautions to take. If we already have a measurement of each student's normal reading speed, then we do not have to worry too much about the length of the text(s) used for scanning. Scanning may seem to require texts of substantial length, which beginning students might find exhausting to read carefully. However, texts used for scanning and careful reading should probably be similar in terms of familiarity and difficulty.

The number of items to be looked for in such a test is presumably a matter of experience. If dates are used (they might seem suitable as a practice to familiarise students with the activity), then only a small number, i.e. 1 to 3, would seem enough. If the instructions are 'Find the following words or phrases', then 1 or 2 would probably be too small, and easily missed. Ten would seem a possible compromise.

We are not restricted to comparative reading speeds as a means for assessing whether scanning or some other reading behaviour has taken place. In a scanning operation, we see the monitor as set at a simple *Yes/No* standard; i.e. is *x* the word the reader is looking for or not? This is the case in a computer *Find* operation. If the answer is 'No', then the search moves on and the last item examined is dismissed from attention. This means that if a scanning operation has been carried out successfully, not only will all the items requested have been identified, but, in theory at least, nothing else from the text has been recovered, i.e. committed to memory. Gibson and Levin (1974: 539) remark that: 'One can scan for a graphic symbol or a word target very fast, but the scanner remembers almost nothing of what he saw except the target.' An examination of the reader's knowledge of the contents of the text just scanned, carried out, perhaps, a few minutes after the scanning period is complete, should reveal that the reader retains little or nothing of the text. Either an interview or a test can be used for this. We have here the odd case when the lower the reader scores on this test, the better.

Pedagogical implications

We have already indicated some doubts as to whether scanning as we have defined it is reading at all. As stated above, Rayner and Pollatsek had doubts as to whether editing tasks had 'implications for normal reading', i.e. whether conclusions based on behaviour on such tasks had any relevance to discussions of normal reading. We think that scanning **is** relevant to L2 reading in two ways.

The first way is partly methodological. In our experience, some L2 readers insist on one style of reading – a relentless, slow plod through the text, beginning at the top left-hand corner, and continuing to the end, the process only broken up in some cases by frequent recourse to a dictionary or to the teacher as a dictionary equivalent. This form of reading behaviour, which can be quite hard to break, may be an epiphenomenon, i.e. a product of previous experience in the classroom. A ruthless insistence on scanning on the part of the teacher may help break this pattern.

The second way is more basic. We have already seen in Section 2.2 the importance that is now attached to automatic word recognition in reading. It is arguable that what makes scanning easy for a good L1 reader is just such recognition; the monitor is able, very quickly, to provide its 'Yes/No' answer. The L2 reader, on the other hand, being less able to distinguish between, say, *blip, flip, bleet, fleet*, etc., is likely to find scanning much more difficult. In fact, it is again arguable that such readers will have to consult the context of a target word in order to identify it. Thus scanning can, at the very least, be used as a useful test of word recognition, not only of the target items but the surrounding items in the text.

Skimming

The reader is referred back to the relevant text of Sections 2.4, 3.2 and 4.3 where we have discussed these strategies in some detail. In Section 2.4 we provided initial working definitions which were then developed in Section 3.2 on testing. In Section 4.3 we tried to break each down further into its constituent enabling operations for use in classroom learning tasks. We define *skimming* as 'expeditious reading carried out for the purpose of extracting gist'. It thus contrasts strongly with our description of *scanning* (see also Appendix 1 for working definitions used in the Chinese Advanced English Reading Test).

Authors **are** in agreement as to the value of skimming. Nuttall considers that skimming (together with scanning) enables the reader 'to select the texts, or the portions of a text, that are worth spending time on', thus suggesting that skimming is a preliminary to careful reading. Rayner and Pollatsek (1989: 447) remark that:

> Skimming . . . is a very important skill in our society. In careers that depend on the written word, there is simply too much information to be assimilated thoroughly, and we are constantly forced to select what we look at. Those unable to skim material would find they spend their entire day reading.

Rayner and Pollatsek equate 'speed reading' with skimming, and say that:

> speed readers appear to be intelligent individuals who already know a great deal about the topic they are reading and are able to successfully skim the material at rapid rates and accept the lowered comprehension that accompanies skimming.   (p. 448)

The *gist* which we mentioned above should be something like a reduced form of Kintsch and van Dijk's macrostructure. A look at the model will suggest that, in the process of skimming, even if an entire sentence is processed, the reader will not necessarily proceed to the next text sentence. The process is therefore selective, some parts of the text being omitted. In turn, and keeping in mind Kintsch and van Dijk's model, this means that coherence relations between different propositions in the text are likely to be sacrificed in the act of skimming. It follows from this that, if the product of the skimming is to be coherent, then background knowledge is going to have to play an increased role in the build up of the macrostructure. Rayner and Pollatsek consider that the successful speed reader (i.e. skimmer) already knows a lot about the topic.

It seems to us, then, that the efficiency with which L2 readers skim a text is likely to depend crucially on their knowledge, either of the topic of the text being skimmed, or the structure of the text, or both, and that this is likely to be even more the case than with careful reading. This familiarity may come either from previous reading in the L2, or from their previously acquired literacy in the L1.

Given that tasks aiming to induce skimming can be framed with sufficient clarity, and that the readers are familiar with what is expected of them, more than one hypothesis can be derived from the above discussion.

- On the same text, or on texts of equivalent length and difficulty, reading speed when in skimming mode will be significantly faster than when in careful reading mode.
- Macrostructure built up on the basis of skimming should be significantly less detailed than that acquired through careful reading. If the skimming is efficient, however, the propositions omitted from the macrostructure should be the lower level, more detailed ones.
- Skimming performance should be significantly reduced if the readers are exposed to texts of unfamiliar structure.

Obviously experimental work designed to test these hypotheses would incorporate timed reading, as well as recall protocols elicited after the reading was complete. A useful controlled exercise in teaching skimming consists of students being given very general, high-level questions before they read, for example 'give a title for the passage'. This method could be used together with while-reading observation of students to find out how they proceeded to answer the questions. Signs of skimming might be rapid movement between pages, possible regression back across pages, as well as rapid completion of the exercise. Self-report protocols might also provide insightful data (see Cohen, 1998).

Careful reading

With careful reading, we are in a somewhat different position concerning speculation as to what strategies are available to students. It would be the view of many teachers of reading that students are definitely able to read carefully both locally and globally, whereas this might not be the case for our other posited types of reading. This may or may not be a valid assumption. The hypothesis would be that students would perform significantly better on questions aimed at careful reading than on other types of reading (see Section 5.3 below). Also, their speed of reading in the former would be similar to their speed when timed during 'normal reading' sessions.

Kintsch and van Dijk (1978: 371) speculate that:

> If a long text is read with attention focused mainly on gist comprehension, the probability of storing individual propositions of the text base should be considerably lower than when a short paragraph is read with immediate recall instructions.

Their first case concerns skimming, in our terms; the second is an instance of what we would refer to as careful local reading.

When comparing our two types of careful reading (global and local), it is obvious that speed is not going to be an issue. We can concentrate on other aspects of the reading process, an important one being performance on tasks (see Section 5.3 below). In Section 3.2 we reported evidence of L2 students performing better on global as opposed to local questions. It looks as if some L2 readers, at least, are using background knowledge to compensate for linguistic deficiencies when reading for global meaning. An attractive area of research here would be to locate such students, then investigate in detail their reading behaviour at low levels as described in the model, i.e. lexical access, syntactic and semantic processing, and establishment of cohesive links.

Conclusion

The pedagogic literature frequently refers to careful reading, skimming, scanning, as well as 'intensive' and 'extensive' reading. We have indicated that we do not think these types have been defined with sufficient clarity in the literature. We have attempted in Chapters 2, 3 and 4 to clarify the differences and establish operational definitions for the five 'main' skill and strategy groupings. It is our hope that if a number of researchers can be persuaded to work in the areas discussed above, and if they publish their results with due attention paid to texts and methods used, together with full description of the students involved, we may acquire a solid set of empirical data support and help to develop pedagogical practice.

We now turn from general considerations of theory and how this might be developed to a particular area in the pedagogy of reading that we feel is in urgent need of investigation by teachers, testers and researchers. In our discussion of how to investigate the relationship between the teaching of grammar and its impact on reading ability, close attention is paid to the definition of terms as the authors feel this to be the *sine qua non* of acceptable research.

5.2 READING AND THE TEACHING OF GRAMMAR

Introduction

As the research topic related to the teaching of reading, we are suggesting an investigation of the relationship between the teaching of reading in the classroom and the teaching of grammar. We have chosen this topic for a number of reasons. First, we do not believe it has ever been systematically investigated. We share Bernhardt's surprise that there has been so little work in this area (Bernhardt, 1991a). Secondly, it would probably be generally agreed that the processing of syntax, as part of the wider processing of written information, is a 'low level' skill, and, as Eskey (1988) has argued, such skills have tended to be neglected in the teaching of reading in a foreign language. Thirdly, it seems to us that many FL teachers have an interest in and knowledge of grammar, so that the topic should be accessible to them.

A pedagogical approach

We should make clear that, in proposing this topic, we are not querying the view that knowledge of grammar plays a part in the reading process. All the models of reading reviewed in Section 2.1 either assert or assume that syntactic knowledge is a component, and we see no reason to question this. What we are proposing is an investigation into whether the *teaching* of grammar in the L2 classroom has a discernible effect on the students' ability to read the L2. The research is thus pedagogically focused.

Having chosen this research topic, the most obvious focus of interest concerns whether a conscious, taught knowledge of grammar has an effect, hopefully beneficial, on students' reading performance. There are, however, other areas of interest involving grammar which it would be worth while to examine, e.g. whether there are particular areas of grammatical knowledge which seem to correlate positively with reading performance.

What follows is not intended to be an outline of a specific research programme, rather an indication of how we think research might be carried out in a particular area. Because we have criticised other writers for lack of clarity in the use of terms, we shall spend rather longer than perhaps expected in discussing terms, particularly the term 'grammar'. We are strongly of the opinion that, unless the researcher has a clear idea of what is meant by this term, any results obtained will be immediately open to criticism.

Grammar and the reading syllabus

Over the past fifty years, the relationship between grammar and reading in the EFL syllabus, at least, has tended to resemble the man and woman in the old-fashioned devices forecasting weather: when one is in, the other is out, and vice versa. In the era when structural linguistics was an important influence on L2 theory, skills such as reading were hardly considered to form part of the syllabus. The assumption was that students should be taught the structures of the language, or at least the most important of them. Then they would, of their own accord, presumably, use their know-ledge of these structures, together with their knowledge of vocabu-lary (which was also a rather down-played area) to speak, write, read and listen. Reading, if considered at all as an issue, was seen as a matter of transfer, whether in the L1 or L2 domain. This is the position adopted by Fries (see p. 22). When a structuralist such as Lado approached the question of language testing, his first concern was to divide the language tested into three linguis-tic areas – phonological, lexical and syntactic – together with a catch-all area referred to as 'cultural' (Lado, 1961, cited in Baker, 1989). And while Lado then proceeded to describe four areas of language use – namely, reading, writing, listening and speaking – structuralism had little or nothing to contribute to use areas. It is true that Fries *did* make a contribution, by describing the parallel-ism between phonemic and graphemic contrasts; this is, however, basically all the contribution that he could make which was par-ticular to reading. Structuralism had (and has) little or nothing to say about such topics as levels of information, inferencing, strat-egies, or the part played by background knowledge.

As Baker (1989: 37) points out, tests in the structuralist tradi-tion gradually developed into

> a 'diluted' version of the original in which the rigid and system-atic testing of elements at each level has given way to a more homely collection of categories: 'reading comprehension', 'grammar', 'vocabulary', etc.

The same development was true of the teaching syllabus, with 'structures' forming the core, and other elements such as 'reading comprehension' added without any theoretical justification in terms of linguistics. Much the same might be said of teaching material which remained uninfluenced by the structuralist tradition; we often find in textbooks passages labelled 'reading comprehension', along with some test questions, accompanied by grammatical and vocabulary exercises. There is often little obvious relationship between the text and grammar. At best, and this is by no means always the case, the text can be seen as supplying data for the grammar.

When communicative language teaching became fashionable, the study of syntax as a separate component was downgraded for at least two reasons: (a) with a concentration on skills, syntax, not being classed as a communicative skill, tended to be omitted; (b) it was argued that since all the skills incorporated syntax, a separate course component was unnecessary. Talking about Communicative Language Teaching (CLT) in general, James, in Johnson and Porter (1983: 110), says:

> The teaching of structure was condemned early on. Indeed, many of the CLT persuasion saw it as axiomatic that they should not teach the structures of the target language (TL) but something else, something rather less tangible, usually its 'functions'. If you think this an exaggeration, recall that an early CLT course, Abbs et al. (1975), was condemned as being 'cryptostructural' simply because it contained discernible structural content.

For syllabuses focusing exclusively on macro-skills areas such as reading and writing, the position taken by those criticised by James is intellectually tenable. Alderson (1993) claims that there has recently been a move back to teaching grammar, but the best way of combining grammatical elements with reading in a syllabus still needs considerable thought.

The meaning of 'grammar'

We have been talking as if 'grammar' was an unambiguous term. This is not, however, the case, as will be discussed below. The problem can be illustrated initially by reference to an example of a grammatical test item from Heaton (1988: 9):

A: ....does Victor Luo ....?
B: I think his flat is on the outskirts of Kuala Lumpur.

There are a number of problems about this item viewed as a test of grammatical knowledge. The obvious way of completing A's utterance is:

'**Where** (does Victor Luo) **live**(?)'

and no doubt this is the response favoured by the tester. But the question arises as to what kind of knowledge is involved in producing this answer. Even if we accept the item in the spirit in which it is offered, it is hard to see how a response like 'Why does Victor Luo commute?' could be rejected. A much more general objection is that the semantics of the lexical items plays an important part in the formulation of the 'correct' answer: one could argue that on strictly 'grammatical' grounds the selection of **any** 'wh-' interrogative word to fill the first gap, and/or **any** intransitive verb, e.g. *eat, drink, cope, ululate*, to fill the second gap, would be difficult to reject. Probably most important of all, any appropriate completion of A's utterance involves recognition that the two utterances form an *adjacency pair*, and that the first part must be completed in such a way that it forms an appropriate question to which the second utterance is the answer. This, however, is not what is normally considered to be 'grammar'. If we used a number of such items as a 'grammar' test in our research, we would be very vulnerable to the charge that what we were testing was a lot more than 'just grammar'.

There are two well-known uses of the term 'grammar' in modern linguistics. The first use is the traditional one adopted by Crystal (1997), namely 'just one branch of language structure, distinct from phonology and semantics' (p. 89). This is the use probably most familiar to teachers in L2 and is the one adopted here. The other use is that of Chomsky and other writers in the transformational tradition, where it means all the systematic patterns of language, e.g. Cook (1988: 29):

> ... the grammar must show how the sentence is pronounced – the sequence of sounds, the stress patterns, the intonation, and so on; what it actually means – the individual words, the syntactic structures, and so on; and how these are related via various syntactic devices.

Such writers use the term 'syntax' as their equivalent to the traditional use of 'grammar' Here we shall use 'grammar', in the traditional sense, to refer either to syntax or to syntax and grammatical morphology, what Quirk et al. (1972) refer to as 'morpho-syntax'.

We still are faced with the problem of deciding on the scope of syntax, i.e. what comes under 'syntax' and is therefore to be included in our research, and what is outside, a different language level. Here we find problems since, while many linguists will agree that language can be divided into different components, and even on the components themselves in general, the boundaries between them vary between different models and between different versions of the same model over time. Horrocks (1987: 24) points out that 'there is no general agreement about the location of the boundary between morphology and syntax'. Since we are including both under 'grammar', this may not be a major problem, but where to place the boundary between syntax and semantics definitely is one. Again, Horrocks (1987: 30) remarks:

> There is thus every reason to expect that the 'borders' between different components will be drawn in different places at different times and that a phenomenon confidently described as syntactic will come to be regarded as semantic or lexical at a later date.

Examples include the inclusion in the 'Aspects' model of transformational grammar (Chomsky, 1965) of selectional restrictions, so that a sentence like '*John elapsed' would be considered as grammatically – as opposed to semantically or lexically – ill-formed; case grammars contain far more 'semantic' information than other, more syntactically based models; a trend over a number of years, in several models, has been the inclusion in the lexicon of operations which would previously have been left to the syntactic component (see Brown, 1984).

Defining syntax

Such divergences can also be found in pedagogical texts. Some pedagogical grammars, e.g. Allen (1974), Berman (1979), Shepherd et al. (1984) include '*Reported Speech*' among obviously syntactic structures such as the *Passive, Defining/Non-defining clauses* (Berman), *Infinitive and Gerund* (Allen). By contrast, in Morgan and Batchelor (1959) '*Direct and Indirect Speech*' is a separate component from '*Grammatical Study*', being placed beside '*Punctuation*' and '*Style and Vocabulary*'. Thus in the early textbook, *Reported Speech* is clearly (and correctly) not being viewed as a strictly syntactic phenomenon. More generally, the grammar by Downing and Locke (1992) contains far more 'communicative' information than does that of Quirk and Greenbaum (1973) which, while eclectic, is more determinedly structural.

Definitions

Sampson (1975) defines syntax as '. . . how words are put together to form sentences'. According to Horrocks (1987: 24):

> Syntax is concerned with the principles according to which words can be combined to form larger meaningful units, and by which larger units can be combined to form sentences.

For Crystal (1997) syntax is 'the way in which words are arranged to show relationships of meaning within (and sometimes between) sentences'. As aspects of sentence syntax, he mentions hierarchy, grammatical function, concord, and transformations (pp. 94–7). Even in these brief definitions there appear to be some significant divergences. For example, Horrocks, to some extent, and Crystal, in particular, seem to attach much more importance to meaning than does Sampson. Crystal's inclusion of relationships between sentences would be rejected by many. Hence it may be useful to examine, rather than definitions, writers' accounts of general aspects of syntax.

General principles

Bolinger (1975) considers that 'the first rule of syntax . . . is that things belonging together will be together'. As well as this principle (which is certainly true for English, but seems less true for, say, classical Latin), he cites, as coming inside the scope of syntax, operators, both grammatical morphemes and function words, the structure of phrasal constituents, word classes (even though he claims the classes are 'basically semantic'), grammatical, logical and psychological functions (e.g. 'subjects', 'objects', etc.), the grammatical functions of sentences (e.g. declarative, imperative, transformations), and 'higher sentences' (e.g. performatives).

Horrocks and Crystal both refer explicitly to meaningful syntactic relationships. As will be seen later, just how much meaning is involved in syntax is an important question for the type of research we are investigating, and will be reviewed later. In Halliday and Hasan (1976) there is a suggestion that the difference between grammatical and lexical meaning is a question of generality, grammatical items being more general than lexical ones, e.g.

The general words (e.g. 'thing', 'person', 'idea') . . . are on the bor-
derline between lexical items and substitutes.

(p. 280; our parentheses)

Bolinger returns on more than one occasion to the notion that
grammar (syntax and morphology) is primarily concerned with
intra-language relationships (an example is the role of the com-
plementiser 'that' which functions to show that a following clause
is embedded), whereas semantics is concerned with 'real-world'
relationships. A similar notion can be found in Halliday and Hasan,
where *reference* relations are 'semantico-pragmatic' while *substitution*
acts at the 'lexico-grammatical' level (pp. 88ff). Bolinger, however,
points out that the distinction is difficult to maintain. In the phrase,
'Jane's house', the possessive morpheme refers to a relationship
in the real world: Jane either owns or occupies the house. In the
phrase 'Jane's cooking', on the other hand, the same morpheme
serves to show that 'Jane' is the grammatical subject of the verb
'cooking'. Hence the distinction, while undeniably there, is of
little use in determining what is syntactic and what is semantic.

General principles, while interesting, appear to be insufficient
to decide with some degree of precision what does or does not
constitute 'grammar' or 'syntax'. Faced with this problem, we have
two choices: either we can define, say, 'syntax' operationally, saying,
in effect, 'this is what we consider to be syntax for the purposes of
this research', or we can adopt a particular model, saying, in effect,
'this is a model of syntax; anything described by the model therefore comes within the bounds of syntax'.

A formal model

At this point we ought to come clean and state that what we are
really looking for is a 'formal', 'structuralist' model, with as little
recourse to 'meaning' or 'communicative value' as possible. Given
the general popularity in recent language teaching of approaches
stressing meaning or communication, this would seem a rather
strange, even perverse, approach to take. And in taking it, we are
not, of course, decrying the importance of meaning or of communication. We have, in fact, two reasons for our preference. The
first is related to what we discussed earlier with reference to the
Heaton example: unless we are very clear about what we mean
about grammar, our research will be open to criticism that it

incorporated a lot more than just grammar. We believe that adopting a formal approach minimises this danger.

Our second reason will become clearer as we progress, but concerns the fact that we see one aspect of the research as correlating performance on grammar/syntax tests with performance on reading tests. It seems clear that the more text-focused or 'communicative' our grammar model is, the closer our grammar tests based on this model will be to tests of low-level reading skills. There is, however, little point in correlating such tests with reading tests: little can be learned by correlating A with A. Therefore, we would argue, we should begin, at least, with seeing whether we can find a correlation between linguistic competence, measured by a test of formal syntax, and linguistic and communicative performance, measured by a reading test.

Choosing a model

We are looking, then, for a formal model of grammar, one which sets out to describe the permissible (grammatical) sequences of words or formatives in the sentences of whichever language we are concerned with. However, we quickly run into a major problem: while there is no shortage of theoretical formal grammars, particularly in the Chomskyan tradition, they have evolved to a point where they have major disadvantages for the classroom experimenter, being either very difficult and abstract, and hence inaccessible, or insufficiently developed at a descriptive level, or both.

Pedagogical grammars, on the other hand, are predictably less abstract, and are far more accessible to teachers and researchers. However, for understandable pedagogical reasons, they do not limit their description to syntactic structures. For example, in *A University Grammar of English*, Quirk and Greenbaum (1973) provide a quite detailed description of formal aspects of the English verb phrase, but accompany this description with information about the use of verb forms, e.g.:

> In indicating that the action is viewed as in process and of limited duration, the progressive can express incompleteness even with a verb like *stop* whose action cannot in reality have duration; thus *the bus is stopping* means that it is slowing down but has not yet stopped. The progressive (usually with an adverb of high frequency) can also be used of habitual action, conveying an emotional colouring such as irritation.   (p. 41)

Similarly, the *Cobuild English Grammar* (Sinclair, 1990), and related volumes, combines very formal lists of verb patterns with distinctly non-formal information such as:

> You can also use 'be possible to' with 'it' as the subject to say that something is possible. You usually use this expression to say that something is possible for people in general, rather than for an individual person. (p. 239)

Thus theoretical grammars are formal, but inaccessible, while pedagogical grammars are accessible but contain much non-structural information.

As a compromise, we propose that researchers allow a theoretical grammar to set the limits of formal syntax, while filling in the descriptive details from pedagogical grammars. If we choose Government/Binding Theory, for example (see Horrocks, 1987), the Base Component, which includes the Lexicon, will define as syntax the following:

(i)   The structure of lexical phrases, and of the sentence, including embedded sentences.

(ii) Transformations relating, say, Interrogative and other Wh-constructions to declarative structures.

(iii) A huge variety of syntactic restrictions included in the Lexicon. In addition, the morphological component will include information about the parallelism of structures such as 'Newton developed the theory' and 'The development of the theory by Newton'.

It is, of course, a major feature of G/B Theory that it contains a number of subtheories designed to filter out deviant sentences which the Base Component has allowed to be generated. On the whole we do not think these subtheories are relevant to our needs, so we do not detail them.

With the fundamentals of syntax thus outlined by the theory, we can now go to the pedagogical grammars to flesh out the descriptive detail. *A University Grammar of English* appears to be very suitable for details of lexical phrases and embeddings, while the *Cobuild English Grammar,* or the *Cobuild Grammar Patterns 1: Verbs* (Francis et al., 1996) appears highly suitable for verb patterns. This combination description can then be used, at least initially, as the basis for grammar tests in the research outlined below.

Correlational studies

The easiest way of investigating whether a relationship exists in L2 between reading and grammar is to measure students' performance on tests of grammar and reading and then correlate the results. Alderson (1993) did this with a specially constructed 'grammar' test and various modules of the IELTS test then being constructed. He found, in general, high correlations between the grammar test and the different modules. In fact, correlations were high between virtually all the tests:

> The relationship between Reading and Listening is as close as or closer than the relationship between one reading test and other reading tests!   (p. 213)

He concludes that 'the results, then, appear to show that a (vaguely defined) generalized grammatical ability is an important component in reading in a foreign language' (p. 218). It is important to stress that correlational studies of this sort do not point to a causal relationship. Alderson's results, as he himself makes clear, could be interpreted as meaning either that grammatical ability improves reading, or that reading ability improves performance on a grammar test, or that the relationship is the result of a third factor, which he terms 'language proficiency'. Indeed, given the high correlations between all his tests, this last might seem to be the most likely explanation. Moreover, from the point of view of the research being suggested here, correlational studies involve testing but not necessarily teaching. Alderson's tests are proficiency tests, unrelated to any particular teaching syllabus. Nevertheless such studies do highlight certain aspects of the problem which we shall examine before moving on to more pedagogically oriented studies.

First, the test of grammar used must, as far as possible, be just that, i.e. it must relate to a clear definition of what constitutes grammar; hence the extended discussion above. Alderson's test consisted of six subsections: (i) vocabulary; (ii) morphology; (iii) prepositions, pronouns, etc., along with rather vaguely termed 'lexical sets'; (iv) verb forms, etc.; (v) transformations; and (vi) 'reference and cohesion'. In our definition of 'grammar', subsection (i) must be eliminated; the 'lexical sets' of subsection (iii) are doubtful. As far as subsection (vi) is concerned, 'reference' is normally treated as a form of cohesion; the latter, if it concerns relationships outside the sentence, will not be classed as syntactic, while identifying pronominal links between cohesive items and their referents, etc., has more to do with pragmatics than syntax. Secondly, as Alderson makes clear, the grammar and reading tests should be as separate from each other as possible. Since most grammar tests involve the students in reading, this is not an easy task. A grammar test can be viewed as a specialised reading test. However, there are a number of steps we can take to reduce the resemblance. We have already said that syntax, in most definitions, is sentence-bound. Comparatively little written text is similarly sentence-bound. Therefore we can achieve some measure of difference by making our grammar test consist of decontextualised sentences or phrases. This will tend to rule out the use of continuous text, as in cloze procedure, or the gap-filling of continuous text recommended by Heaton (1988) and used by Alderson.

It was largely this wish to have the widest possible distance between grammar and reading that influenced the discussion above in the direction of strictly formal, as opposed to more functional or semantic, grammars. Alderson classes the test he used as 'communicative' on the grounds that 'we wished to test a student's ability to process and produce appropriate and accurate forms in meaningful contexts', justifying this on the grounds that 'the ability to manipulate form without attention to meaning is of limited value and probably rather rare' (p. 218). In general we would agree, but consider that this argument is irrelevant for our research; in **reading** we would require a student to process appropriate forms in meaningful contexts. What we are investigating is whether a knowledge of formal syntax is of help in this activity.

Alderson refers to 'meaningful contexts' and the undesirability of teaching 'form without attention to meaning'. The question of meaning is a particular problem in the context we are discussing. Since reading involves the extraction of meaning, it is clear that any grammar test involving a heavy emphasis on meaning is likely to overlap with reading tests. When listing a number of grammar test-types, Heaton remarks that they test 'the ability to recognize or produce correct forms of language rather than the ability to use language to express meaning, attitude, emotions etc.' (p. 34). However, one of his types involves matching sentences like 'Tom ought not to have told me' with possible paraphrases. From the viewpoint of G/B Theory, this looks like the interface between syntax and semantics. Significantly, Heaton (1988: 35) remarks that 'such an item may be included either in a test of reading comprehension or in a test of grammar'. We would like to restrict such items **either** to grammar tests **or** to reading tests, and would suggest that if they are included in grammar tests, care should be taken to exclude inferences, together with the referential and sense meanings of lexical items.

Beyond correlations

Correlations, if they exist, between performance on syntactic and reading tests are interesting and worth while examining. However, the research design touched on above involves what have traditionally been termed proficiency tests, i.e. they are not constructed with reference to a particular syllabus. This conflicts with our stated aim at the beginning of this section, namely to investigate the relationship between reading and a taught syntactic component. In addition, as pointed out above, correlations do not establish causes, only relationships. If we want to test whether a taught grammar course has a measurable effect on subsequent reading performance, we need a different research design.

A pedagogically more relevant research design would involve comparison between one group, the experimental group, and an equivalent group, the control group. Both groups are given a reading *pre-test* at the beginning of the experimental period. Ideally there should not be a significant difference between the means of the two groups, but this is not strictly necessary. During the experimental period, which would probably extend over a term or semester, the experimental group is taught grammar, according to a grammar syllabus based on the topics outlined above. Normal reading instruction could continue, but should be kept separate from the grammar instruction. During this time the control group gets the same reading instruction, but is not given the grammar classes, having some other activity, preferably not related to reading, put in their place. At the end of the experimental period, both groups are given a reading *post-test*. The null-hypotheses are: (a) if there was no significant difference between the groups on the pre-test, there should be no significant difference on the post-test; (b) neither group should show a significant improvement in scores on the post-test as compared to the pre-test. If, on the other hand, either of the null-hypotheses was overturned, this would be evidence that grammar teaching had the effect of improving reading performance. We should perhaps add, as a third possibility, that a significant effect may be found, but will be negative, i.e. that the grammar teaching had a detrimental effect on reading. Care would have to be taken that the grammar component was taught as formal grammar, i.e. that 'communicative' elements were excluded as much as possible. Given the emphasis placed nowadays (probably rightly) on the value of such communicative emphasis, this might be a problem for some teachers. However, our own experience has been that students are quite receptive to formal grammar, so this may not be a major problem. It should be noted that in this research design, a grammar test is not strictly necessary, though it could be included.

A number of such experiments, conducted with different groups of students in different places, should establish whether the teaching of formal syntax, at least, had a beneficial effect on reading performance.

Refining the grammar syllabus

So far, we have not attempted to distinguish different items of what we earlier defined as syntax. In the research projects outlined above, we have assumed that any item on our list is a valid one for inclusion in a syntactic test or syllabus. However, it may be that, for reading, certain parts of the syntax component are more important than others. Discussing the relationship between language elements and communication, Heaton (1988: 10) comments:

> There is also at present insufficient knowledge about the weighting which ought to be given to specific language elements. How important are articles, for example, in relation to prepositions or pronouns?

We can focus Heaton's general query on reading in particular. For adequate comprehension of the quotation above, how important is the presence of the single article '*the*'? In fact, how important are articles at all for reading comprehension? If, following Heaton's line, we were to eliminate prepositions from the quotation, then it becomes much more difficult to read (admittedly the original quotation contains six prepositions as opposed to one article). To pursue this argument would be to attempt to devise a grammar syllabus focused on reading, as opposed to, say, one focused on writing or speaking, a *receptive* as opposed to *productive* syllabus.

It has to be admitted that producing such a syllabus would be a fairly impressionistic endeavour. (It is worth while also pointing out that the grammar syllabuses to which we are accustomed in textbooks may well be biased towards written language already (cf. Brown and Yule, 1983), and that, in terms of language teaching in general, a really innovative aim would be to produce a grammar dedicated to *spoken* language.) However, it may well be worth the attempt to devise a grammar syllabus specifically with reading in mind. First thoughts might include decisions to give priority to prepositions over articles, declaratives over interrogatives, and simple as opposed to continuous verb forms. More generally, such a syllabus might include a heavy focus on constituent structure of phrases, clauses and sentences. Given the suggestion, often made, that a primary task in sentence-processing is to find subject and verb, exercises practising this and similar tasks might well be made prominent. An alternative, or additional, focus might be placed on distinguishing heads from modifiers and complements. Given what has been said above about the role of syntactic restrictions in the lexicon, yet another focus might be to focus more on vocabulary from a syntactic perspective, directing the students' attention to, for example, the types of complement taken by a wide range of different verbs.

Grammar and texts

The suggestion made above that declaratives and simple verb forms are more relevant than interrogatives and continuous forms is based on the fact that, in the case of, say, expository study texts, interrogatives and continuous forms are comparatively rare. This raises the question of whether a grammar course could be focused on a particular written *genre*. We claimed in Chapter 3 that the grammar exercises commonly found accompanying texts in conventional textbooks often showed little sign of having been designed to help the students read the texts. It remains to be seen whether a more focused approach would have a wider and transferable effect.

Grammar and different kinds of reading

Inspection of the reading model we put forward in Chapter 2 suggests that grammatical competence will be involved in different degrees in different kinds of reading. In the Just and Carpenter model on which our model is based, each sentence is processed grammatically before the next sentence is accessed. In our speculative description of different reading behaviours, we suggested that this need not always be the case. With *scanning*, for example, it seems possible that no grammatical processing need take place at all. All that is necessary for success in extreme cases is for a word or phrase to be recognised. At the other end of the scale, *careful local reading* would seem to depend heavily on successful syntactic processing. *Careful global reading* might seem to come in between these extremes, since the larger part played by background knowledge might compensate for at least some local grammatical processing.

A teacher or researcher could investigate these hypotheses by organising a syntax course, followed by a series of tests aimed at testing students' performance on different kinds of reading. It is suggested at the level of test design that different tests should take place at different times; the use of a single test requiring a number of different reading types would probably result in contamination of results. The aim would be to measure correlations between a syntax test and tests of scanning, careful local reading, etc. The use of a control group, i.e. another class or group of students, would not be necessary here since the main focus of interest would be on differences between correlations. If our hypothesis is correct, and grammar affects different types of reading differentially, then we would expect a score on scanning to correlate least with a score on the syntax text, etc.

Conclusions

Grammar is a component of reading which has been almost ignored in the research. It seems to us that this is an interesting and potentially valuable research area which L2 teachers and applied linguists are in a good position to investigate.

5.3   THE USE OF TESTS TO INVESTIGATE COMPONENTIALITY IN READING RESEARCH

In the previous section we have stressed the importance of defining terms clearly and adequately as the basis for valid and reliable research. In addition to a clear idea of what is to be investigated, research needs to be credible to an outside audience in terms of design, sampling, methodological procedures, analysis and reporting. It should be logical with clear progression from research questions through data collection, analysis, conclusions and recommendations. Crucially it should be systematic with clearly stated procedural rules not only to guard against threats to validity and reliability but also to allow replicability by other researchers.

Davies (1990) has described language testing as the cutting edge of applied linguistics. He supports this argument by suggesting that one of the single most effective measurement tools for exploring the nature of language proficiency or language acquisition is the language test. We share the view and believe that language tests offer a reliable and rigorous means for exploring the componentiality of reading though we are also well aware that there are a number of qualitative procedures that can produce data that complement those generated by language tests.

Language tests tell us little of the processes that underly reading and we need to employ different methodological procedures to investigate these. In particular, introspective methods may help shed light on underlying thought process (see Cohen, 1987; Cohen et al., 1979; and Rankin, 1988). Olson et al. (1984) point out a number of problems associated with the method, such as the time taken to administer and analyse, limited sampling and sensitivity to instructional variables. However, methods such as introspection and retrospection may offer insights into the perceived processes that take place during different types of reading and help us understand the nature of the differences in processing as well as the existence of such differences.

In this section we are limited by space. Our concern is thus with the latter, i.e. componentiality, the issue of the divisibility of the construct, rather than unpacking the mental processes. The discussion below is, accordingly, for the most part limited to testing. This should not be taken to signify that we consider other methodological procedures, or the investigation of process, as being any less important.

Research is only as good as the tools that are used to operationalise constructs. Inadequacies or limitations in these will constrain the value of any research. In order to investigate the componentiality of reading systematically, we need to develop maximally valid operationalisations of what we believe to be the important elements of that construct in the form of texts and associated tasks. This is not just the concern of researchers. Anyone who teaches reading in the language classroom is putting into practice his or her view of the construct of reading every time reading-connected activities are carried out by their students. Any of these activities are open to investigation to evaluate their worth in relation to impact on students' reading abilities.

We propose below a number of *a priori* and *a posteriori* procedures, which constitute a systematic approach to investigating the componentiality of the reading ability of students principally through testing. They should help illuminate whether reading is a unitary activity or whether it is made up of separable components, for example: expeditious types of reading as in search reading, skimming, scanning for specifics, and careful reading at the global and local levels. They will tell us about the relative contribution of the posited skills and strategies to the overall picture of a student's reading ability. They will tell us about the relationship between these components and inform us of the relative weaknesses and strengths of our students. Whether for formative or summative purposes, such evaluation can impact on whole educational systems as well as individual classrooms.

These procedures (*mutatis mutandis*) should be applicable to the development of any reading test from national to classroom level. Within the constraints of the classroom all of the procedures may not be practical at one particular point in time, but every teacher should be aware that, to produce the most accurate picture of a student's transitional performance in reading, all have a contribution to make. The data from these procedures are all grist to the construct validity mill. They can all shed light on what it is we are measuring and how well we are doing this. The more of these we can embrace in our research investigations into reading the better founded might be our findings.

There are no short cuts in rigorous research. This does not mean it is the preserve of the few or the well resourced. Small-scale research systematically carried out can be synthesised to provide real advances. What is required, however, is a comprehensive

but common framework of description of what is to be investigated available to researchers, teachers and testers as well as the
development of systematic procedures that allow full comparison
across studies. Language testing encourages explicitness in specification and through its potential systematicity offers the possibility
of generalising beyond a particular study.

An overview of the research methodology to investigate the componentiality of reading is presented below. The exemplification
is from our investigations into EAP reading in China (see Appendix 1) and in Egypt (see Khalifa, 1997). However, the methods
and approach are generic and should for the most part apply to
all reading situations.

A METHODOLOGY FOR INVESTIGATING THE EAP READING CONSTRUCT

Stage 1: Specification of the construct

STRATEGIES AND SKILLS and the CONDITIONS under which these activities are
performed might be established through:

- Target situation analysis
- Theoretical literature
- Research literature
- Document analysis: course-books/tests

Stage 2: Development of pilot tests to operationalise EAP reading specification

2.1 A priori *validation*
  2.1.1 *Systematic mindmapping of appropriate texts*
  2.1.2 *Produce pilot version of test(s)*
  - Decide format
  - Allow for attrition in texts and items
  - Ensure intelligibility of rubrics
  - Empirically establish timing
  - Consider order of questions/process dimension
  - Check layout
  - Trial on small samples
  - Produce first draft of mark scheme
  - Moderate tasks and mark scheme in committee

2.2 A posteriori *validation*
2.2.1 *Trial on reasonable sample*
2.2.2 *Item analysis*
  ■ Facility values
  ● Discrimination
2.2.3 *Estimates of reliability*
  ■ Marker reliability
2.2.4 *Estimates of internal validity*
  ■ Internal consistency
  ● Correlations
  ■ Principal component analyses
  ■ Level: Means, *t*-tests and cross-tabulation
2.2.5 *Estimates of external validity*
  ■ Qualitative expert judgement of items
  ■ Qualitative introspection/retrospection by test-takers
  ■ Feedback from test-takers (interview/questionnaire)
2.2.6 *Revise*
  ■ Administrator's instructions
  ■ Items
  ■ Timing
  ■ Rubrics
  ■ Mark schemes
  ■ Re-trial any new items

Stage 3: Research study proper
Administration of Revised Version of test(s) to a representative sample
of intended population.

3.1 *Item analysis*
  ■ Facility values
  ● Discrimination
  ■ Internal consistency
  ■ Descriptive statistics, *t*-tests, cross-tabulations

3.2 *Estimates of internal validity*
  ■ Correlations
  ■ Principal component analyses
  ■ Measures of level

3.3 *Estimates of external validity*
  ■ Correlation with other established measures of the construct
    (including teachers' estimates)
  ■ Feedback from test takers.

Specification of operations and performance conditions in an EAP reading construct

There are a number of steps that we can take to try to ensure that we come closer to achieving construct validity in our measuring instruments in terms of mirroring the skills/strategies underlying the various types of reading whose empirical existence we wish to establish.

- We need to be clear about the nature of such type(s) of reading in terms of a framework of operations and performance conditions established from the theoretical and research-based literature and document analysis.
- We have to establish, for selected text(s) we are considering using in a test, what would constitute an understanding of that text given closely defined purposes for reading it, arrived at on the basis of target situation analysis.
- Finally we have to establish appropriate test development procedures to establish test items that were most likely to elicit those reading behaviours in a testing mode.

Example

To establish a specification of operations and performance conditions to be tested we pursued a number of avenues in the development of the Advanced English Reading Test (AERT) for undergraduates in China (see Appendix 1 for background to the project and for details of the specification). The following tasks were carried out:

- A needs analysis of reading in the EAP context through document inspection, interviews, group discussion and questionnaire demonstrated the need for expeditious reading strategies/skills as well as careful reading; for coping with longer (1000–3000 word texts) as well as shorter texts (<1000). It emphasised the need to select texts from journals and books rather than newspapers.
- A review of theories of the reading process and available research findings (together with the needs analysis) showed the need for embracing a wider view of reading which would take into account expeditious reading as well as the more usual careful reading and for considering comprehension at the global as well as the local level.

- An analysis of current learning tasks used in teaching materials in reading English for Academic Purposes demonstrated the need to go beyond the traditional concern with slow careful reading to include tasks focusing on quick, efficient, selective reading and raised the issue of prediction activities in relation to activating existing schemata.

- An analysis of test tasks used in assessing reading English for Academic Purposes showed, among other things, the importance of providing a purpose for each reading activity; the importance of controlling time spent on each activity; the importance of establishing a minimal and maximal level of topic familiarity; the types of format that lent themselves to the testing of the various operations.

These data clarified the nature of reading operations across discipline areas in the Chinese academic context and led to the specification in Appendix 1. These investigations also provided data on the conditions for reading activities in EAP. The specifications for performance conditions in the Chinese AERT are also listed in Appendix 1. Once appropriate operations and conditions are established these have to be implemented in a test.

A priori validation

Textmap content of texts to establish content to be extracted according to purpose for reading

Potentially appropriate texts for a test population should initially be selected by a moderating committee from a bank of such texts on the basis of as close a match as possible with the performance conditions laid out in the specifications (see Section 3.3 for a discussion of these conditions). The committee would at the same time need to confirm that the texts selected allowed the testing of the intended operations.

A practical method of doing this is to establish the content that might be extracted from a text in line with the established purpose for reading it. Various systems of text analysis are proposed in the literature (see Section 2.2, *text structure*) but, though impressive in their attention to detail and replicability/reliability, they consume inordinate amounts of time and the end results do not necessarily enable the researcher or test developer to decide which are the important ideas in a text for testing. A more utilisation-focused procedure is to try to establish the main ideas of a passage through expeditious or careful 'textmapping' procedures (see Buzan, 1974; Geva, 1980, 1983; Nuttall, 1996; Pearson and Fielding, 1991).

In each textmapping procedure an attempt should be made to replicate a single type of reading on a single text, e.g. *reading a text slowly and carefully to establish the main ideas.* The product of the particular reading of a text can be compiled in the form of a spidergram or as a linear summary. This is first done individually and then the extent of consensus with colleagues who have followed the same procedure is established. The objective of the procedure is to examine whether what we have decided is important, is in line with the specified type of reading activity and matches what colleagues consider important (see Sarig, 1989, for an interesting empirical investigation of this procedure).

This is a crucial first step in trying to ensure the validity of our tests. We would be concerned that the answers to the questions we then wrote revealed the important information in the text that could be extracted by the particular type of reading being assessed. An ability to answer the items should indicate that the candidate has understood the passage in terms of successful performance of the specified operation(s).

To illustrate the technique of textmapping and to demonstrate how this can help to summarise in note form the products of reading a text for a variety of purposes, we give an example in Appendix 2 of the procedure for textmapping a text for developing a test of careful reading.

The procedure would remain the same for other skills and strategies but the key conditions of

- time allowed for the textmapping
- length of text

would alter in line with discussion on performance conditions presented in Section 3.3 above.

The parts of the EAP reading construct in the exemplification below are expeditious and careful reading at both global and local levels (see Section 3.2 and 4.3 above for a discussion of these issues). We would, therefore, want to test these strategies/skills using different passages (to ensure the independence of items and to avoid the possibility of muddied measurement). For this reason a different set of procedures is necessary for each to reflect as closely as possible the processing behind each of those skills or strategies.

It is important to note that the time for the textmapping task provides a benchmark for the actual test time. All too often test constructors take considerable periods of time reading and re-reading texts and they peel off deeper and deeper levels of meaning. They then give candidates 20 minutes or so to reach the same depth of understanding under exam conditions. This is obviously a nonsense. The candidates would not normally be expected to find answers to questions in a shorter period than it has taken the test setter. Conversely, if one wishes to test expeditious strategies then the time/text length ratio should not allow test takers to process in a careful non-selective fashion.

The textmapping procedure represents a principled way of avoiding this particular threat to the test's validity. If it can be done with students who are at a suitable level of reading ability drawn from the population who will eventually take the test, this may be even more valid than using language or subject specialists to perform this activity.

Produce pilot version of tests(s)

Decide format

Procedures such as textmapping should enable us to determine in a principled fashion what we might wish to test. However, the format, which acts as the vehicle for testing reading activities, may constrain the operations and conditions we attempt to include. Therefore, as well as carefully specifying the latter we need to consider carefully the method we are going to use so as to minimise the influence of method on measurement of the trait (see Section 3.4 above for a detailed discussion of methods available). The cardinal rule remains, however. We must first decide what types of reading we want to test and develop systematic procedures for deciding the micropropositions and/or macropropositions that we would expect candidates to extract from texts in performing these types of reading. Only then do we consider test formats and decide which will most faithfully mirror the procedures and allow the appropriate propositions to be extracted. No matter how neat or efficient the format, if it compromises what we are trying to test it must be rejected. Any threat to the validity of the measurement must be resisted.

Write more questions, and use more texts, than you will need

The textmapping procedure will provide the content for each section of the test. It will also show whether the passage is suitable for its intended reading purpose. Where it is possible to produce a consensus textmap this, then, needs to be converted into appropriate test items in the format selected. Where consensus is not achieved or the textmapping produces too few items, these texts must be rejected!

Wherever possible it is advisable to write more items than are needed in case some of them do not work. One cannot tell in advance of empirical trialling those items that will work and those that will not. It is best to trial items on small numbers initially, because it may well take two or three attempts before problems in wording are resolved. Try the test on colleagues or a few students at a time. If the test is piloted on all immediately accessible candidates to begin with, then this could be problematic. The important trialling on larger numbers should not take place until it is reasonably certain that the items are working well and any obvious problems have been eliminated.

Careful attention needs to be given to:

- *Rubric*: Are the instructions clear, accessible and unequivocal?
- *Timing*: Is the timing for each reading type on each passage appropriate given the length of the text and the activities we are expecting test takers to perform on it?
- *Order of questions/process dimension*: Do the order of the questions set on a particular passage and the order of the reading types in the test as a whole encourage the reading behaviours we are hoping to test?
- *Layout*: Does the layout help the students to work efficiently through each subtest; does it appear elegant and neat?

Produce first draft of mark scheme

It is important in the piloting to draw up a comprehensive mark scheme of acceptable responses to questions, particularly if a short-answer question format is employed, where variation of wording used in answers has to be accommodated. It is frustrating when later administering the test to the sample proper if an acceptable response arises which necessitates remarking hundreds/thousands of scripts because it has not been included in the mark scheme.

Moderate tasks and mark scheme in committee

It is crucial to set aside time and elicit the co-operation of informed colleagues in closely moderating the test and the mark schemes. This is a key stage of the test development process and failure to go through this procedure is a serious threat to a test's validity. We are too close to the tests, which we develop for research or assessment purposes, and after a while we may not be able to see the flaws.

A *posteriori* validation

Trial on reasonable sample

Once the necessary development preliminaries described above are completed, it is important to trial the test on as broad a sample of the intended population, in terms of ability, as possible and then subject the results to statistical analysis to establish the test's value as a measuring instrument.

It is important at the trialling stage to administer the research instrument to as normally distributed a sample as possible. This might mean purposefully sampling from top, medium and lower universities, institutions, schools and classes within these. Normally distributed data allow the researcher to apply the statistical analysis recommended below to establish how the items in the subtests are functioning. A skewed sample, where the majority of students are too strong or too weak, will not allow the researcher to do this. This is why samples of less than 30 are normally not recommended. The distribution of scores achieved by the sample on the test should allow two standard deviations to fit in either side of the mean. In Figure 5.1 the test is out of 60, the mean is 32.9 and the standard deviation is 9.91. So in this data set we can get two standard deviations (2×9.91) easily either side of the mean. This tells us that we have a distribution approximating to normal and we can continue with the further analysis discussed below.

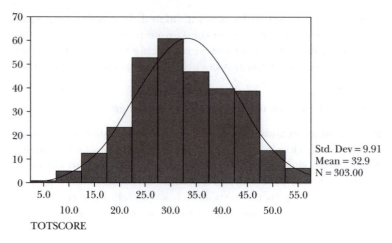

Figure 5.1   Histogram of a reading test.

Statistical analysis

Facility values (mean)

This is based on the percentage of people getting an item right and is usually reported on a scale between 0 and 1 (see column labelled 'Mean' in Table 5.1(a)). If an item is too easy most people will get it right, and if it is too difficult most people will get it wrong. The variance in performance on these items is usually less. This is indicated by the 'SD' column. Item 06 is too easy with 87 per cent of candidates getting it right and there is far less variance associated with this item than the others (SD = 0.33). These items will not usually contribute a great deal to the overall reliability of the test. Item 06 in Table 5.1(a) would appear to require some attention.

In test development it is conventional to use items whose facility values lie between 0.2 and 0.8. Having established the facility value of each item the next step is to examine whether the items discriminate between stronger and weaker candidates.

Discrimination

A discrimination index (see '**Corrected item – total correlations**' in Table 5.1(b)) shows how well an item discriminates between the strong candidates (based on overall performance) and weak candidates on each item. The index is based on a scale from 0 to

Table 5.1(a)   Descriptives of AERT Section 1 Careful reading

Number of valid observations (listwise) = 303.00
Number of items = 15

Variable	Mean	SD	Minimum	Maximum	Valid N
ITEM 01	0.73	0.45	0.00	1.00	303
ITEM 02	0.72	0.45	0.00	1.00	303
ITEM 03	0.36	0.48	0.00	1.00	303
ITEM 04	0.67	0.47	0.00	1.00	303
ITEM 05	0.57	0.50	0.00	1.00	303
ITEM 06	0.87	0.33	0.00	1.00	303
ITEM 07	0.71	0.45	0.00	1.00	303
ITEM 08	0.71	0.45	0.00	1.00	303
ITEM 09	0.51	0.50	0.00	1.00	303
ITEM 10	0.48	0.50	0.00	1.00	303
ITEM 11	0.64	0.48	0.00	1.00	303
ITEM 12	0.61	0.49	0.00	1.00	303
ITEM 13	0.26	0.44	0.00	1.00	303
ITEM 14	0.25	0.43	0.00	1.00	303
ITEM 15	0.69	0.46	0.00	1.00	303

1 and 0.2 is often taken as the cut-off point for acceptable discrimination. Items 02 and 06 are not discriminating very well and both would need to be considered carefully for exclusion.

Discrimination is important in developing the reading test battery because it demonstrates that an item can reliably discriminate between a person who has the ability and a person who does not. It may well be that, on samples of students who take the test later because they are all good or weak, such discrimination is lacking. This does not matter if the item has been shown to discriminate in the piloting on a normally distributed representative sample of the large potential population.

There may be cases where an item tests comprehension of an important idea and we have to decide whether we can accept a low facility value and a lower positive index of discrimination. A negative discrimination index is never acceptable. The validity of what we are testing must always come first. If the main idea of a passage proves easy to extract, so be it. The text has been selected as representative of the domain the respondent has to cope with on a principled basis.

Table 5.1(b)   Reliability analysis: scale (alpha)

Statistics for scale

Mean	Variance	SD	No. of variables
8.7888	8.8095	2.9681	15

Item – total statistics

	Scale mean if item deleted	Scale variance if item deleted	Corrected item – total correlation	Alpha if item deleted
ITEM 01	8.0627	7.9331	0.2690	0.6711
ITEM 02	8.0693	8.1442	0.1802	0.6820
ITEM 03	8.4257	7.8148	0.2832	0.6695
ITEM 04	8.1155	7.8177	0.2935	0.6681
ITEM 05	8.2145	7.6128	0.3481	0.6605
ITEM 06	7.9142	8.3039	0.2069	0.6776
ITEM 07	8.0792	7.8215	0.3072	0.6663
ITEM 08	8.0792	7.7354	0.3429	0.6618
ITEM 09	8.2739	7.8684	0.2459	0.6748
ITEM 10	8.3069	7.5843	0.3536	0.6597
ITEM 11	8.1452	7.7868	0.2960	0.6677
ITEM 12	8.1815	7.8643	0.2573	0.6730
ITEM 13	8.5314	7.8459	0.3146	0.6656
ITEM 14	8.5413	7.9776	0.2642	0.6717
ITEM 15	8.1023	7.6021	0.3869	0.6558

Reliability coefficients: No. of cases = 303.0;   Alpha = 0.6836;
No. of items = 15

Internal consistency

These estimates are often cited as indicators of reliability, but they are just as useful in exploring the construct validity of a subtest. They evidence that items within a subtest are measuring a construct in a similar fashion. Table 5.1(b) provides some data on the internal consistency of a pilot version of a subtest designed to measure careful reading for main idea extraction. You can see the internal consistency data in the column headed 'Alpha if item deleted'. The alpha for the data is given at the bottom of Table 5.1(b) at 0.6836. The 'Alpha if item deleted' column tells us whether an item is contributing to the overall internal consistency of the test. In this case the overall alpha for this component would not be improved by removing any item although it is noticeable that items 02 and 06 are contributing the least among the 15 items.

The data on facility value, discrimination and internal consistency can all help the researcher to take decisions on how to select items which provide the best measure of the construct they wish to investigate through the test(s).

Estimate of reliability

Marker reliability

It is also important to demonstrate that the data have been marked reliably, otherwise the reliability of the results themselves will be affected. It is usual to xerox a number of answer sheets, 30 plus, and to have these marked by all the markers involved in the study. Ideally markers should themselves receive the same set of sheets at a later stage for remarking to establish intra-marker reliability. The reliability of a test is a combination of its internal consistency, inter- and intra-marker reliability. Formulae exist for combining these to provide an overall reliability estimate which will help the reader of the research to understand the extent to which one can depend on the results.

Estimates of internal validity

Correlations

We have suggested that each part of the test should be designed to operationalise a component of the reading process. When the data are available from trialling, the totals for each subtest can be correlated with each other to see the extent to which they overlap. One might also expect that individual items should correlate more with their own subtest than with other subtests. If subtests correlate highly with each other (0.8 and above) this might offer an initial indication that the constructs are overlapping.

To be sure of the relationship between items and components, factor analysis provides a further method for giving a clearer picture of the structure of the underlying data. A commonly used form of this is principal components analysis (PCA).

Principal components analysis

In Table 5.2 you will see an example of PCA that was carried out on data on two reading subtests. Items 1–15 are careful reading items testing global understanding in three passages (we looked at the item analyses of these above) and items 46–60 are careful reading items testing local comprehension in three passages.

The discerning reader will note that items 1–15 load positively on the second factor, whereas items 46–60 all load negatively. This is partial evidence supporting the view that the reading construct may well differ in respect of these two components. Such data indicate that the two types of reading the test designers intended to test do appear to load on different factors, and this is contributory evidence for the separability of these two skills.

Level: means, *t*-tests and cross-tabulation

Correlations tell us about the relationship, the degree of 'overlap', between constructs but they do not tell us about levels of ability in the respective constructs. Two abilities may be distributed in a similar fashion across a population but proficiency in one may be much higher or lower than in another.

Analysis does not always have to be highly sophisticated. The purpose of statistics is to lay out the data set so as to facilitate interpretation. We could examine the descriptive statistics related to one subset of items and compare it with another. The **mean** scores would tell us the levels obtained in both and **t-tests** would tell us whether the differences were significant, i.e. if they had been achieved by chance or whether they represented a real difference in performance.

In Table 5.3 two subtests (TOTCARE, items 1–15, and TOTLEXI, items 46–60) are compared in terms of the means of the whole sample (303). In this example the candidates are performing significantly better on the global (TOTCARE) as against the local comprehension items (TOTLEXI) by almost one and a half points. Such overall means tell us how the population is behaving.

In Figure 5.2 (p. 287) there is a cross-tabulation of the performance at the individual level on TOTCARE, the careful reading global items (1–15), as against TOTLEXI, the careful reading local items (46–60), which clearly illustrates that respondents had

Table 5.2 Principle component analysis

Careful global (Section 1) vs Careful
local (Section 5)
Extraction 1 for analysis: 1, Principal
Components Analysis (PCA)
PC extracted.   3 factors

Factor matrix:

	Factor 1	Factor 2	Factor 3
Item 01	0.35419	0.07147	0.24566
Item 02	0.25198	0.02516	0.32407
Item 03	0.39938	0.04971	0.32812
Item 04	0.36344	0.19864	0.09796
Item 05	0.35125	0.41042	0.43283
Item 06	0.22666	0.13507	0.46428
Item 07	0.38603	0.19247	0.20150
Item 08	0.37549	0.34387	−0.09751
Item 09	0.20756	0.48369	0.19068
Item 10	0.47791	0.09945	−0.01514
Item 11	0.41513	0.03979	−0.05306
Item 12	0.35698	0.20657	−0.57466
Item 13	0.42686	0.12114	−0.16013
Item 14	0.31132	0.29858	−0.26518
Item 15	0.42710	0.42185	−0.42105
⋮			
Item 46	0.43179	−0.33806	0.11272
Item 47	0.50645	−0.31203	0.11268
Item 48	0.30775	−0.09041	0.09677
Item 49	0.24747	−0.07246	0.26668
Item 50	0.33496	−0.23607	−0.01828
Item 51	0.42613	−0.13725	0.04570
Item 52	0.32176	−0.34385	−0.03447
Item 53	0.27668	−0.41138	−0.06872
Item 54	0.24263	−0.14900	0.06010
Item 55	0.37222	−0.31271	−0.14617
Item 56	0.47017	−0.11028	−0.10293
Item 57	0.38027	−0.03741	−0.18228
Item 58	0.38288	−0.30800	−0.01056
Item 59	0.51289	−0.01229	−0.19782
Item 60	0.41676	−0.02467	−0.07180

Final statistics:

Factor	Eigenvalue	% of Var.	Cum. %
1	4.19728	14.0	14.0
2	1.77580	5.9	19.9
3	1.60594	5.4	25.3

Table 5.3   TOTCARE and TOTLEXI compared through a t-test

Variable	No. of pairs	Corr	2-tail Sig	Mean	SD	SE of Mean
TOTCARE				8.7888	2.968	0.171
	303	0.442	0.000			
TOTLEXI				7.3696	3.094	0.178

| Paired differences | | | | | |
Mean	SD	SE of Mean	t-value	df	2-tail Sig
1.4191	3.203	0.184	7.71	302	0.000
95% CI (1.057, 1.781)					

greater difficulty with the latter than with the former. These cross-tabulated data are summarised in Figure 5.3 which provides an even clearer view of the potentially differing performance abilities in these two areas. With a notional pass mark of 60 per cent (9/15) substantially more would fail the local but pass the global careful reading test (85) than vice versa (31).

If these data reported in the analyses above were to be repeated using differing measures and different samples, then we might begin to synthesise an argument for the divisible nature of the reading construct.

Estimates of external validity

Internal statistical measures are necessary but not sufficient to establish the nature of the reading abilities under investigation. We need to get a closer idea of what is actually happening during the test experience to accumulate evidence that the test is performing in an ecologically valid fashion, i.e. in answering the items the students are processing as the test developer/researcher intends them to. For example, if test takers were using test-taking strategies to avoid skimming or search reading through faulty item construction, the test statistics would not necessarily tell us this. We need to generate data on the process as well as the product. We shall examine a number of ways in which this might be done including survey, introspection and retrospection.

| | TOTLEXI | | | | | | | | | | | | | | | | |
TOTCARE	0.00	1.00	2.00	3.00	4.00	5.00	6.00	7.00	8.00	9.00	10.00	11.00	12.00	13.00	14.00	15.00	Total
0.00										1							3
1.00			1		2												3
2.00				1			2		1								8
3.00			1	2	3												11
4.00		1	1	2	2	2	2	1	1	1							18
5.00		1	1	2	1	1	2	3	4	1	1						26
6.00	1	1	4	6	5	3	3	5	2	2	2	1					28
7.00	1	1	6	2	5	5	7	5	2	2	2				1		40
8.00		1	2	2	4	5	5	7	5	3	3	4	1				38
9.00			3	3	4	4	4	5	3	2	2						40
10.00			2	1	4	5	4	6	9	4	2	2	1				40
11.00				2	2	1	4	3	2	4	5	3	2	1			26
12.00				2	2	2	3	2	4	3	5	3	1	2			25
13.00			1		4	2	5	5	2	1	2	3	2	2			23
14.00					1	2	2	2	2	1							13
15.00																	1
Total	2	4	10	24	22	24	28	41	36	33	29	24	12	5	9	0	303

Figure 5.2 Cross-tabulation of total careful reading and total lexical items.

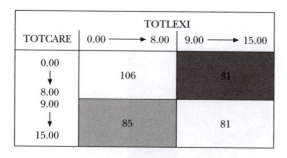

Figure 5.3   Summary of cross-tabulation in Figure 5.2.

Structured feedback from test takers

The intentions of the test developer are always mediated by the response of the test takers. Their attitude to facets of the test are as important as the evidence arising from the statistical data as it can often explain why things have happened in a certain way.

In a feedback questionnaire one might wish to establish test takers' perceptions of, for example,

- topic familiarity
- difficulties with language in a text
- domain specificity of content
- domain accessibility
- familiarity with formats
- value of formats
- sufficiency of time
- clarity of rubrics
- length of test
- whether test likely to achieve its objectives.

An extract of a pilot questionnaire used in the Advanced English Reading Test (AERT) project in China is shown in Figure 5.4 (pp. 290–1).

Data from structured questionnaires of this type are important because they give us a broad based view of how the sample is responding to the test. A lot of the features examined through these sample questionnaires might impact adversely on the measurement of the construct if we have not done a proper job at the development stage. They act as a check on our ability to faithfully implement the test specification. As well as this broad-spectrum data we also need more in-depth information on our test items.

This is provided by qualitative research procedures such as introspection, retrospection and expert judgement. As well as data relating to students' perceptions of the instruments, texts and tasks, we are also interested in their views on what they thought the items in the test were actually getting them to perform in terms of the skills and strategies in our posited construct. Qualitative data obtained from introspection, retrospection and questionnaire survey would provide us with process information on what the test takers thought the test was testing. This would usefully complement the quantitative data obtained through test administration.

Introspection

An introspection study into the students' process of reading texts and answering the questions should be carried out to find out what skills and strategies students are using in completing each section of the test. A procedure for this was developed with Shanghai Jiaotong University staff in the AERT project, PRC. The students were trained to think aloud onto tapes in a language laboratory while taking the test. Before the test, a training session was necessary to demonstrate what they were expected to do during the test. Students should be allowed to use L1 if appropriate if necessary in their verbal reports. The data are then transcribed and content analysed in terms of the test operations.

Retrospection

A separate retrospection study enables the researchers to obtain a larger data set (than is possible through the time-consuming spoken protocols) to establish student perceptions of the skills and strategies used in the process of taking the test. This can be carried out in the large-scale trialling of the test. It can be incorporated into the process of doing the test by providing a checklist for candidates to tick after they finish each section of the test (see Table 5.4).

Experts' judgements

Apart from students' introspection and retrospection, language testing experts and reading experts should be asked to give their professional opinion of the constructs being tested. Table 5.4 is

Figure 5.4 Extract from the test feedback questionnaire used in the AERT project in China.

QUESTIONNAIRE TO CANDIDATES

Name: _____   University: _____

Discipline: _____   Candidate No: _____

1. About the passages

Passages	Language difficulty			Topic familiarity			Subject sepcificity			Appropriate discipline		
	H	M	L	N	H	M	L	N	H	M	L	N	AH	ST	ML
1															
2															
3															
...															

H = high;   M = medium;   L = low;   N = no;
AH = arts and humanities;   ST = science and technology;   ML = medical and life science

Figure 5.4 (Cont'd)

2. About time limits

Section	More than enough	Just enough	Not quite enough	Not enough at all
1 Careful reading				
2 Skimming				
3 Search reading				
4 Scanning				
5 Lexical items				

3. General satisfaction with the test

	High	Medium	Low	No
Formats				
Content				
Length				
Time				
Design				
Rubrics				

Table 5.4 Student retrospection/expert judgement sheet

What skill/strategy do you think is tested in each section?
- Please double tick (✓✓) for the primary focus of the skill/strategy tested.
- Please tick (✓) for the secondary focus of the skill/strategy tested if you think there is one.

	Section 1		Section 2		Section 3		Section 4	
	Primary	Secondary	Primary	Secondary	Primary	Secondary	Primary	Secondary
Reading carefully for main ideas								
Reading quickly to get the overall idea of a text								
Reading quickly to search for information on main ideas								

Table 5.4 (Cont'd)

Reading quickly to find specific information: words/numbers/symbols			
Carefully working out meaning of words from context			
Others (please specify)			

an example of the type of proforma that might be used to collect their opinion on the construct validity of the test (designed with Jin Yan and Luo Peng for the AERT in China).

Revision

As a result of the qualitative and quantitative investigations described above the researcher is well equipped to make any necessary amendments to the pilot version of the research instruments to make them more valid operationalisations of the intended construct.

On the basis of the procedures discussed above we would have sufficient data to help us revise our test instruments to ensure that they come closer to performing the job intended.

Using the test to explore the construct reading

Stage 3: Research study proper

When the test instrument(s) have gone through the rigorous development phase described above, we can use them to investigate the nature of reading for the purposes and audience we have in mind. We would administer the Revised Version of test(s) to a representative sample of intended population and then subject the data to the same procedures outlined above in connection with the earlier trialling:

3.1 *Item analysis*
   - Facility values
   - Discrimination
   - Internal consistency
   - Descriptive statistics, *t*-tests and cross-tabulations.

3.2 *Estimates of internal validity*
   - Correlations
   - Principal component analyses
   - Measures of level.

3.3 *Estimates of external validity*
   - Correlations with other established measures of the construct (including teachers' estimates)
   - Feedback from test takers.

These investigations would help provide insight into the nature of the reading construct as defined by the specification and operationalisation in the test(s). They should tell us about

- the unidimensionality or multidivisibility of the reading construct under investigation
- the relative contribution the different parts of the test were making to the measurement of an individual's reading ability
- the relative strengths of the sampled population in the different parts of the reading test
- the nature of individual differences in performance on each of the components.

Conclusion

None of this is easy to follow through. Not all of these things are possible for the teacher in the classroom except over an extended period of time. What is clear, however, is that the more rigorous and comprehensive we can be in our investigations, the clearer the account that is likely to emerge of the nature of reading. Clear specification of what we are trying to teach or test, and soundly conceived methodologies for investigating components and processes, are essential. It is hoped that this book is of some value in this endeavour.

Notes

1. Richard Joung, November 1997.
2. One of the authors teaches British undergraduates, who regularly assure him that the initial sequence [kn] is impossible to pronounce, a judgement that might have seemed strange to their ancestors.
3. This is a broader definition than that used by Bernhardt, who restricts her attention to examination of the reading process.
4. Only for a moment, though. The effect of such analogies is to give a spurious impression of precision regarding fairly vague and ill-understood processes.

Appendix 1

THE DEVELOPMENT OF A SPECIFICATION FOR THE ADVANCED ENGLISH READING TEST (AERT) IN THE PEOPLE'S REPUBLIC OF CHINA

The Advanced English Reading Test (AERT) project was conceived in the context of the teaching of reading in English for Academic Purposes carried out in the third year of Chinese universities. It was clear that the EAP reading was not receiving sufficient attention from university authorities, teachers and students as required by the National College English Teaching Syllabus (NCETS).

The NCETS promulgated in 1985 on the basis of a nationwide comprehensive needs analysis stipulates that the ultimate goal of Chinese EFL learners at the undergraduate level is to gain access to scientific and technical literature through the medium of English. To achieve the goal, an EAP reading course is required for the third-year students who have completed the foundation stage study. However, the course has never been accorded sufficient attention and is sometimes neglected. The lack of an adequate and appropriate assessment tool was seen as a major contributory factor in this neglect.

The aim of the project is to develop an EAP reading test for Chinese third- and fourth-year undergraduates. This should enable universities to monitor and evaluate students' performance in EAP reading over a long period of time. Furthermore, it is hoped that it will bring about a much-needed beneficial backwash effect on the teaching of EAP reading in China.

As we described in Section 5.3 (p. 274), the first step in test development was to investigate the construct of EAP reading through:

1. a literature review of
   (a) the componentiality of reading
   (b) the ESP issue in reading;
2. a survey of Chinese undergraduates' EAP reading needs; and
3. an analysis of EAP reading-teaching materials and test papers
   in terms of task types and text types.

On the basis of these investigations, a taxonomy of EAP reading skills and strategies, and the conditions under which these are performed was specified. In Table A1.1, the **conditions** part of the specification considered facets such as topic familiarity, text length, propositional content, time constraints, and rhetorical structure of texts; the **operationalisations** part of the specification in Table A1.2 comprised the expeditious reading strategies of skimming, search reading and scanning and the skills of careful reading for local comprehension and careful reading for global comprehension.

TEXT SELECTION: SPECIFICATION OF THE CONDITIONS FOR AERT

Here we are concerned with the conditions under which reading activities should be carried out. The needs analysis, the survey of the literature, previous empirical studies, the analysis of existing teaching and testing tasks for EAP reading, and discussions with the AERT management team and reading specialists in the UK have indicated that the following performance conditions would need to be built into the test:

Table A1.1 Requirements for selecting texts for AERT

Conditions	Descriptions
Purpose(s) of reading	To test students' ability to comprehend academic texts and to extract important information from those texts.
Nature of texts	Texts written for a non-specialist audience with informative and interesting ideas.
Source of texts	Chapters from textbooks, journal articles, abstracts.
Rhetorical organisation	Mainly expository texts with rhetorical organisations of comparison, collection of descriptions, problem/solution, and causation.
Propositional features Lexical range	Normally no technical jargon: approximately 7000 words (root forms; functional and subtechnical lexis); academic semi-technical words defined in the syllabus for Section 5.
Topic area	Familiar to students: humanity and management/science and technology/biology and medicine.
Background knowledge	Within students' background knowledge but not totally given; students should not be able to answer test questions from background knowledge without recourse to the text.
Illocutionary features	To inform, to explain, to describe, to advise, to persuade.
Channel of presentation	Normally textual. Some texts might contain graphics.

Table A1.1 (Cont'd)

Conditions	Descriptions
Size of input/length of text	3 short passages (approx. 600–900) for careful reading (global) 15 items 3 short passages (approx. 250–500) for careful reading (local) 15 items 3 long passages (approx. 1000–1800) for expeditious reading (global) 15 items 3 long passages (approx. 1000) for expeditious reading (local) 15 items
Speed of processing	144 minutes for a total of 12 passages: about 60–90 wpm for careful reading; 100–150 wpm for expeditious reading.
Control over skills/strategies	Three passages for each skill/strategy, one from arts and humanities, one from science and technology, one from life and medical science. For careful reading, passages are short and may sometimes have relatively implicit text structure. For expeditious reading, passages are long and may sometimes have relatively explicit text structures.
Control over time spent	Time is strictly controlled both for each section and for each passage within the section. Careful reading (global): 60 minutes, 20 for each passage; Expeditious reading (skimming): 15 minutes, 5 for each passage; Expeditious reading (search reading): 21 minutes, 7 for each passage; Expeditious reading (scanning): 18 minutes, 6 for each passage; Careful reading (local): 30 minutes, 10 for each passage.
Amount of help	General instructions (in Chinese) to candidates are provided 15 minutes before the test. Instructions for each section are clearly written on a separate page in the question booklet and students are reminded to read instructions before texts. Example provided for the truth/false/justification items since candidates are not familiar with format.
Number and ordering of tasks	Order for the five sections: careful reading (global), skimming, search reading, scanning, careful reading (local).
Method factor/response mode	Formats include: SAQ, true/false, table/flow chart/sentence/text completion.
Question/answer in L1/TL	Mainly in English but could be in Chinese if necessary.
Receptive/productive	Mainly receptive, some limited writing involved in SAQ but only brief answers will be required; no more than 10 words.
Explicitness of weighting	All items equally weighted

Table A1.2 A taxonomy of skills and strategies in reading for academic purposes

Types of reading strategies and skills	Expeditious reading strategies		
	Skimming	Search reading	Scanning
Purpose	Processing a text selectively to get the main idea(s) and the discourse topic as efficiently as possible – which might involve both expeditious and careful reading. ■ To establish a general sense of the text; ■ To quickly establish a macropropositional structure as outline summary without decoding all the text; ■ To read more efficiently; ■ To decide the relevance of texts to established needs.	Locating information on predetermined topic(s) (e.g., in the form of questions set on main idea(s) in a text). This normally goes beyond mere matching of words (as in scanning). The process is selective but is likely to involve careful reading once relevant information has been located.	Looking quickly through a text – not necessarily following the linearity of the text – to locate a specific symbol or group of symbols: e.g., a particular word, phrase, name, figure, or date.
Operationalisations	Where appropriate to text-type: ■ Reading title and subtitles quickly. ■ Reading abstract carefully. ■ Reading introductory and concluding paragraph carefully. ■ Reading first and last sentence of each paragraph carefully. ■ Glancing at words or phrases.	■ Keeping alert for words in the same or related semantic field (not certain of precise form of these words). ■ Using formal knowledge for locating information. ■ Using titles and subtitles. ■ Reading abstract where appropriate. ■ Glancing at words or phrases.	Looking for (matching): ■ specific words/phrases ■ figures, percentages ■ dates of particular events ■ specific items in index ■ names.

Table A1.2   (Cont'd)

Types of reading strategies and skills	Expeditious reading strategies		
	Skimming	Search reading	Scanning
Focus	Both global and local.	Both global and local.	Local.
Text coverage	Selective reading to establish important propositions of a text.	Selecting information relevant to predetermined topic(s).	Ignoring most of the text.
Rate of reading	Rapid with some careful reading.	Rapid with careful reading when information is located.	Rapid with some careful reading.
Direction of processing	Sequencing observed.	Sequencing not always observed.	Sequencing not observed.
Relationship with the underlying process(es)	Interactive process involving both top-down and bottom-up processing.	Interactive process. ■ There is more observance of the linearity and sequencing as compared with scanning. ■ Involves some top-down processing, i.e., using formal knowledge. The periods of close attention to the text tend to be more frequent and longer than in scanning. ■ Also bottom-up involved because of close attention to the selected part(s) of the text. The periods of close attention to the text may be less frequent than skimming because of the predetermined searching.	Surface level rather than deep processing of a text. Mainly a bottom-up process: ■ exhibiting a mixture of rapid inspection of the text with an occasional closer inspection; ■ finding a match between what is sought and what is given in a text, very little information [being] processed for long-term retention or even for immediate understanding. (Pugh, 1978: 53) But for some items the top-down process may be involved (i.e. using formal knowledge to look for specific information in a fixed-pattern text, or to draw upon previous understanding established through skimming).

Types of reading strategies and skills	Careful reading skills		
	Understanding a text	Understanding lexis	Understanding syntax
Purpose	Processing a text carefully and thoroughly in order to comprehend main idea(s) and supporting information. To decode all in order to comprehend all. To carefully establish a macro structure for the text.	Lexical inferences are of three kinds: the resolution of lexical ambiguity; the prediction of the meaning of unknown words; the identification of pronominal reference. (Chikalanga, 1991)	When faced with a text whose meaning they cannot untangle, [readers] may be able to identify the constituents of its sentences, e.g. the subject, the verb, and to analyse these if they are complex. (Nuttall, 1996: 78)
Operationalisations	▪ Separating explicitly stated main idea(s) from supporting details through (a) recognising topic sentence(s) (b) recognising lexical indicator(s) ▪ Generating a representation of a text as a whole ▪ Understanding the development of an argument and/or logical organisation	▪ Making **propositional inferences**. Propositional inference is made when the reader uses explicit statements in the text to come to a conclusion that is not explicitly stated, without recourse to knowledge from outside the text. (Chikalanga, 1991)	▪ **Resolving lexical ambiguity**: the reader makes a choice between two or more meanings of a lexical item. ▪ **Predicting the meaning of unknown words**: the reader infers the meaning of unknown words from the context in a text.	▪ **Removing** all the optional elements of complex sentences systematically until only the essentials remain and the bare structure of the sentence is clear. ▪ **Paraphrasing** optional elements of complex sentences one by one, and fitting them into the whole structure to make sense of them.

Table A1.2 (Cont'd)

Types of reading strategies and skills	Careful reading skills		
	Understanding a text	Understanding lexis	Understanding syntax
	■ Distinguishing generalisations and examples	■ **Identifying pronominal reference**: the reader identifies the pronominal anaphoric and cataphoric links within a text.	
	Where appropriate to the text-type:		
	■ Making **propositional informational inferences** which are either referential typically answering questions beginning with *what* and *which*, or spatio – temporal (typically answering questions beginning with *where* and *when).*		
	■ Making **propositional explanatory inferences** which are concerned with motivation, cause and consequences, and enablement, and will often answer questions beginning with *why* and *how*. All the information needed to make propositional inferences is recoverable from the text.		

Types of reading strategies and skills	Careful reading skills			
	Understanding a text		Understanding lexis	Understanding syntax
		These may involve: ■ discovering writer's intention ■ understanding writer's attitude to the topic ■ identifying the addressee ■ distinguishing fact from opinion.		
Focus	Both global and local.	Both global and local.	Mainly local, occasionally global.	Local.
Text coverage	Reading from beginning to end.	Will vary but will be selective.	Normally use of immediate context and on occasion wider context.	Use of immediate context.
Rate of reading	Reading the whole text carefully.	Reading the selected parts carefully.	Reading the selected part(s) carefully.	Reading the selected part carefully.
Direction of processing	Linear and sequential, with regressions if needed.	Not necessarily sequential.	Sequencing not observed.	Sequential with some regression.
Relationship with the underlying process(es)	Mainly text-based bottom-up sequential process with limited top-down process.	Text based. Initially use bottom-up process to identify information from the text and then top-down process kicks in as needed to activate knowledge schemata to help make inferences based on the text.	Mainly bottom-up process. Occasionally with the help of top-down process.	Bottom-up process.

Appendix 2

MAPPING A TEXT – I

Time for the mapping activity should not exceed the actual test time. The aim is to identify items that can be used to test **careful reading at the global level**, that is those which test main ideas.

Text length, c.600 words

(A) Individual work

Stage I: 10–15 minutes

- Read the text carefully to establish the main ideas. Notes may NOT be taken (*see below*).

Stage II: 5 minutes

- Without looking back at the text, write out these ideas as clearly as you can on a sheet of paper.
- Try as far as possible to organise the points in the order you think they appeared in the text.
- Number the points you have made.

(B) Group work

Stage I

- On a master sheet of paper, list the main ideas on which the group members agree.

- Write the number of people who agreed on them, e.g. 4/5 (4 out of 5 agreed).
- Normally agreement of $N-1$ is necessary, i.e. if there are 5 people in the group, at least 4 must have included the point for a consensus.

Notes may not be taken: The aim is to extract only the main ideas/ the macropropositions and to avoid jotting down micropropositions or minor detail. If careful reading is an incremental process then arguably we cannot establish the macrostructure until we have read all the text. By not allowing notes to be taken we are trying to avoid experiences in the past where mindmappers have written down a lot of peripheral detail. If we only transfer important information from working memory to long-term storage then this might be a way of achieving that. Mental rehearsal/monitoring of what is important is an indicator of good reading.

References

Abbs, B.A., Ayton, A. and Freebairn, I. 1975. *Strategies*. London: Longman.

Alderson, J.C. 1978. *A study of the cloze procedure with native and non-native speakers of English*. PhD Thesis. University of Edinburgh.

Alderson, J.C. 1984. Reading in a foreign language: a reading problem or a language problem? In Alderson, J.C. and Urquhart, A.H. (eds), pp. 1–24.

Alderson, J.C. 1990a. Testing reading comprehension skills (Part one). *Reading in a Foreign Language*, **6**, 425–38.

Alderson, J.C. 1990b. Testing reading comprehension skills: getting students to talk about taking a reading test (Part two). *Reading in a Foreign Language*, **7**, 465–503.

Alderson, J.C. 1993. The relationship between grammar and reading in an English for academic purposes test battery. In Douglas, D. and Chappelle, C. (eds), pp. 203–14.

Alderson, J.C. and Hughes, A. (eds) 1981. *Issues in Language Testing* ELT Documents 111. London: The British Council.

Alderson, J.C. and Lukmani, Y. 1989. Cognition and reading: cognitive levels as embodied in test questions. *Reading in a Foreign Language*, **5**, 253–70.

Alderson, J.C. and Urquhart, A.H. (eds) 1984. *Reading in a Foreign Language*. London: Longman.

Alderson, J.C. and Urquhart, A.H. 1985. The effect of students' academic discipline on their performance on ESP reading tests. *Language Testing*, **2**, 192–204.

Allen, J.P.B. and H.G. Widdowson (eds) 1973. *English in Focus*. London: OUP.

Allen, W.S. 1974. *Living English Structure* (5th edn). London: Longman.

Alvermann, D.E. and Moore D.W. 1991. Secondary school reading. In Barr, R. et al. (eds), pp. 951–83.

Anderson, N.J., Bachman, L., Perkins, K. and Cohen, A. 1991. An exploratory study into the construct validity of a reading comprehension test: triangulation of data sources. *Language Testing.* **8**, 41–66.

Anderson, R.C. and Freebody, P. 1981. Vocabulary knowledge technical. *Report No 136.* Urbana: University of Illinois, Centre for the Study of Reading.

Anderson, R.C. and Pearson, P.D. 1988. A schema-theoretic view of basic processes in reading comprehension. In Carrell, P.L. et al. (eds), pp. 36–55.

Anderson, T.H. and Armbruster, B.B. 1984. Studying. In Pearson, P.D. et al. (eds), pp. 657–79.

Aulls, M.W. 1986. Actively teaching main idea skills. In Baumann, J.F. (ed.), pp. 96–132.

Bachman, L.F. 1990. *Fundamental Considerations in Language Testing.* Oxford: Oxford University Press.

Bachman, L.F. and Palmer, A.S. 1981. The construct validity of the FSI oral interview. *Language Learning,* **31**, 67–86.

Back, E. and Harms, R.T. (eds) 1968. *Universals in Linguistic Theory.* New York: Holt.

Baker, D. 1989. *Language Testing: A Critical Survey and Practical Guide.* London: Edward Arnold.

Baker, L. and Brown, A.L. 1984. Cognitive monitoring in reading. In Flood, J. (ed.), pp. 21–44.

Bamford, J. 1984. Extensive reading by means of graded readers. *Reading in a Foreign Language,* **2**, 218–60.

Barnett, M. 1986. Syntactic and lexical/semantic skill in foreign language reading: importance and interaction. *Modern Language Journal,* **70**, 343–9.

Barr, R. and Dreeben, R. 1991. Grouping students for reading instruction. In Barr, R. et al. (eds), pp. 885–910.

Barr, R., Kamil, M.L., Mosenthal, P. and Pearson, P.D. (eds) 1991. *Handbook of Reading Research,* Vol II. New York: Longman.

Bartlett, B.J. 1978. *Top Level Structure as an Organizational Strategy for Recall of Classroom Text.* Unpublished Ph.D. Dissertation. Arizona State University.

Bartlett, F.C. 1932. *Remembering: A Study in Experimental and Social Psychology.* Cambridge: Cambridge University Press.

Baten, L. and Cornu, A.M. 1984. Reading strategies for LSP texts: a theoretical outline on the basis of text function, with practical application. In Pugh, A.K. and Ulijn, J.M. (eds), pp. 190–201.

Baumann, J.F. (ed.) 1986. *Teaching Main Idea Comprehension.* Newark, Delware: IRA.

Baynam, M. 1995. *Literacy Practices.* London: Longman.

Beck, I. 1981. Reading problems and instructional practices. In Mackinnon, G.E. and Waller, T.G. (eds), pp. 55–99.

Beck, I. and McKeown, M. 1991. Conditions of vocabulary acquisition. In Barr, R. et al. (eds), pp. 789–814.

Bensoussan, M. and Kreindler, I. 1990. Improving advanced reading comprehension in a foreign language: summaries versus short-answer questions. *Journal of Research in Reading,* **13**, 55–68.

Bensoussan, M. and Laufer, B. 1984. Lexical guessing in context in EFL reading comprehension. *Journal of Research in Reading,* **7**, 15–31.

Berg, P.C. 1973. Evaluating reading abilities. In McGinitie, W.H. (ed.), pp. 27–34.

Berman, M. 1979. *Advanced Language Practice for EFL.* London: Hodder & Stoughton.

Berman, R.A. 1984. Syntactic components of the foreign language reading process. In Alderson, J.C. and Urquhart, A.H. (eds), pp. 139–59.

Bernhardt, E.B. 1991a. *Reading Development in Second Language: Theoretical, Empirical and Classroom Perspectives.* New Jersey: Ablex Publishing Corporation.

Bernhardt, E.B. 1991b. A psycholinguistic perspective on second language literacy. In Hulstijn, J.H. and Matter, J.F. (eds), pp. 31–44.

Bloom, B.S., Engelhart, M.D., Furst, E.J., Hill, W.H. and Kratwohl, D.R. (eds) 1956. *Taxonomy of Educational Objectives: Cognitive Domain.* New York: David McKay. (See also Bloom, B.S. et al. (eds), Taxonomy of educational objectives. *Handbook I: Cognitive Domain.* London: Longman, 1974.)

Bloome, D. and Greene, J. 1984. Directions in the sociolinguistic study of reading. In Pearson, P.D. et al. (eds), pp. 395–421.

Bloom, D. 1985. Procedural Display. Unpublished manuscript. University of Massachusetts. Amherst MA.

Bloor, M. 1985. Some approaches to the design of reading courses in English as a foreign language. *Reading in a Foreign Language,* **3**: 341–61.

Bolinger, D. 1975. *Aspects of Language* (2nd edn). New York: Harcourt Brace Jovanovich.

Bransford, J., Stein, B. and Shelton, T. 1984. Learning from the perspective of the comprehender. In Alderson, J.C. and Urquhart, A.H. (eds), pp. 28–44.

Bright, J.A. 1965. *Patterns and Skills in English*, Books 1 and 3. Nairobi: Longman.

Bright, J.A. and McGregor, G.P. 1970. *Teaching English as a Second Language*. London: Longman.

Britton, B.K. and Black, J.B. (eds) 1985. *Understanding Expository Text: A Theoretical and Practical Handbook for Analyzing Explanatory Text*. Hillsdale, NJ: LE.

Bronfenbrenner, U. 1976. The experimental ecology of education. *Educational Researcher*, 5, 5–15.

Brooks, C. and Warren, R.P. 1952. *Fundamentals of Good Writing*. London: Dennis Dobson.

Brown, A.L. and Day, J.D. 1983. Macrorules for summarizing texts: the development of expertise. *Journal of Verbal Learning and Verbal Behavior*, 22, 1–14.

Brown, G. and Yule, G. 1983. *Discourse Analysis*. Cambridge: Cambridge University Press.

Brown, K. (1984) *Linguistics Today*. Fontana.

Brown, P.J. and Hirst, S.B. (1983) Writing reading courses: the interrelationship of theory and practice. In Brumfit, C.J. (ed.), pp. 135–51.

Brumfit, C.J. (ed.) 1983. *Language Teaching Projects for the Third World*. ELT Documents 116. Oxford: Pergamon Press, in association with The British Council.

Brutten, S.R., Perkins, K. and Upshur, J.A. 1991. Measuring growth in ESL reading. Paper presented at the 13th Annual Language Testing Research Colloquium. Princeton, New Jersey.

Buck, G. 1990. *The testing of second language listening comprehension*. Unpublished Ph.D. Thesis. University of Lancaster.

Buzan, T. 1974. *Use Your Head*. London: BBC.

Calfee, R.C. and Curley, R. 1984. Structures of prose in content areas. In Flood, J.S. (ed.), pp. 161–80.

Calfee, R. and Hiebert, E. 1991. Classroom assessment of reading. In Barr, R. et al. (eds), pp. 281–310.

Candlin, C. 1984. *Preface*. In Alderson, J.C. and Urquhart, A.H. (eds), pp. ix–xiii.

Candlin, C. and Murphy, D. (eds) 1987. *Language Learning Tasks*. Englewood Cliffs, NJ: Prentice Hall.

Cangiano, V.J. 1992. *Bilingual and ESL approaches to deaf education: perspectives on the reading process.* Master's Thesis. Hunter College, City University of New York.

Carnine, D. and Silbert, J. 1979. *Direct Instruction Reading.* Columbus, Ohio: Merrill.

Carr, T.H. 1985. The development of reading skills. *New Directions for Child Development,* No. 27. San Francisco: Jossey-Bass.

Carr, T.H. and Levy, B.A. (eds) 1990. *Reading and Its Development: Component Skills Approaches.* San Diego: Academic Press.

Carrell, P.L. 1983a. Three components of background knowledge in reading comprehension. *Language Learning,* 33, 183–207.

Carrell, P.L. 1983b. Some issues in studying the role of schemata, or background knowledge in second language comprehension. *Reading in a Foreign Language,* 1, 81–92.

Carrell, P.L. 1983c. Some classroom implications and applications of recent research into schema theory and EFL/ESL reading. First Rough Draft of a Paper to be Presented at the Colloquium on Research in Reading in a Second Language at the 1983 TESOL Convention. Toronto, March 17.

Carrell, P.L. 1983d. Background knowledge in second language comprehension. *Language Learning and Communication,* 2, 25–34.

Carrell, P.L. 1984. The effects of rhetorical organisation on ESL readers. *TESOL Quarterly,* 18, 441–69.

Carrell, P.L. 1988. Interactive text processing: implications for ESL/second language classrooms. In Carrell, P.L. et al. (eds), pp. 239–59.

Carrell, P.L. 1988a. Introduction, in Carrell, P.L. et al. (eds), pp. 1–7.

Carrell, P.L. 1991. Second language reading: reading ability or language proficiency. *Applied Linguistics,* 12, 159–79.

Carrell, P.L. and Eisterhold, J.C. 1988. Schema theory and ESL reading pedagogy. In Carrell, P.L. et al. (eds), pp. 73–92.

Carrell, P.L., Devine, J. and Eskey, D.E. (eds) 1988. *Interactive Approaches to Second Language Reading.* Cambridge: Cambridge University Press.

Carrell, P.L., Pharis, G.B. and Liberto, J.C. 1989. Metacognitive strategy training for ESL reading. *TESOL Quarterly,* 23, 647–75.

Carroll, J.B. 1972. Defining language comprehension: some speculations. In Freedle, R.O. and Carroll, J.B. (eds), pp. 1–29.

Carroll, J.B. and Freedle, R.O. (eds) 1972. *Language Comprehension and the Acquisition of Knowledge.* Washington: Wiley.

Carter, R. and McCarthy, M. (eds) 1988. *Vocabulary and Language Teaching*. London: Longman.

Carver, R.P. 1985. How good are some of the world's best readers? *Reading Research Quarterly*, **20**, 389–419.

Carver, R.P. 1992. What do standardized tests of reading comprehension measure in terms of efficiency, accuracy and rate? *Reading Research Quarterly*, **27**, 347–59.

Cavalcanti, M.C. 1983. *The pragmatics of FL reader–text interaction. Key lexical items as source of potential reading problems*. Unpublished PhD Thesis, University of Lancaster.

Chackray, C. 1979. *Growth in Reading*. London: Ward Lock Educational.

Chafe, W.L. 1972. Discourse structure and human knowledge. In J.B. Carroll and R.O. Freedle (eds), pp. 41–69.

Chall, J.S. 1979. The great debate. Ten years later, with a modest proposal for reading stages. In Resnick, L.B. and Weaver, P.A. (eds), pp. 29–55.

Chall, J.S. 1983. *Stages of Reading Development*. New York: McGraw-Hill.

Chall, J.S. 1984. Readability and prose comprehension continuities and discontinuities. In Flood, J.S. (ed.), pp. 233–46.

Chapman, J. (ed.) 1981. *The Reader and the Text*. London: Heinemann.

Chapman, L.J. 1979a. Confirming use of cohesion ties in text: pronouns. *The Reading Teacher*, **33**, 317–22.

Chapman, L.J. 1979b. Pedagogical strategies for fluent reading. In Chackray, C., pp. 147–154.

Chihara, T., Oller, J. and Chavez-Oller, M.A. 1977. Are cloze tests sensitive to constraints across sentences? *Language Learning*, **27**, 143–51.

Chikalanga I.W. 1990. *Inferencing in the reading process*. Unpublished PhD Thesis. University of Reading.

Chikalanga, I.W. 1992. A Suggested taxonomy of inferences for the reading teacher. *Reading in a Foreign Language*, **8**, 697–710.

Chikalanga, I.W. 1993. Exploring inferencing ability of ESL readers. *Reading in a Foreign Language*, **10**, 932–52.

Chomsky, N. 1965. *Aspects of the Theory of Syntax*. Cambridge, Mass.: MIT Press.

Clapham, C. 1990. Is ESP testing justified? Paper Given at the Language Testing Research Colloquium, San Francisco.

Clapham, C. 1994. *The effect of background knowledge on EAP reading test performance.* Unpublished PhD Thesis. Lancaster University.

Clapham, C. 1996a. *The Development of IELTS: A Study of the Effect of Background Knowledge on Reading Comprehension.* Cambridge: University of Cambridge Press.

Clapham, C. 1996b. What makes an ESP reading test appropriate for its candidates? In Cumming, A. and Berwich, R. (eds), pp. 171–94.

Clarke, D.F. and Nation, I.S.P. 1980. Guessing the meaning of words from context: strategy and techniques. *System,* **8**, 211–220.

Clarke, M. 1979. Reading in Spanish and English: evidence from adult ESL students. *Language Learning,* **29**, 121–50.

Clarke, M.A. 1980/1988. The short circuit hypothesis of ESL reading – or when language competence interferes with reading performance. In Carrell, P.L. et al. (eds), 1988, pp. 114–124.

Clymer, T. (ed.) 1968. *Innovation and Change in Reading Instruction.* Chicago: University of Chicago Press.

Coady, J. 1979. A psycholinguistic model of the ESL reader. In Mackay, R. et al. (eds), pp. 5–12.

Cohen, A. 1987. Using verbal reports in research on language learning. In Faerch, C. and Kasper, G. (eds), pp. 82–96.

Cohen, A. 1998. *Strategies in Learning and Using a Second Language.* London: Longman.

Cohen, A.D., Glasman, H., Rosenbaum-Cohen, P.R., Ferrara, J. and Fine, J. 1979. Discourse analysis and the use of student informants. *TESOL Quarterly.* **13**, 551–64.

Cohen, A.D., Glasman, H., Rosenbaum-Cohen, P.R., Ferrara, J. and Fine, J. 1988. Reading English for specialized purposes: discourse analysis and the use of student informant. In Carrell, P.L. et al. (eds), pp. 152–67.

Collins, A.M. and Quillian, M.R. 1969. Retrieval time from semantic memory. *Journal of Verbal Learning and Verbal Behavior,* **8**, 240–7.

Conant, J.B. 1934. Notes and news: President Conant speaks again. *Modern Language Journal,* **19**, 465–6.

Cook, V.J. 1988. *Chomsky's Universal Grammar.* Oxford: Blackwell.

Cook, V.J. 1992. *Chomsky's Universal Grammar.* Oxford: Blackwell.

Cornu, A.M., van Parijs, J., Delahye, M. and Baten, L. (eds) 1986. *Beads or Bracelet: How Shall We Approach ESP?* Leuven: OUP.

Coulthard, M. (ed.) 1994. *Advances in Written Text Analysis.* London: Routledge.

Cowan, J.R. 1974. Lexical and syntactic research for the design of EFL reading materials. *TESOL Quarterly*, **8**, 388–99.

Cowan, J.R. 1976. Reading, perceptual strategies and contrastive analysis. *Language Learning*, **26**, 95–109.

Criper, C. and Davies, A. 1988. *English Language Testing Service. Research Report 1 (i) ELTS Validation Project Report*. The British Council and the University Examinations Syndicate.

Crookes, G. and Gass, S.M. 1993a. *Tasks and Language Learning*. Clevedon: Multilingual Matters.

Crookes, G. and Gass, S.M. (eds) 1993b. *Tasks in a Pedagogical Context*. Clevedon: Multilingual Matters.

Crothers, E.J. 1972. Memory structure and the recall of discourse. In Freedle, R.O. and Carroll, J.B. (eds), pp. 247–83.

Crothers, E.J. 1978. Inference and coherence. *Discourse Processes*, **1**, 51–71.

Crystal, D. 1997. *The Cambridge Encyclopedia of Language* (2nd edn). Cambridge: Cambridge University Press.

Cumming, A. and Berwich, R. (eds) 1996. *Validation in Language Testing*. Clevedon: Multilingual Matters.

Cziko, G.A. 1978. Differences in first and second language reading: the use of syntactic, semantic and discourse constraints. *Canadian Modern Languages Review*, **34**, 473–89.

Cziko, G.A. 1980. Language competence and reading strategies: a comparison of first and second language oral reading errors. *Language Learning*, **30**, 101–14.

Dansereau, D.F., Collins, K.W., McDonald, B.A., Holley, C.D., Garland, J., Dickhoff, G. and Evans, S.H. 1979. Development and evaluation of a learning strategy program. *Journal of Educational Psychology*, **71**, 64–73.

Davies, A. 1983. The validity of concurrent validation. In Hughes, A. and Porter, D. (eds), pp. 141–5.

Davies, A. 1990. *Principles of Language Testing*. Oxford: Blackwells.

Davies, F. 1995. *Introducing Reading*. London: Penguin Group.

Davies, F. and Greene, T. 1980. *Reading for Learning in the Sciences*. Edinburgh: Oliver & Boyd.

Davis, C. 1995. Extensive reading: an expensive extravagance? *ELT Journal*, **49**, 329–36.

Davis, F.B. 1944. Fundamental factors of comprehension in reading. *Psychometrika*, **9**, 185–97.

Davis, F.B. 1968. Research in comprehension in reading. *Reading Research Quarterly*, **3**, 499–545.

Davis, F.B. 1972. Psychometric research on comprehension in reading. *Reading Research Quarterly*, **7**, 628–78.

Day, R., Omura, C. and Hiramatsu, M. 1991. Incidental vocabulary learning and reading. *Reading in a Foreign Language*, **7**, 541–53.

de Beaugrande, R. 1980. *Text, Discourse and Process: Toward a Multidisciplinary Science of Texts*. London: Longman.

de Beaugrande, R. 1981. Design criteria for process models of reading. *Reading Research Quarterly*, **16**, 261–315.

DeFrancis, J. 1984. *Visible Speech: The Diverse Oneness of Writing Systems*. Honolulu: University of Hawaii Press.

de Leeuw, M. and de Leeuw, E. 1965. *Read Better, Read Faster*. Harmondsworth: Penguin.

de Leeuw, M. and de Leeuw, E. 1990. *Read Better, Read Faster* (new edition). Harmondsworth: Penguin

Devine, J. 1987. General language competence and adult second language reading. In Devine, J. et al., pp. 73–87.

Devine, J. 1988. The relationship between general language competence and second language reading proficiency: implications for teaching. In Carrell, P.L. et al. (eds), pp. 260–77.

Devine, J., Carrell, P. and Eskey, D.E. (eds) 1987. *Research in Reading in English as a Second Language*. Washington: TESOL.

Dhaif, H. 1990. Reading aloud for comprehension. *Reading in a Foreign Language*, **7**, 457–64.

Dornic, S. (ed.) 1977. *Attention and Performance VI*. New York: Academic Press.

Douglas, D. and Chappelle, C. (eds) 1993. *A New Decade of Language Testing Research*. Washington: TESOL.

Downing, A. and Locke, P. 1992. *A University Course in English Grammar*. New York: Prentice Hall.

Downing, J. and Leong, K.L. 1982. *Psychology of Reading*. New York: Macmillan.

Dubin, F., Eskey, D.E. and Grabe, W. (eds) 1986. *Teaching Second Language Reading for Academic Purposes*. Reading, Mass.: Addison-Wesley.

Duffy, G. and Anderson, L. 1981. *Final Report: Conceptions of Reading Project*. Unpublished report. Institute for Research on Teaching, Michigan State University, East Lansing, MI.

Elley, W. 1991. Acquiring literacy in a second language: the effect of book based programmes. *Language Learning*, **41**, 375–411.

Elley, W.B. and Mangubhai, F. 1983. The impact of reading on second language learning. *Reading Research Quarterly*, **19**, 53–67.

Ellis, G. and Mcrae, J. (eds) 1991. *Extensive Reading Handbook for Secondary Teachers.* London: Penguin.

Ellis, R. and Tomlinson, B. 1988. *Reading Advanced.* Oxford: Oxford University Press.

Entwhistle, N., Hanley, M. and Hounsell, D. 1979. Identifying distinctive approaches to studying. *Higher Education,* **8**, 365–80.

Eskey, D.E. 1988. Holding in the bottom: an interactive approach to the language problems of second language readers. In Carrell, P.L. et al. (eds), pp. 93–100.

Faerch, C. and Kasper, G. (eds) 1986. The role of comprehension in foreign language learning. *Applied Linguistics,* **7**, 257–74.

Faerch, C. and Kasper, G. (eds) 1987. *Introspection in Second Language Research.* Clevedon: Multilingual Matters.

Fairclough, N. (ed.) 1992. *Critical Language Awareness, No. 16.* London: Longman.

Fairclough, N. 1995. *Critical Discourse Analysis.* London: Longman.

Fanselow, J.H. and Crymes, R.H. (eds) 1976. *On TESOL 76.* Washington: TESOL.

Farr, R.C. 1968. The convergent and discriminant validity of several upper level reading tests. *Yearbook of the National Reading Conference,* **17**, 181–91.

Farr, R.C., Carey, R. and Tone, B. 1986. Recent theory and research into the reading process: implications for reading assessment. In Orasanu, J. (ed.), pp. 134–49.

Ferguson, N. 1977. The mind's eye: non-verbal thought in technology. *Science,* **197**, 827–36.

Feuerstein, R.P., Klein, P.S. and Tannenbaum, A.J. 1991. *Mediated Learning Experience: Theoretical, Psychological and Learning Implications.* London: Freund.

Fillmore C.J. 1968. The case for case. In Back, E. and Harms, R.T. (eds), pp. 1–88.

Fillmore, C.J. and Kay, P. 1983. *Text Semantic Analysis of Reading Comprehension Tests (Final report, NIE).* Berkeley: University of California, Institute of Human Learning.

Fingeret, A. 1983. Social network: a new perspective on independence and illiterate adults. *Adult Education Quarterly,* **33**, 133–46.

Fingeret, A. 1990. Literacy for what purpose? A response. In Venezky, R.L. et al. (eds), pp. 35–8.

Flood, J.S. (ed.) 1984. *Understanding Reading Comprehension: Cognition, Language, and the Structure of Prose.* Newark, DE: IRA.

Francis, G., Hunston, S. and Manning, E. (eds) 1996. *Cobuild Grammar Patterns 1: Verbs.* London: Harper Collins.

Fransson, A. 1984. Cramming or understanding? Effects of intrinsic and extrinsic motivation on approach to learning and test performance. In Alderson, J.C. and Urquhart, A.H. (eds), pp. 86–121.

Freebody, P. and Luke, A. 1990. Literacies, programs: debates and demands in cultural context. *Prospect,* **5**, 7–16

Freedle, R.O. and Carroll, J.B. (eds) 1972. *Language Comprehension and the Acquisition of Knowledge.* Washington: Winston, V.H. & Sons.

Fries, C.C. 1963. *Linguistics and Reading.* New York: Holt, Rinehart & Winston.

Fry, E. 1963. *Teaching Faster Reading: A Manual.* Cambridge: Cambridge University Press.

Fyfe, R. and Mitchell, E. 1985. *Reading Strategies and their Assessment.* London: NFER Nelson.

Gates, A.I. 1926. A study of the role of visual perception, intelligence and certain associative processes in reading and spelling. *Journal of Educational Psychology,* **17**, 433–45.

Geddes, M. and Sturtridge, G. 1982. *Reading Links.* London: Heinemann Educational.

Gee, J. 1990. *Social Linguistics and Literacies: Ideology in Discourses.* Brighton: Falmer Press.

Geva, E. 1980. *Meta textual notions and reading comprehension.* Unpublished PhD Thesis. University of Toronto.

Geva, E. 1983. Facilitating reading comprehension through flow-charting. *Reading Research Quarterly,* **18**, 384–405.

Gibson, E.J. and Levin, H. 1974. *The Psychology of Reading.* Cambridge, Mass.: MIT Press.

Glendinning, E. 1974. *English in Mechanical Engineering.* London: Oxford University Press.

Glendinning, E. and Holmström, B. 1992. *Study Reading – A Course in Reading Skills for Academic Purpose.* Cambridge: Cambridge University Press.

Glushko, R. 1979. The organization and activation of orthographic knowledge in reading aloud. *Journal of Experimental Psychology: Human Perception and Performance,* **5**, 674–91.

Goodman, K.S. 1967. Reading: a psycholinguistic guessing game. *Journal of the Reading Specialist,* **6**, 126–35.

Goodman, K.S., Goodman, Y. and Flores, B. 1979. *Reading in the Bilingual Classroom: Literacy and Biliteracy.* Rosslyn, Va.: National Clearinghouse for Bilingual Education.

Goodman, K.S. and Fleming, J.T. (eds) 1969. *Psycholinguistics and the Teaching of Reading*. Newark, DE: IRA.

Goody, J. (ed.) 1968. *Literacy in Traditional Societies*. Cambridge: Cambridge University Press.

Goody, J.R. and Watt, I. 1968. The consequences of literacy. In Goody, J. (ed.), pp. 27–68.

Gough, P.B. 1972. One second of reading. In Kavanagh, F.J. and Mattingly, G. (eds), pp. 331–58.

Grabe, W. 1988. Reassessing the term 'interactive'. In Carrell, P.L. et al. (eds), pp. 56–70.

Grabe, W. 1991. Current developments in second language reading research. *TESOL Quarterly*, **25**, 375–406.

Grabe, W. and Kaplan, R.B. 1996. *The Theory and Practice of Writing: An Applied Linguistic Perspective*. London: Longman.

Graves, M.F. and Cook, C.L. 1980. Effects of previewing difficult short stories for high school students. *Research on Reading in Secondary Schools*, **6**, 38–54.

Graves, M.F., Cook, C.L. and LaBerge, H.J. 1983. Effects of previewing difficult short stories on low-ability junior high school students' comprehension, recall and attitude. *Reading Research Quarterly*, **18**, 262–76.

Grellet, F. 1981. *Developing Reading Skills*. Cambridge: Cambridge University Press.

Griffin, P. 1990. *Adult Literacy and Numeracy Competency Scales*. Victoria, Australia: Assessment Research Centre, Phillip Institute of Technology.

Grimes, J.E. 1975. *The Thread of Discourse*. The Hague: Mouton.

Grundin, E.H. and Grundin, H.U. 1984. *Reading: Implementing the Bullock Report*. London: Ward Lock International.

Guthrie, J.T. (ed.) 1977. *Cognition, Curriculum, and Comprehension*. Newark, DE: International Reading Association.

Guthrie, J.T. and Kirsch, I.S. 1987. Distinctions between reading comprehension and locating information in text. *Journal of Educational Psychology*, **79**, 220–97.

Guthrie, J.T. and Mosenthal, P. 1987. Literacy as multidimensional: locating information and reading comprehension. *Educational Psychologist*, **22**, 279–97.

Hafiz, F.M. and Tudor, I. 1989. Extensive reading and the development of language skills. *ELT Journal*, **43**, 4–13.

Hafiz, F.M. and Tudor, I. 1990. Graded readers as an input medium in L2 learning. *System*, **18**, 31–42.

Haines, S. 1987. *Reading 3*. London: Cassell.

Haines, S. 1988. *Reading 4.* London: Cassell.

Halliday, M.A.K. and Hasan, R. 1976. *Cohesion in English.* London: Longman.

Hamp-Lyons, L. 1984. Developing a course to teach extensive reading skills to university-bound learners. *System,* 11, 303–12.

Hamp-Lyons, L. 1985. Two approaches to teaching reading: a classroom based study. *Reading in a Foreign Language,* 3, 363–73.

Handscombe, J., Orem, R.A. and Taylor, B.P. (eds) 1984. *On TESOL 83: The Question of Control.* Washington, D.C.

Harri-Augstein, S. and Thomas, L. 1984. Is comprehension the purpose of reading? In Grundin, E.H. and Grundin, H.U., pp. 250–76.

Harris, T.L. and Hodges, R.E. 1981. *A Dictionary of Reading and Related Terms.* Newark: IRA.

Hartman, D. 1992. Eight readers reading: the intertextual links of able readers using multiple passages. *Reading Research Quarterly,* 27, 122–3.

Hayes, J.R. (ed.) 1970. *Cognition and the Development of Language.* New York: Wiley.

Haynes, M. 1984. Patterns and perils of guessing in second language reading. In Handscombe, J. et al. (eds), pp. 163–76.

Haynes, M. 1993. Patterns and perils of guessing in second language reading. In Huckin, T. et al., pp. 46–62.

Haynes, M. and Carr, T.H. 1990. Writing system background and second language reading: a component skills analysis of English reading by native speakers of Chinese. In Carr, T.H. and Levy, B.A. (eds), pp. 375–421.

Heaton, J.B. 1988. *Writing English Language Tests* (2nd edn). London: Longman.

Hedge, T. 1985. *Using Graded Readers in Language Teaching.* London: Macmillan.

Hegarty, M., Carpenter, P.A. and Just, M.A. 1991. Diagrams in the comprehension of scientific texts. In Barr, R. et al. (eds), pp. 641–68.

Hill, D.R. 1992. *The EPER Guide to Organising Programmes of Extensive Reading.* Edinburgh: The Institute of Applied Language Studies, University of Edinburgh.

Hill, D.R. and Reid-Thomas, H. 1988a. Survey review: graded readers (Part 1). *English Language Teaching Journal,* 42, 44–82.

Hill, D.R. and Reid-Thomas, H. 1988b. Survey review: graded readers (Part 2). *English Language Teaching Journal,* 42, 124–36.

Hill, D.R. and Reid-Thomas, H. 1989. Survey review: seven series of graded readers. *English Language Teaching Journal*, **43**, 221–31.

Hill, D.R. and Reid-Thomas, H. 1993. Seventeen series of graded readers. *English Language Teaching Journal*, **48**, 250–6.

Hillocks, G. and Ludlow, L.H. 1984. A taxonomy of skills in reading and interpreting fiction. *American Educational Research Journal*, **21**, 7–24.

Hoey, M. 1983. *On the Surface of Discourse*. London: George Allen & Unwin.

Hoffman, J.V. 1991. Teacher and school effects in learning to read. In Barr, R. et al., pp. 911–50.

Holcomb, T. and Peyton, J. 1992. *ESL Literacy for a Linguistic Minority: The Deaf Experience*. Washington, DC: National Clearinghouse on Literacy Education.

Hoover, W.A. and Tunmer, W.E. 1993. The components of reading. In Thompson, J.B. et al., pp. 1–19.

Horrocks, G. 1987. *Generative Grammar*. London: Longman.

Hosenfeld, C. 1984. Case studies of ninth grade readers. In Alderson, J.C. and Urquhart, A.H. (eds), pp. 231–49.

Householder, F. 1971. *Linguistic Speculations*. Cambridge: Cambridge University Press.

Howatt, A.P.R. 1984. *A History of English Language Teaching*. Oxford: Oxford University Press.

Huckin, T., Haynes, M. and Coady, J. 1993. *Second Language Reading and Vocabulary Learning*. Norwood, NJ: Ablex.

Hudson, T. 1982. The effects of induced schemata on the 'short circuit' in L2 reading: non-decoding factors in L2 reading performance. *Language Learning*, **32**, 3–31.

Hudson, T. 1988. The effects of induced schemata on the 'short-circuit' in l2 reading: non-decoding factors in L2 reading performance. In Carrell, P.L. et al. (eds), pp. 183–205.

Huey, E.B. 1968. *The Psychology and Pedagogy of Reading*. Cambridge, Mass.: MIT Press.

Hughes, A. (ed.) 1988. *Testing. English for University Study*. ELT Documents 127. Oxford: Modern English Press.

Hughes, A. 1989. *Testing for Language Teachers*. Cambridge: Cambridge University Press.

Hughes, A. 1993. Testing the ability to infer when reading in a second or foreign language. *Journal of English and Foreign Languages*, **10/11**, 13–20.

Hughes, A. and Porter, D. (eds) 1983. *Current Developments in Language Testing*. London: Academic Press.

Hulstijn, J.H. and Matter, J.F. (eds) 1991. Reading in two languages. *AILA Review*, **8** (Amsterdam).

Inman, M. 1978. Lexical analysis of scientific and technical prose. In Todd, M. et al. (eds), pp. 242–56.

Ja'far, W.M. 1992. *The Interactive Effects of background knowledge on ESP reading comprehension proficiency tests*. Unpublished PhD Thesis. University of Reading.

James, C. 1983. A two stage approach to language teaching. In Johnson, K. and Porter, D. (eds), pp. 109–25.

Jarvis, D.K. and Jensen, D.C. 1982. The effect of parallel translations on second language reading and syntax acquisition. *Modern Language Journal*, **66**, 18–23.

Jimenez, R.T., Garcia, E. and Pearson, P.D. 1996. The reading strategies of bilingual Latina/o students who are successful English readers: opportunities and obstacles. *Reading Research Quarterly*, **31**, 90–112.

Johns, T. and Davies, F. 1983. Text as a vehicle for information. *Reading in a Foreign Language*, **1**, 1–19.

Johnson, D.M. and Reynolds, F. 1941. A factor analysis of verbal ability. *Psychological Record*, **4**, 183–95.

Johnson, K. and Porter, D. (eds) 1983. *Perspectives in Communicative Language Teaching*. London: Academic Press.

Johnston, P.H. 1983. *Reading Comprehension Assessment: A Cognitive Basis*. Newark, DE: International Reading Association.

Johnston, P.H. 1984. Assessment in reading. In Pearson, P.D. et al. (eds), pp. 147–85.

Johnston, P. and Allington, R. 1991. Remediation. In Barr, R. et al., pp. 984–1012.

Jones, B., Palincsar, A., Ogle, D. and Carr, E. 1987. Strategic Teaching and Learning: Cognitive Instruction in the Content Area. Alexandria, VA: Association of Supervision and Curriculum Development.

Juel, C. 1991. Beginning reading. In Barr, R. et al. (eds), pp. 759–88.

Just, M. and Carpenter, P.A. (eds) 1977. *Cognitive Processes in Comprehension*. Hillsdale, NJ: Erlbaum.

Just, M.A. and Carpenter, P.A. 1980. A theory of reading: from eye fixation to comprehension. *Psychological Review*, **87**, 329–54.

Just, M.A. and Carpenter, P.A. 1987. *The Psychology of Reading and Language Comprehension*. Boston, Mass.: Allyn & Bacon.

Kamil, M.L., Smith-Burke, M. and Rodrigue-Brown, F. 1986. The sensitivity of cloze to intersentential integration of information in Spanish bilingual populations. In Niles, J.A. and Lalik, R.V. (eds), pp. 334–8.

Kant, I. 1781/1787/1963. *Critique of Pure Reason* (1st edn; 2nd edn; translated by N. Kemp Smith). London: Macmillan.

Katz, S., Lautenschlager, G., Blackburn, A. and Harris, F. 1990. Answering reading comprehension items without passages on SAT. *Psychological Science*, **1**, 122–7.

Kavanagh, F.J. and Mattingly, G. (eds) 1972. *Language by Ear and by Eye.* Cambridge, MA: MIT Press.

Khalifa, H. 1997. *A study in the construct validation of the reading module of an EAP proficiency test battery: validation from a variety of perspectives.* PhD Thesis. University of Reading.

Kieras, D.E. and Just, M.A. (eds) 1984. *New Methods of Reading Comprehension Research.* Hillsdale, NJ: Lawrence Erlbaum.

King, P. 1989. The uncommon core: some discourse features of students' writing. *System*, **17**, 13–20.

Kintsch, W. 1974. *The Representation of Meaning in Memory.* New York: Wiley.

Kintsch, W. and Keenan, J.M. 1973. Reading rate and retention as a function of the number of propositions in the base structure of sentences. *Cognitive Psychology*, **5**, 257–79.

Kintsch, W. and van Dijk, T.A. 1978. Toward a model of text comprehension and production. *Psychological Review*, **85**, 363–94.

Kintsch, W. and Yarborough, J.C. 1982. Role of rhetorical structure in text comprehension. *Journal of Educational Psychology*, **74**, 828–34.

Klare, G.M. 1984. Readability. In Pearson, P.D. et al. (eds), pp. 681–744.

Kobayashi, M. 1995. *Effects of text organisation and test format on reading comprehension test performance.* PhD Thesis. Thames Valley University.

Koda, K. 1987. Cognitive strategy transfer in second language reading. In Devine, J. et al., pp. 125–44.

Koh, M.Y. 1985. The role of prior knowledge in reading comprehension. *Reading in a Foreign Language*, **3**, 375–80.

Kolers, P.A. 1969. Reading is only incidentally visual. In Goodman, K.S. and Fleming, J.T. (eds) *Psycholinguistics and the Teaching of Reading.* Newark, DE: IRA, pp. 8–16.

Koran, M.L. and Koran, J. 1980. Interaction of learner characteristics with pictorial adjuncts in learning from science text. *Journal of Research in Science Teaching*, **17**, 477–83.

Krashen, S. 1993. *The Power of Reading*. Englewood, CO: Libraries Unlimited.

Krashen, S.D. and Terrell, T.D. 1983. *The Natural Approach*. Oxford: Pergamon.

Kretovics, J.R. 1985. Critical theory: Challenging the assumptions of mainstream educational theory. *Journal of Education*, **2**, 50–62.

Lado, R. 1961. *Language Testing*. London: Longman.

Langer, J.A. 1981. Pre-reading plan (PReP): Facilitating text comprehension. In Chapman, J. (ed.), pp. 125–30

Langer, J.A. 1984. Examining background knowledge and text comprehension. *Reading Research Quarterly*, **19**, 468–81.

Lass, N. (ed.) 1982. *Speech and Language: Advances in Basic Research and Practice*, Vol. 7. New York: Academic Press.

Laufer, B. 1989. What percentage of text lexis is essential for comprehension? In Lauren, L. and Nordman, M. (eds), pp. 316–23.

Lauren, L. and Nordman, M. (eds) 1989. *Special Language: From Human Thinking to Thinking Machines*. Clevedon: Multilingual Matters.

Lee, J.F. 1986. On the use of the recall task to measure L2 reading comprehension. *Studies in Second Language Acquisition*, **8**, 201–11.

Lee, J.F. and Musumeci, D. 1988. On hierarchies of reading skills and text types. *The Modern Language Journal*, **72**, 173–87.

Lefevre, C.A. 1964. *Linguistics and the Teaching of Reading*. New York: McGraw-Hill.

Legg, S. and Algina, J. (eds) 1990. *Cognitive Assessment of Language and Math Outcomes*. Norwood, NJ: Ablex.

Lesgold, A., Pelligreno, J., Fokkema, S. and Glaser, R. (eds) 1978. *Cognitive Psychology and Instruction*. New York: Plenum.

Lesgold, A. and Perfetti, C. (eds) 1981. *Interactive Processes in Reading*. Hillsdale, NJ: Erlbaum.

Levelt, W.J.M. 1989. *Speaking: From Intention to Articulation*. Cambridge, Mass.: MIT Press.

Lewkowicz, J.A. 1997. *Investigating authenticity in language testing*. Unpublished PhD Thesis. University of Lancaster.

Lucas, C. (ed.) 1990. *The Sociolinguistics of the Deaf Community*. San Diego: Academic Press.

Lumley, T.J.N. 1993. Reading comprehension sub-skills: teachers' perceptions of content in an EAP test. *Melbourne Papers in Applied Linguistics*, **2**, 25–55.

Lund, R.J. 1991. A comparison of second language listening and reading comprehension. *Modern Language Journal*, **75**, 196–204.

Lunzer, E. and Gardner, K. (eds) 1979. *The Effective Use of Reading.* London: Heinemann Educational.

Lunzer, E., Waite, M. and Dolan, T. 1979. Comprehension and comprehension tests. In Lunzer, E. and Gardner, K. (eds), pp. 37–71.

Lyons, J. 1968. *Introduction to Theoretical Linguistics.* Cambridge: Cambridge University Press.

Macias, R.F. 1990. Definitions of literacy: a response. In Venezky et al. (eds), pp. 17–22.

McCarthy, M.J. 1990. *Vocabulary.* Oxford: Oxford University Press.

McCormick, S. 1992. Disabled readers' erroneous responses to inferential comprehension questions: description and analysis. *Reading Research Quarterly*, **27**, 54–77.

McGinitie, W.H. (ed.) 1973. *Assessment Problems in Reading.* Newark, DE: International Reading Association.

McGovern, D., Mathews, M. and Mackay, S.E. 1994. *English for Academic Study: Reading.* Prentice Hall International (UK) Ltd.

Mackay, R., Barhman, B. and Jordan, R.R. (eds) 1979. *Reading in a Second Language.* Rowley, Mass.: Newbury House.

Mackay, R. and Mountford, A. 1979. Reading for information. In Mackay, R. et al. (eds), pp. 106–41.

Mackinnon, G.E. and Waller, T.G. (eds) 1981. *Reading Research: Advances in Theory and Practice*, Vol 2. London: Academic Press.

McNamara, T. 1996. *Measuring Second Language Performance.* Longman: London.

McNamara, T.P., Miller, D.L. and Bransford, J.D. 1991. Mental models and reading comprehension. In Barr, R. et al. (eds), pp. 490–511.

Mahon, D. 1986. Intermediate skills: focusing on reading rate development. In Dubin, F. et al. (eds), pp. 77–102.

Markham, P. 1985. The rational deletion cloze and global comprehension in German. *Language Learning*, **35**, 423–30.

Marslen-Wilson, W. (ed.) 1989. *Lexical Representation and Process.* Cambridge, Mass.: MIT Press.

Marton, J.R. 1976. Teaching academic vocabulary to foreign graduate students. *TESOL Quarterly*, **10**, 91–9.

Matthews, M. 1990. Skill taxonomies and problems for the testing of reading. *Reading in a Foreign Language*, **7**, 511–17.

Mattingly, G. and Kavanagh, F.J. 1972. The relationships between speech and reading. *The Linguistic Reporter*, **14**, 1–4.

Mead, R. 1982. Review of Munby: communicative syllabus design. *Applied Linguistics*, **3**, 70–8.

Menyuk, P. 1984. Language development and reading. In Flood, J.S. (ed.), pp. 101–19.

Meyer, B.J.F. 1975. *The Organization of Prose and its Effect on Memory.* Amsterdam: North-Holland.

Meyer, B.J.F. 1985. Prose analysis: purposes, procedures, and problems. In Britton, B.K. and Black, J.B. (eds), pp. 11–64.

Meyer, B.J.F. and Freedle, R.O. 1984. The effects of different discourse types on recall. *American Educational Research Journal*, **21**, 121–43.

Meyer, B.J.F. and Rice, G.E. 1982. The interaction of reader strategies and the organisation of text. *Text 2*, **1**, 155–92.

Meyer, B.J.F. and Rice, G.E. 1984. The structure of text. In Pearson, P.D. et al. (eds), pp. 319–52.

Mikulecky, L. 1990. Literacy for what purpose? In Venezky et al. (eds), pp. 24–34.

Miller, J.R. and Kintsch, W. 1980. Readability and recall for short passages: a theoretical analysis. *Journal of Experimental Psychology: Human Learning and Memory*, **6**, 335–54.

Mohammed, M.A.H. and Swales, J.M. 1984. Factors affecting the successful reading of technical instructions. *Reading in a Foreign Language*, **2**, 206–17.

Moore, J. 1980. *Reading and Thinking in English.* Oxford: Oxford University Press.

Moran, C. and Williams, E. 1993. Survey review: recent materials for the teaching of reading at intermediate level and above. *ELT Journal*, **47**, 64–84.

Morgan, J. O'C and Batchelor, E.M. 1959. *The Approach to School Certificate English.* London: Academic Press.

Morrow, K.E. 1980. *Skills for Reading.* Oxford: Oxford University Press.

Munby, J. 1978. *Communicative Syllabus Design.* Cambridge: Cambridge University Press.

Nation, I.S.P. 1990. *Learning and Teaching Vocabulary.* New York: Newbury House.

Nation, P. 1997. The language learning benefits of extensive reading. *The Language Teacher*, **21**, 13–16.

Neal, E.A. and Foster, I. 1926. A program of silent reading. *Elementary School Journal*, **27**, 275–80.

Nesi, H. and Meara, P. 1991. How using dictionaries affects performance in multiple choice EFL tests. *Reading in a Foreign Language*, **8**, 631–43.

Neville, M.H. and Pugh, A.K. 1982. *Towards Independent Reading.* London: Heinemann Educational.

Nevo, N. 1989. Test-taking strategies on a multiple-choice test of reading comprehension. *Language Testing*, **6**, 199–215.

Newman, A.P. and Beverstock, C. 1990. *Adult Literacy: Contexts and Challenges.* Newark: IRA and Bloomington.

Nicholson, T. 1993a. The case against context. In Thompson, G.B. et al. (eds), pp. 91–104.

Nicholson, T. 1993b. Reading without context. In Thompson, G.B. et al. (eds), pp. 105–22.

Nickel, G. (ed.) 1976. *Proceedings of the 4th International Congress of Applied Linguistics*, Vol 1. Stuttgart Hochschulverlag.

Niles, J.A. and Lalik, R.V. (eds) 1986. *Thirty-fifth Yearbook of the National Reading Conference.* Rochester, NY: National Reading Conference.

Nisbet, J. and Shucksmith, J. 1991. *Learning Strategies.* New York: Routledge.

Nunan, D. 1985. Content familiarity and the perception of textual relationship in second language reading. *RELC Journal*, **16**, 34–51.

Nunan, D. 1989. *Designing Tasks for the Communicative Classroom.* Cambridge: Cambridge University Press.

Nunan, D. 1993. Task based syllabus design: selecting, grading and sequencing tasks. In Crookes, G. and Gass, S.M. (eds), pp. 55–68.

Nuttall, C. 1982. *Teaching Reading Skills in a Foreign Language.* London: Heinemann Educational.

Nuttall, C. 1985. Recent materials for the teaching of reading. *ELT Journal*, **39**, 198–207.

Nuttall, C. 1996. *Teaching Reading Skills in a Foreign Language* (rev. edn). London: Heinemann Educational.

Olshavsky, J.E. 1977. Reading as problem solving: an investigation of strategies. *Reading Research Quarterly*, **12**, 654–74.

Olson, G.M., Duffy, S.A. and Mack, R.L. 1984. Thinking-out-loud as a method for studying real-time comprehension processes. In Kieras, D.E. and Just, M.A. (eds), pp. 253–86.

O'Neill, T., Snow, P. and Webb, R. 1996. *Crescent English Course: Teacher's Book.* Beirut: OUP.

Orasanu, J. (ed.) 1986 *Reading Comprehension: From Research to Practice.* Hillsdale, NJ: Erlbaum.

Orlek, J. 1996. *A theoretical and empirical exploration of main ideas in reading.* Unpublished MA TEFL Dissertation. CALS, University of Reading.

Oxford, R. and Crookall, D. 1989. Research on language learning strategies: methods, findings, and instructional issues. *The Modern Language Journal,* **73**, 404–19.

Paap, K.R., Newsome, S.L., McDonald, J.E. and Schaneveldt, R.W. 1982. An activation-verification model for letter and word recognition: the word superiority effect. *Psychological Review,* **89**, 573–94.

Padden, C.A. 1990. *Deaf Children and Literacy. Literacy Lessons.* Geneva: International Bureau of Education.

Palincsar, A. and Brown, A. 1984. Reciprocal teaching of comprehension fostering and comprehension monitoring activities. *Cognition and Instruction,* **1**, 117–75.

Paran, A. 1991. *Reading Comprehension.* Limassol, Cyprus: Burlington Books.

Paran, A. 1993. *Points of Departure.* Ra'anana: Eric Cohen Books.

Paran, A. 1996. Reading in EFL: facts and fictions. *ELT Journal,* **50**, 25–34.

Paris, S.G., Wasik, B.A. and Turner, J.C. 1991. The development of strategic readers. In Pearson, P.D. et al. (eds), pp. 609 – 40.

Pask, G. 1976. Styles and strategies of learning. *British Journal of Educational Psychology,* **46**, 12–48.

Pearson, P.D. and Fielding, L. 1991. Comprehension instruction. In Barr, R. et al. (eds), pp. 815–60.

Pearson, P.D. and Johnson, D.D. 1978. *Teaching Reading Comprehension.* New York: Holt, Rinehart & Winston.

Pearson, P.D. et al. (eds) 1984. *Handbook of Reading Research.* New York: Longman.

Pegolo, C. 1985. The role of rhythm and intonation in the silent reading of French as a foreign language. *Reading in a Foreign Language,* **3**, 313–27.

Perfetti, C.A. 1977. Language comprehension and fast decoding: some psycholinguistic prerequisites for skilled reading comprehension. In Guthrie, J.T. (ed.), pp. 141–83.

Perfetti, C.A. 1985. *Reading Ability.* New York: Oxford University Press.

Perfetti, C.A. and McCutchen, D. 1982. Speech processes in reading. In Lass, N. (ed.), pp. 237–69.

Perkins, K. and Brutten, S. 1988. An item discriminality study of textually explicit, textually implicit and scriptally implicit questions. *RELC Journal*, **19**, 1–11.

Pettit, N.T. and Cockriel, I.W. 1974. A factor study on the literal reading comprehension test and the inferential reading comprehension test. *Journal of Reading Behavior*, **6**, 63–75.

Pitts, M., White, H. and Krashen, S. 1989. Acquiring second language vocabulary through reading: a replication of the clockwork orange study using second language acquirers. *Reading in a Foreign Language*, **5**, 271–6.

Pollitt, A. and Hutchinson, C. 1986. The validity of comprehension tests: what makes questions difficult?. In Vincent, D. et al. (eds), pp. 41–61.

Posner, M.I. 1986. *Chronometric Explorations of Mind*. Hillsdale, NJ: Erlbaum.

Pressley, M., Ghatala, E.S., Woloshyn, V. and Pirie, J. 1990. Sometimes adults miss the main ideas and do not realize it: confidence in responses to short-answer and multiple choice comprehension questions. *Reading Research Quarterly*, **25**, 232–49.

Pritchard, R. 1990. The effects of cultural schemata on reading processing strategies. *Reading Research Quarterly*, **25**, 273–95.

Pugh, A.K. 1976. Implications of problems of language testing for the validity of speed reading courses. *System*, **4**, 29–39.

Pugh, A.K. 1978. *Silent Reading*. London: Heinemann Educational.

Pugh, A.K. and Ulijn, J.M. (eds) 1984. *Reading for Professional Purposes: Studies and Practices in Native and Foreign Languages*. London: Heinemann Educational.

Pyrczak, F. 1975. Passage dependence of reading comprehension questions: examples. *Journal of Reading*, **18**, 308–11.

Quirk, R. and Greenbaum, S. 1973. *A University Grammar of English*. London: Longman.

Quirk, R., Greenbaum, S., Leech, G. and Svartvik, J. 1972. *A Grammar of Contemporary English*. London: Longman

Ramsey, C.L. 1990. Language planning in deaf education. In Lucas, C. (ed.), pp. 123–46.

Randall, M. and Meara, P. 1988. How Arabs read Roman letters. *Reading in a Foreign Language*, **4**, 133–45.

Rankin, M.J. 1988. Designing think-aloud studies in ESL reading. *Reading in a Foreign Language*, **4**, 119–32.

Rayner, K. and Pollatsek, A. 1989. *The Psychology of Reading.* Englewood Cliffs, NJ: Prentice Hall.

Reder, L.M. and Anderson, J.R. 1980. A comparison of texts and their summaries: memorial consequences. *Journal of Verbal Learning and Verbal Behavior,* **19**, 121–34.

Rendell, R. 1977. *A Judgement in Stone.* London: Hutchinson.

Resnick, L.B. and P.A. Weaver (eds) 1979. *Theory and Practice of Early Reading.* Hillsdale, NJ: Erlbaum.

Richards, J.C. 1989. Profile of an effective L2 reading teacher. *Prospect,* **4**, 13–29.

Ridgway, T. 1996. Reading theory and foreign language reading comprehension. *Reading in a Foreign Language,* **10**, 55–76.

Ridgway, T. 1997. Thresholds of the background knowledge effect in foreign language reading. *Reading in a Foreign Language,* **11**, 151–68.

Rigg, P. 1988. The Miscue-ESL project. In Carrell, P.L. et al. (eds), pp. 206–20.

Robb, T.N. and Susser, B. 1989. Extensive reading versus skills building in an EAP context. *Reading in a Foreign Language,* **5**, 239–51.

Roberts, J.R. 1997. *Language Teacher Education.* London: Arnold.

Robinson, H.M. (ed.) 1960. *Sequential Development of Reading Ability.* Chicago: University of Chicago Press.

Robinson, P. 1991. *ESP Today: A Practitioner's Guide.* London: Prentice Hall.

Rodrigo, V. 1995. Does a reading program work in a foreign language classroom? Paper presented in the Extensive Reading Colloquium at the American Association of Applied Linguistics. Long Beach, CA.

Roehler L.R. and Duffy, G.G. 1991. Teachers' instructional actions. In Barr, R. et al. (eds), pp. 861–84.

Roller, C.M. 1990. The interaction between knowledge and structure variables in the processing of expository prose. *Reading Research Quarterly,* **25**, 79–89.

Rosch, E. 1975. Cognitive representations of semantic categories. *Journal of Experimental Pschology (General),* **104**, 192–233.

Rosch, E., Mervis, C.B., Gray, D., Johnson, D.M. and Boyes-Braem, P. 1976. Basic objects in natural categories. *Cognitive Psychology,* **8**, 383–439.

Rosenshine, B.V. 1980. Skill hierarchies in reading comprehension. In Spiro, R.J. et al. (eds), pp. 535–54.

Rost, D.H. 1993. Assessing the different components of reading comprehension: fact or fiction. *Language Testing*, **10**, 79–92.

Rost, M. 1990. *Listening in Language Learning*. London: Longman.

Royer, J.M. and Cunningham, D.J. 1978. *On the Theory and Measurement of Reading Comprehension* (Tech. Rep. No. 91). Urbana: University of Illinois, Center for the Study of Reading.

Rudzka-Ostyn, B. 1986. Vocabulary teaching: a cognitive approach. In Cornu, A.M. et al. (eds), pp. 98–106.

Rumelhart, D.E. 1977. Toward an interactive model of reading. In Dornic, S. (ed.), pp. 573–603.

Rumelhart, D.E. 1980. Schemata: the building blocks of cognition. In Spiro, R.J. et al. (eds), pp. 123–56.

Ryan, A. and Meara, P. 1991. The case of the invisible vowels: Arabs reading English words. *Reading in a Foreign Language*, **7**, 531–40.

Sadoski, M., Paivio, A. and Goetz, E.T. 1991. A critique of schema theory in reading and a dual coding alternative. *Reading Research Quarterly*, **27**, 463–89.

Saljo, R. 1975. Qualitative differences in learning as a function of the learner's conception of the task. *Acta Universitatis Gothoburgensis*. Goteborg.

Sampson, G. 1975. *The Form of Language*. London: Weidenfeld and Nicholson.

Sampson, G. 1980. *Schools of Linguistics*. London: Hutchinson.

Sampson, G. 1985. *Writing Systems*. London: Hutchinson.

Sampson, G. 1994. Chinese script and the diversity of writing systems. *Linguistics*, **32**, 117–32.

Sampson, G. 1997. *Educating Rita*. London: Cassell.

Samuels, S.J. and Kamil, M.L. 1988. Models of the reading process. In Carrell, P.L. et al. (eds), pp. 22–37.

Saragi, T., Nation, I.S.P. and Meister, G.F. 1978. Vocabulary learning and reading. *System*, **6**, 72–8.

Sarig, G. 1987. High-level reading in the first and in the foreign language: some comparative process data. In Devine, J. et al. (eds), pp. 105–20.

Sarig, G. 1989. Testing meaning construction: can we do it fairly? *Language Testing*, **6**, 77–94.

Shanahan, T., Kamil, M. and Tobin, A. 1982. Cloze as a measure of intersentential comprehension. *Reading Research Quarterly*, **17**, 229–55.

Shen, Z., Weir, C.J. and Green, R. 1998. *The Test for English Majors Validation Project*. Shanghai: Foreign Languages Education Press.

Shepherd, D. 1978. *Comprehensive High School Reading Methods* (2nd edn). Columbus, OH: Charles E. Merrill.

Shepherd, J., Rossner, R. and Taylor, J. 1984. *Ways to Grammar: a Modern English Practice Book.* London: Macmillan.

Shohamy, E. 1984. Does the testing method make a difference? The case of reading comprehension. *Language Testing,* **1**, 147–70.

Siedow, M.D., Memory, D.M. and Bristow, P.S. 1985. *Inservice Education for Content Area Teachers.* Newark, DE: International Reading Association.

Silberstein, S. 1994. *Techniques and Resources in Teaching Reading.* New York: Oxford University Press.

Sim, D.D. and Laufer-Dvorkin, D. 1982. *Reading Comprehension Course: Selected Strategies, Collins Study Skills in English.* Glasgow: Collins.

Sinclair, J. (ed.) 1990. *Collins Cobuild English Grammar.* London: Collins.

Singer, H. and Ruddell, R.B. (eds) 1970. *Theoretical Models and Processes of Reading.* Newark, DE: International Reading Association.

Skehan, P. 1996. A framework for the implementation of task based instruction. *Journal of Applied Linguistics,* **17**, 38–62.

Skehan, P and Foster, P. 1995. Task type and task processing conditions as influences on foreign language performance. *Thames Valley University Working Papers in English Language Teaching,* **3**, 139–89.

Smith, C.B. 1988. Does it help to write about your reading? *Journal of Reading,* **32**, 276–85.

Smith, F. 1971. *Understanding Reading: A Psycholinguistic Analysis of Reading and Learning to Read.* New York: Holt, Rinehart & Winston.

Smith, F. 1973. *Psycholinguistics and Reading.* New York: Holt, Rinehart & Winston.

Spearritt, D. 1972. Identification of subskills in reading comprehension by maximum likelihood factor analysis. *Reading Research Quarterly,* **8**, 92–111.

Spiegel, D.L. and Fitzgerald, J. 1990. Textual cohesion and coherence in children's writing revisited, *Research in the Teaching of English,* **24**, 48–64.

Spilich, G.J., Vesonder, G.T., Chiesi, H.L. and Voss, J.F. 1979. Text processing of domain-related information for individuals with high and low domain knowledge. *Journal of Verbal Learning and Verbal Behavior,* **18**, 275–90.

Spiro, R.J., Bruce, B.C. and Brewer, W.F. (eds) 1980. *Theoretical Issues in Reading Comprehension*. Hillsdale, NJ: Erlbaum.

Spiro, R.J. and Myers, A. 1984. Individual differences and underlying cognitive processes in reading. In Pearson, P.D. et al. (eds), pp. 471–504.

Spolsky, B. 1995. *Measured Words*. Oxford: Oxford University Press.

Stahl, S.A. and Fairbanks, M.M. 1986. The effects of vocabulary instruction: a model based meta-analysis. *Review of Educational Research*, **56**, 72–210.

Stanley, R.M. 1984. The recognition of macrostructure: a pilot study. *Reading in a Foreign Language*, **2**, 148–53.

Stanovich, K.E. 1980. Toward an interactive compensatory model of individual differences in the development of reading fluency. *Reading Research Quarterly*, **16**, 32–71.

Stanovich, K.E. 1981. Attentional and automatic context effects in reading. In Lesgold, A. and Perfetti, C. (eds), pp. 241–67.

Stanovich, K.E. 1991. Word recognition: changing perspectives. In Barr, R. et al. (eds), pp. 418–52.

Stanovich, K.E., Cunningham, A. and Feeman, D.J. 1984. Intelligence, cognitive skills, and early reading progress. *Reading Research Quarterly*, **19**, 278–303.

Steffensen, M.S. 1988. Changes in cohesion in the recall of native and foreign texts. In Carrell, P.L. et al. (eds), pp. 140–51.

Steffensen, M.S. and Joag-Dev, C. 1984. Cultural knowledge and reading. In Alderson, J.C. and Urquhart, A.H. (eds), pp. 48–61.

Steffensen, M.S., Joag-Dev, C. and Anderson, R.C. 1979. A cross-cultural perspective on reading comprehension. *Reading Research Quarterly*, **15**, 10–29.

Steinert, J. 1978. Allgemeiner deutscher Sprachtest (German general language test). Braunschweig/Göttingen: Westermann/Hogrefe.

Sticht, T.G. 1972. Learning by listening. In Freedle, R.O. and Carroll, J.B. (eds), pp. 285–314.

Sticht, T.G. 1980. *Literacy and Human Resource Development at Work*. Alexandria, VA.: Human Resources Research Organization.

Sticht, T.G. 1984. Rate of comprehending by listening or reading. In Flood, J.S. (ed.), pp. 140–60.

Sticht, T.G. and James, J.H. 1984. Listening and reading. In Pearson, P.D. et al. (eds), pp. 293–318.

Stoker, H.W. and Kropp, R.P. 1960. The predictive validities and factorial content of the Florida state-wide ninth grade testing program. *Florida Journal of Educational Research*, **2**, 105–14.

Storey, P. 1995. *A process approach to reading test validation.* Unpublished PhD Thesis. University of Reading.

Street, B.V. 1995. *Social Literacies: Critical Approaches to Literacy in Development, Ethnography and Education.* London: Longman.

Strother, J.B. and Ulijn, J.A. 1987. Does syntactic rewriting affect ESL for science and technology (EST) text comprehension? In Devine, J. et al. (eds), pp. 89–101.

Suarez, A. and Meara, P. 1989. The effects of irregular orthography on the processing of words in a foreign language. *Reading in a Foreign Language*, **6**, 349–56.

Sulzby, E. and Teale, W. 1991. Emergent literacy. In Barr, R. et al. (eds), pp. 727–58.

Swaffar, J.K. 1981. Reading in a foreign language classroom: focus on process. *Unterrichtspraxis*, **14**, 176–94.

Swales, J.M. 1990. *Genre Analysis: English in Academic and Research Settings.* Cambridge: Cambridge University Press.

Sweet, H. 1954. *Anglo-Saxon Primer* (9th edn; rev. Davis, N.). Oxford: Oxford University Press.

Taylor, I. and Olson, D.R. (eds) 1995. *Scripts and Literacy: Reading and Learning to Read Alphabets, Syllabaries and Characters.* Dordrecht: Kluwer Academic Publishers.

Taylor, W.L. 1953. Cloze procedure: a new tool for measuring readability. *Journalism Quarterly*, **9**, 206–23.

Taylor, S.E. 1965. Eye movements in reading: facts and fallacies. *American Educational Research Journal*, **2**, 187–202.

Thomas, L.F. and Augstein, E.S. 1972. An experimental approach to the study of reading as a learning skill. *Research in Education*, **8**, 28–46.

Thompson, G.B., Tunmer, W.E. and Nicholson, T. 1993. *Reading Acquisition Processes.* Clevedon: Multilingual Matters.

Thorndike, E.L. 1917. Reading as reasoning: a study of mistakes in paragraph reading. *Journal of Educational Psychology*, **8**, 323–32.

Thorndike, R.L. 1973. *Reading Comprehension Education in Fifteen Countries.* New York: Wiley.

Todd, M. et al. (eds) 1978. *English for Specific Purposes: Science and Technology.* Corvallis, OR: English Language Institute, Oregon State University.

Tomlinson, B. and Ellis, R. 1988. *Reading Advanced.* Oxford: Oxford University Press.

Trzeciak, J. and Mackay, S.E. 1994. *Study Skills for Academic Writing.* Hemel Hempstead: Prentice Hall International.

Tudge, C. 1987. To read or not to read. *New Scientist,* **1569**, 70–1.

Ulijn, J.M. and Kempen, G.A.M. 1976. The role of the first language in second language reading comprehension: some experimental evidence. In Nickel, G. (ed.), pp. 495–507.

Unger, J.M. and J. DeFrancis 1995. Logographic and semasiographic writing systems: a critique of Sampson's classification. In Taylor, I. and Olson, D.R. (eds), pp. 45–58.

Urquhart, A.H. 1976. *The Effect of Rhetorical Organization in the Readability of Study Texts.* Unpublished PhD Thesis. University of Edinburgh.

Urquhart, A.H. 1987. Comprehensions and interpretations. *Reading in a Foreign Language,* **3**, 387–409.

Urquhart, A.H. 1996. Identifying the good reader. *Triangle 14: To Read in a Foreign Language.* Paris: Didier-Erudition, pp. 17–34.

Van Dijk, T.A. 1977. Semantic macrostructure and knowledge frames in discourse comprehension. In Just, M. and Carpenter, P.A. (eds), pp. 1–32.

Van Dijk, T.A. 1980. *Macrostructures.* Hillsdale, NJ: Erlbaum.

Van Dijk, T.A. and Kintsch, W. 1983. *Strategies of Discourse Comprehension.* New York: Academic Press.

Venezky, R.L. 1984. The history of reading research. In Pearson, P.D. et al. (eds), pp. 3–38.

Venezky, R.L. 1990. Definitions of Literacy. In Venezky R.L. et al. (eds), pp. 2–16.

Venezky, R.L. and Calfee, R.C. 1970. The reading competency model. In Singer, H. and Ruddell, R.B. (eds), pp. 273–91.

Venezky, R.L., Wagner, D.A. and Cilberti, D.S. 1990. *Towards Defining Literacy.* Newark, DE: International Reading Association.

Vernon, P.E. 1962. The determinants of reading comprehension. *Educational and Psychological Measurement,* **22**, 269–86.

Vincent, D. 1985. *Reading Tests in the Classroom: An Introduction.* Windsor: NFER Nelson.

Vincent, D., Pugh, A.K. and Brooks, G. (eds) 1986. *Assessing Reading: Proceedings of the UKRA Colloquium on the Testing and Assessment of Reading.* London: Macmillan Educational Books.

Vygotsky, L.S. 1962. *Thought and Language.* Cambridge, Mass.: MIT Press.

Vygotsky, L.S. 1978. *Mind in Society.* Cambridge, Mass.: MIT Press.

Walker, C. 1987. Individualising reading. *ELT Journal,* **46**, 46–50.

Wallace, C. 1988. *Learning to Read in a Multicultural Society.* New York: Prentice Hall.

Wallace, C. 1992a. *Reading.* Oxford: Oxford University Press.

Wallace, C. 1992b. Critical literacy awareness in the ESL classroom. In Fairclough, N. (ed.), pp. 59–92.

Wallace, C. 1996. Critical reading in the foreign language classroom. *Triangle,* **14**, 80–101.

Wardhaugh, R. 1969. The teaching of phonics and comprehension: a linguistic evaluation. In Goodman, K.S. and Fleming, J.T. (eds), pp. 79–90.

Weaver, C.A. and Kintsch, W. 1991. Expository text. In Barr, R. et al. (eds), pp. 230–45.

Weakley, S. 1993. *Procedures in the content validation of an EAP proficiency test of reading comprehension.* Unpublished MATEFL Dissertation. CALS, University of Reading.

Weir, C.J. 1981. A reply to Morrow. In Alderson, J.C. and Hughes, A. (eds), pp. 26–37.

Weir, C.J. 1983a. *Identifying the language needs of overseas students in tertiary education in the United Kingdom.* PhD Thesis. Univerity of London, Institute of Education.

Weir, C.J. 1983b. The associated examining board's test in English for academic purposes: an exercise in content validation. In Hughes, A. and Porter, D. (eds), pp. 147–53.

Weir, C.J. 1990. *Communicative Language Testing.* London: Prentice Hall.

Weir, C.J. 1993. *Understanding and Developing Language Tests.* London: Prentice Hall.

Weir, C.J. 1994. Reading as multi-divisible or unitary: between Scylla and Charybdis. Paper presented at RELC, Singapore, April.

Weir, C.J. and Roberts, J.R. 1994. *Evaluation in ELT.* Oxford: Blackwell.

Weir, C.J., Hughes, A. and Porter, D. 1990. Reading skills: hierarchies, implicational relationships and identifiability. *Reading in a Foreign Language,* **7**, 505–10.

Weir, C.J. and Porter, D. 1996. The multi-divisible or unitary nature of reading: the language tester between Scylla and Charybdis. *Reading in a Foreign Language,* **10**, 1–19.

Wenden, A. 1987a. Conceptual background and utility. In Wenden, A. and Rubin, J. (eds), pp. 3–13.

Wenden, A. 1987b. Metacognition: an expanded view of the cognitive abilities of L2 learners. *Language Learning*, **37**, 573–97.

Wenden, A. and Rubin, J. (eds) 1987. *Learner Strategies in Language Learning*. Hemel Hempstead: Prentice Hall.

West, R. 1991. Development in the testing of reading. *English as a World Language*, **1**, 60–70.

Widdowson, H.G. 1976. The authenticity of language data. In Fanselow, J.H. and Crymes, R.H. (eds), pp. 261–70.

Widdowson, H.G. 1978. *Teaching Language as Communication*. Oxford: Oxford University Press.

Widdowson, H.G. 1984. Reading and communication. In Alderson, J.C. and Urquhart, A.H. (eds), pp. 213–30.

Widdowson, H.G. 1979. *Explorations in Applied Linguistics*. Oxford: Oxford University Press.

Williams, E. 1984. *Reading in the Language Classroom*. London: Macmillan.

Williams, E. 1987. Classroom reading through activating content-based schemata. *Reading in a Foreign Language*, **4**, 1–7.

Williams, E. 1994. *Reading in Two Languages in African Schools*. ODA Project Report.

Williams, E. 1995. First and second language reading proficiency of year 3, 4 and 6 children in Malawi and Zambia. *Reading in a Foreign Language*, **10**, 915–29.

Williams, E. 1996. Reading in two languages at year five in African primary schools. *Applied Linguistics*, **17**, 182–209.

Williams, E. and Moran, C. 1989. Reading in a foreign language at intermediate and advanced levels with particular reference to English. *Language Teaching*, **22**, 217–28.

Williams, M. and Burden, R.L. 1997. *Psychology for Language Teachers: A Social Constructivist Approach*. Cambridge: Cambridge University Press.

Williams, R. 1983. Teaching the recognition of cohesive ties in reading a foreign language. *Reading in a Foreign Language*, **1**, 35–53.

Wilson, P.T. and Anderson, R.C. 1986. What they don't know will hurt them: the role of prior knowledge in comprehension. In Orasanu, J. (ed.), pp. 31–48.

Winter, E. 1994. Clause relations as information structure: two basic text structures in English. In Coulthard, M. (ed.), pp. 46–68.

Yang, H. 1986. A new technique for identifying science/technology terms and describing science texts. *Literary and Linguistic Computing*, **1**, 93–103.

Zakaluk, B.L. and Samuels, S.J. 1988. *Readability: Its Past, Present, and Future*. Newark, DE: International Reading Association.

Zamel, V. 1992. Writing one's way into reading. *TESOL Quarterly*, **26**, 463–81.

Author Index

Subject Index